THEY HAVE FOUND A FAITH

THEY HAVE FOUND A FAITH

By MARCUS BACH

Essay Index Reprint Series

BOOKS FOR LIBRARIES PRESS
FREEPORT, NEW YORK

Library of Congress Cataloging in Publication Data

Bach, Marcus, 1906-
    They have found a faith.
    (Essay index reprint series)
    1. Sects--U. S. I. Title.
BR516.5.B3 1971   289   74-134049
ISBN 0-8369-2481-9

PRINTED IN THE UNITED STATES OF AMERICA
BY
NEW WORLD BOOK MANUFACTURING CO., INC.
HALLANDALE, FLORIDA 33009

To

RENEE

CONTENTS

THEY HAVE FOUND A FAITH

CHAPTER 1

HOMETOWN

I ALWAYS knew that someday I would write a book on religion, not in the theological or doctrinal sense, but about what religion is and what it does in the lives of people. I can trace this premonition to the time my dad took me to a meeting of the Holy Jumpers up in Waukesha, Wisconsin. When the members of that congregation "got the spirit," they began hopping up and down. Sometimes they stood in one spot, jumping higher and higher; sometimes they skipped up and down the aisles, shouting as they journeyed. I was only a youngster and to me it seemed wonderful. As I watched I was sure that I would never find anything more exciting anywhere in life than what these people found in their religion.

This feeling was intensified by our pilgrimage to a camp meeting. There folks rolled. Their faces took on an out-of-this-world expression because they were "lost in Jesus." They bumped against tables and pews, but without injury. Jesus wiped away the pain, they said, and I believed them.

Why my dad trotted me around to such off-the-beaten-path sects instead of setting me down in the staid surroundings of the Presbyterian church, of which he was a member, I never

11

quite figured out. Was he perhaps on a spiritual quest? And did he take me along as his decoy? If so, it led us on another occasion to the sawdust sanctuary of a tent evangelist who had advertised that he would demonstrate how Jesus walked on the water. The stage was set with a large tank in front of a homemade cross. Calling loudly upon the Lord, the evangelist stepped into the tank with arms extended. The water was about three feet deep, but he sank down only a fraction of an inch. After two or three impressive steps great shouts came from the worshipers: "Bless you, Jesus!...Hallelujah!...Praise the Lord!" Dad moved forward in his chair. Had he finally found the real thing? Just then the water-walker became the object of clutching hands. Down he went. The shouting stopped. An awful calm shot through the meeting, followed immediately by hisses and catcalls from the crowd of unbelievers encircling the tent. The pseudo-Messiah stood dripping in the spot where he had slipped off a concealed plank. I wondered if this was the way Jesus did His miracles. My dad just shook his head and quietly took me home.

This religious gypsying was in amazing contrast to the dignity of my mother's Reformed Church which she attended faithfully without any display of outward emotion. The melodic old church bell was our Sunday morning alarm. The Catholics always rang theirs long and loud for early Mass. We just pulled the blankets over our ears. But the first tap from the steeple of *Friedens Reformirte Kirke* filled our house with frenzied sanctity and set us on our way to third pew front, center section. My uncle, a stocky, severe gentleman with a long white beard, was the pastor. He always wore a little black *mitzi* or skullcap. I never remember seeing him smile—certainly not in church.

When he preached, he ascended a series of twelve steps into the pulpit and closed a little gate behind him. There he stood, high above the heads of the congregation. Looking up at him kept us awake, gave us stiff necks, and reminded us of the direction in which we had to look to see God. It also proved that the minister was nearer heaven than the rest of us poor sinners.

In our church the men sat in one section and the women in another. Boys sat with their fathers, girls with their mothers, and it was considered sinful to let one's eyes wander over to the opposite sex. I went to the services with the expectation of being scolded and I was never disappointed. Even the songs contributed to the chastening, reminding me of my low estate.

> "Alas! and did my Saviour bleed,
> And did my Sovereign die?
> Would He bow that bruised head
> For such a worm as I?"

Just let me be a good worm or a good spider, I thought as I sang. That is about all a fellow should expect out of life!

The communion service was more gratifying. At the old organ Aunt Selma began playing "Break Thou the Bread of Life." The congregation intoned the first verse. During the singing, the men gathered in a semicircle around the table. No woman was allowed at that first serving. Once a man brought his wife with him. Uncle told him to take her back to her pew. The man explained that his wife was ill, and that she could not stand there alone. "Take her back just the same!" Uncle commanded. "She must come up with the women." The man turned and walked up the aisle. He did not stop at his pew. He and his wife went on out of the door and never came back.

Unperturbed, Uncle handed the chalice to the first communicant who sipped gingerly and handed it back. Before giving it to the next man, Uncle turned it a little. He turned it after each sip until the rim of the chalice had been once around. Then he wiped it off with a white napkin, though he thought this was unnecessary. "No germ can live on a communion cup," he always affirmed with the severe authority that accompanied every religious pronouncement. His was the final word of infallibility, and I never thought of God without thinking of Uncle August.

My dad envied my mother for what she had so comfortably and irrevocably found in her faith. He was still a spiritual stray—hunting for the green pastures. Lamblike I followed; and where he didn't lead, I went alone.

Many of my relatives read the violent yellow sheet called *The Menace*. There was enough anti-Catholic bias in my home to make any boy wonder if the priest kept beautiful young girls tied up in the confessional booths and if there was really an arsenal in the church basement. Only once during the liturgical year was there a semblance of religious unity underlying the sectarianism of my home town. On Christmas Eve all the church bells rang at the same time. One night after school—I was in the seventh grade—I climbed up the steps of the forbidding Catholic Church and pulled open one of the big black doors. I stopped short. Standing before me was a mighty angel holding a holy-water basin. Struggling between curiosity and fear, I ventured forward and cautiously dipped in my finger. Nothing happened, so I went on unafraid.

The sanctuary lamp, red and magical; the huge white

altars; the long, finger-shaped windows of stained glass; the stations of the cross—all was taboo, but it made religion visual. I spied a confessional booth. Tiptoeing over, I opened the door. . . . No girls. I went down into the damp, dark basement. . . . No guns. I went up into the balcony. . . . Nothing to fear. It was all silent and impressive. Why did we think all Roman Catholics were going to hell? And why did they think all Reformed members were going there? And how would everybody feel when they all got together? When I went back to the holy-water angel, the door was locked.

I finally got out through a basement window and walked in on my parents, who were in tears. Somebody had suggested dragging the river. When I told my story, my dad said never a word. He just sat there listening and thinking, but my mother told me to go and wash myself "all over."

This passion to keep me unspotted from the great world outside the Reformation continued through my high-school years. Upon graduation I was shipped off to the Mission House College and Seminary near Sheboygan, Wisconsin. In spite of the great emphasis placed on spiritual growth and guidance there, seminary religion was never exciting. The querulous church fathers had built the school out in the country to keep the boys away from temptation. The relentless boredom that pervaded the place made the tavern which was within easy walking distance seem a little corner of paradise. There were also poker games and frequent rolling of the dice, which the professors condemned, condoned, or participated in—depending upon the professor. And, in the eyes of the lonely candidates for the ministry, the kitchen maids were transformed into bewitching sirens luring the boys from Xenophon and Zwingli.

In spite of these forms of escape many dropped out long before graduation to follow other pursuits. The majority, however, plodded through the seven prescribed years of study, married, and launched out to serve churches throughout the Midwest. Usually they fell into a complacent, businesslike ministry according to the gospel of the Reformation.

I felt from the beginning that this would never be my life-work. As the days dragged by at the Mission House, something akin to rebellion stirred within me—youthful rebellion against the cold and formalistic theology which never seemed to touch life. My boyhood impressions of the sincere and sensational disciples within the ranks of America's little-known religions made historic religions seem like dry leaves. Whenever I went home for vacations, my dad prodded me with questions. He wanted to know about the great truth he had hoped I would find. And once he asked if I had seen any miracles. The only ones I could think of were the artful methods students used to get in and out of the dormitories after hours. At the end of my third year I devised means to get out for good and moved into the profane environment of a state university! But my interest in contemporary faiths persisted. As if pointing the way, a traveling fellowship provided an opportunity for personal contact with America's minority religions.

Led by the adventurous spirit of my culting hobby further and further away from the traditional church, I learned to expect anything. In the fantastic and eccentric goings on I

felt the full scale of human emotions. Down in New Mexico
I asked a Penitente why he dragged the heavy, four-hundred-
pound cross until it wore a rough spot on his shoulder and
drew blood. He answered, "The Master said, 'If any man
would be my disciple, let him take up his cross and follow
me.'" The snake handlers of Tennessee coiled hissing rattlers
around their bare arms and cried, "These signs shall follow
them that believe." I made a retreat with the Trappist monks
of Kentucky, those strange and devout men who never speak.
I roamed among the Sons of Freedom, the "spirit wrestlers"
of western Canada, who stage nude parades. I lived with the
Hutterites in South Dakota, the purest and most rigorous com-
munists in the world. The impenetrable hook-and-eye Amish
permitted me to record their music. Among the Basque shep-
herds of Idaho I had many friends. The Voodooists of Louisiana had received me, and the trails of America's utopian
groups had been exciting. Whatever people believed seemed
right because they were convinced that their course was
ordered by divine directives. This assumption is at the heart
of the analysis of every religious sect. Many a farcical revelation has led to a constructive movement and a great faith.
Turn up the sod of every vital religious group and you will
find dreams, visions, and what the followers believe to be
telltale traces of the divine. Whenever these came along they
were interpreted as holy whisperings or wild hallucinations,
depending upon the point of view.

Through all my wanderings the idea for a book on religion
lingered, but it crystallized in a wholly unexpected and dramatic way. One night I was lecturing on the sensationalism

of American communistic, utopian, and folk groups. I concluded with a poem by Ella Wheeler Wilcox:

> "All roads that lead to God are good;
>   What matters it, your faith or mine;
>   Both center at the goal divine
> Of love's eternal brotherhood.
>
> A thousand creeds have come and gone,
>   But what is that to you or me?
>   Creeds are but branches of a tree——"

I had got that far, "Creeds are but branches of a tree," when suddenly a man in the audience shouted, "The hell they are!"

The crowd which had been orderly and interested turned from me to this heckler. As I sought him out I had to admit that his appearance belied such an uncouth interruption. He was well dressed and portrayed a stiff dignity as he came to his feet.

"The trouble with religion," he was saying, "is that we have watered it down until the strength has gone out of it. Nobody knows what to believe. Now you come along and insinuate that one denomination is as good as another. All roads that lead to God are good! What do you mean? Creeds are branches of a tree! Where do you get that idea? Have you ever investigated the commercialized heretical groups that are making inroads into our established churches? They're a threat to true religion! They're taking unfair advantage of the Bill of Rights!"

I had often heard such accusations while on my trek along the eternal roads of what people believe. It was the fire behind this man's words that compelled me to get down to facts. Fifty per cent of our population were church members; less than fifty per cent of these attended services. But the cults were booming. The stream of faith was being divided by a crosscurrent of scathing condemnations. The struggle was between those who wanted to maintain the *status quo* and those who felt that the religious world was ready for reconstruction. While the churches claimed that they were the voice of a glorious and triumphant past, the cults announced the invocation of a new Protestantism.

Suddenly I was no longer concerned with isolated experiments. Before me lay an expanding dominion of *little-known* religions that were becoming altogether too well known. They were putting the pressure on my old Presbyterian church—my old Reformed church—my old Catholic church—jolting them to action or to death.

Perhaps my accuser was right. Would a new investigation disclose leaders who had taken undue advantage of the Bill of Rights? Or were they inspired by a higher courage to break away from ancient moorings to explore with God?

I walked home from that lecture amid a torrent of thoughts—with the Holy Jumpers and the camp-meeting enthusiasts—with the water-walking evangelist and Uncle August—with the angel in the Catholic church—with the quiet, searching questions of my dad—with the earnest seminary fathers and their age-old spiritual ideals—with the spirits of the lowly elect of American folkways.

Somehow, I felt that I must become a representative of the average churchgoer everywhere in America whose heart was with me in my seeking. If Jehovah's Witnesses have some heavenly tip-off that the world is coming to an end in 1973, we want to tell our friends about it in plenty of time! If Father Divine is really God, we want to know about it! If Unity is building a new city down in Missouri, we Americans want to get in on the ground floor! If that man in Moscow, Idaho, talked with God "actually and literally," we have a right to know how it's done!

Certainly these modern movements suggested that there was a vital, if not always coherent, moving force back of them, giving luster and drive to their beliefs. Perhaps we of the old historic faiths had become too self-contained and modifi- able. Once in our church we prayed on our knees, later we stood, then we sat, and now we sit on cushions. Yet none of the tendencies or practices in any religion could vitiate my feeling that everyone who truly sought God had a solemn right to his own seeking.

I would not concern myself so much with the rivalry among groups as with their realization. I would devote myself more to the *way* than to the *why* of their doctrine. What could these precocious isms teach me about keeping alive the eternal fire of the quest? Through what landscapes did these new roads run to reach again the old horizons of an enthusiastic faith? Let others turn ecclesiastical microscopes on them or weigh them in the sensitive scale of final truth; I would content myself with the age-old verdict of Gamaliel, "If this work be of men, it will come to nought; but if it be of God, ye cannot overthrow it."

So, with a spurt of expectation, I decided to set forth on my own with no strings attached, no stipend from any university, no commission from any church, no obligation to any individual or group, no bias, no preconceived judgment, no illusions.

"All roads that lead to God are good." As I began my adventure the fervor of this naïve and youthful conviction rushed over me once more.

CHAPTER II

JEHOVAH'S WITNESSES

WATCHTOWER! CONSOLATION! Get your copy!" I had heard these words on Main Street across the nation, and it always seemed to me that the folks who said them were a rather odd slice of Americana. Artist Grant Wood would have found them engaging subjects. Equally insensitive to drizzling rain and driving wind, they set their faces in the tradition of America's second freedom: the freedom of worship. The summer sun glued them to their chosen spot, a street corner where the races of men pass by. There they stood, self-sufficient in Jehovah God, canvas bags slung over their shoulders, periodicals in their upraised hands. Saturday crowds could not dislodge them. For the law, they had no need. For mankind, generally, they evinced a sovereign aloofness. They would rather be alone with what they considered truth than in league with nameless travelers of the road. It was their business to warn this Armageddon-bound generation of its impending destiny. "The Kingdom is at hand!" was their battle cry and Jehovah God their leader. Jehovah's Witnesses are what they wanted to be, sentinels on the watchtower of time.

"Watchtower! Consolation!"

The words always slowed me down, but one day in the heart of America's Bible Belt they stopped me. The voice of a street-corner Witness was suddenly lost in the angry accusation of a local cleric.

"Damn you, conscientious objector!" he muttered in righteous indignation as he knocked Jehovah's envoy roughly with his elbow.

A shadow crossed the vendor's face. Perhaps he was thinking of his rights under the Constitution, the God-given right of every Witness. But he accepted this offense with a patient, submissive smile—a smile that seemed to say, "Strange how slowly people come to the truth, isn't it?" No doubt he was remembering that he had been assured by Scripture that there would always be opposition from "the children of the Devil Satan." The world, and that included organized religion, was bound to be at enmity with the chosen of the Lord. This was prophecy.

Something drew me nearer. It was the secure and insular expression in the man's deep-set eyes. It was the way he stood there, behind the sturdy wall of his convictions. He was probably thirty-five, tall and thin. From beneath the brim of his dark hat prematurely gray hair showed. His gray suit was worn, but newly pressed. Judging by the appearance of this man, I felt that I had found a contradiction for those who considered the Witnesses an impoverished, anti-intellectual group. And yet, as I took my stand on this street corner to continue my study of this little-known movement, I recognized that the man was cast in the seasoned mold of his organization.

"Watchtower! Consolation!"

In the lavish gallery of American religious history, scenes

from this group are hung in sensational frames. At a St. Louis convention in 1941, one hundred fifteen thousand Witnesses jammed the city and fanned out to knock at the door of every home for a radius of forty miles. Never had I seen delegates at a church convention take time out for anything like this. It was as startling as though a meeting of the American Medical Association had recessed to run down and gratuitously treat the city's sick! Yet this was simply a regular part of the agenda of all Witness work. At a Detroit convention in 1940 the city swimming pool was rented for a baptismal service. Twenty-five hundred converts were dipped under the water in the name of the Lord. In Little Rock, Arkansas, in 1940, a regular meeting of local Witnesses was attacked by a mob of workmen armed with guns, sticks, and lead pipes. Two Witnesses were wounded by bullets, five others so severely beaten they had to be treated at a Little Rock hospital. In Grinnell, Iowa, on May 17, 1942, a band of citizens tipped over the trailers of two Witnesses, who had moved into town to warn the unsuspecting populace that the end of the age was near. Close by Newark, New Jersey, in 1937, authorities jailed a hundred of them because they were "considered dangerous." At a convention in Plainfield, New Jersey, in 1933, police roamed the auditorium with revolvers and shotguns. They said they were protecting the delegates, but the Witnesses felt they were being molested.

When I spoke in Civilian Public Service camps during World War II, I asked, "Where are Jehovah's Witnesses?"

The answer was always the same: "They are in Federal prisons, carrying their C. O. ideas that far."

Yet, according to their belief, they are not conscientious objectors; they are "neutrals." Actually they are *not* nonresistant.

They will fight for Jehovah's truth, but they will have no part in the squabbles among "the children of men or the governments of the earth." Ushers have carried canes at some conventions, and in New Jersey they used them to evict troublemakers. *"Watchtower! Consolation!"* There was a flood of strength behind the words. This was America's most misunderstood religious group. To me, the reason was evident, for I had just returned from Brooklyn where I had tried to ferret out the truth behind the movement. I found the Watchtower Bible and Tract Society at 117 Adams Street an impenetrable organizational headquarters. Perhaps this is as it should be. For the first time in my jaunt up and down America's trails of faith, I found an office that claims to have a leased line to God's great throne. Here was the Theocratic capitol of the universe.

The man-made front for Jehovah's Kingdom consists of two modern brick buildings: the factory and Bethel Home. Marking the entrance to the factory is a huge electric sign of ruby lights: RICHES. It does not mean money; it hints of the unspeakable treasures of the Theocracy. Although the Society has a president, its true director is God and its chief officer is Christ Jesus. He is the rightful King of the world, and Jehovah's Witnesses are the true citizens of Zion.

Such an exorbitant claim to infinite riches makes the earthly history of the movement amazingly incidental. Since its appearance in 1874 as an obscure, tragicomic, date-setting faith, there have been only three leaders: Charles Taze Russell, Joseph Franklin Rutherford, Nathan H. Knorr. Their true personalities were known only slightly to their followers. Scandal surrounded Pastor Russell; mystery, Judge Rutherford; silence,

Brother Knorr. The first two acted as the amanuenses of Jehovah. Their written words were accounted gospel. They dipped their pens into the "inexhaustible reservoir of divine truth" and an almost endless stream of books flowed to Witnesses throughout the world. It was not unusual for one of these publications to have a first printing of ten million copies. When Knorr took over in 1941, publications gradually ceased carrying the author's name. It was as though the new administrator deliberately desired to obscure worldly personalities. Today behind the walls at 117 Adams Street, Gargantuan presses grind out fabulous and unlimited numbers of books with the simple and impressive inscription, "Dedicated to Jehovah and His Messiah." To count or classify the publications of the Watchtower Bible and Tract Society convinces the credulous that God's hand is in the business. The presses are geared to a daily capacity of twenty thousand bound books and one hundred fifty thousand booklets. The annual output soars to the amazing total of twenty million pieces—printed, bound, and mailed from one address. This building also houses the factory for the manufacture of glue, inks, dies, cuts, bindings, portable phonographs, transcriptions, and whatever else is needed to keep seventy thousand distributors active on Main Street, U. S. A.

These factual details I had already dug out of the Society's Yearbook. I had gone to Brooklyn to meet the people but was greeted with "Reporters deliberately garble things." I wanted to sit down with their leader, but "Mr. Knorr is in Europe now."

At near-by Bethel Home my reception was the same. The Witnesses were cordial, but noncommittal. They were of the opinion that the uninitiated could never understand the deeper meaning of the work. They forgot that that meaning was tacitly reflected in the severity of their devotion. They did not know that the questions which they evaded were written in their lives. These pilgrims to paradise seemed to know where they came from, where they were going, and what was happening to them and their fellows along the way.

Bethel Home is a seven-story apartment building facing East River at 124 Columbia Heights. Here, long ago, stood the mansion of Henry Ward Beecher, a giant in the chronicles of American faith. He had nothing to do with the history of Jehovah's Witnesses. In fact, I am sure that Dr. Beecher would blink his eyes at the displacement of his staid old manse by this modern "House of God." It is a self-sustaining, miniature village with living quarters, offices, shops, and a common refectory for the Witnesses who man the factory next door. Food is supplied by farms owned by the Society.

A bell arouses the Witnesses at seven in the morning to begin a day of labor for the Lord. At ten-thirty in the evening the bell rings again and the lights go out. For such a workaday existence these confederates with the Unseen receive ten dollars a month in addition to room and board. It is all they ask, all they want. Beyond the walls of this monastic vocation they have caught a vision of Jehovah's Kingdom. They are secure in the belief that theirs is the only organization on earth that is doing God's will. One Witness assured me that all I needed to do was read a little more, think a little less, and get acquainted with God's true word! She suggested a copy of *The Emphatic Diaglott*, which presents in parallel columns both the Greek and English texts of the New Testament. It is nicely bound in leatherette and embossed in gold.

"You can have it for a contribution of two dollars," she encouraged. "Our books and periodicals are never sold. They are always exchanged for contributions. In many cases we receive less than the cost, but if you want the publications, you can have them."

"What is there in all this for you?" I asked. "Do you think you will always be content here?"

The answer was quick and confident. "Of course! You see, the end of the age is near, almost at hand. Just a little while, then the final battle, Armageddon. After that, we who have fulfilled Jehovah God's requirements will carry out the divine mandate to fill the earth with a righteous race for all eternity. Worth working for? What do you think?"

Without giving me a chance to reply, she continued prophetically, "You see, this unrighteous earth will be dissolved and the wicked will be destroyed. Then we will take over. If the Empire State Building still stands after that great and terrible day, we will walk through the granite corridors and God will tell us what to do. Kings will have died and earthly rulers will be no more. Money will have no value. The only riches will be truth and the only treasures loyalty and service to Jehovah God. In those great days the Witnesses will come into their own and the meek will inherit the earth."

Now she was leading me to a table covered by a veritable cloudburst of "inspired writings" bound in flashy multicolored covers. There was *The Final War* with a blood-red gladiator astride a white horse. *Where Are the Dead?* was illustrated with a lone, haunted figure coming out of a tomb. Masses of humanity fled to the mountains for refuge from Armageddon on *Escape to the Kingdom*. *Intolerance* depicted the Witnesses condemned by an unjust judge.

I decided to adjudge them innocent until further investigation. Perhaps that is why on this Midwestern street, I dug into my pocket for a nickel and said, "I'll take a *Watchtower*."

"It's Jehovah's true message."

He spoke mechanically, synchronizing his words with the act of placing the periodical into my hands. I had bought copies of the *Watchtower* many times, but again I was struck by the boldness of the claim made on its cover page. Stamped against the conventional background of God's throne and the stronghold of His Witnesses was the persistent "Announcing Jehovah's Kingdom."

"Everyone should have a chance to accept or reject it," he added.

"Is that your mission, to give everyone a chance?"

"In my territory, yes," he averred.

"A great responsibility," I admitted casually. "What if you miss somebody?"

"We don't miss," he insisted.

"How can you be so sure?" I asked.

"We take our message directly to the people in their homes."

"And if they're out?"

"We call again until we find them."

"How long have you been working this town?"

"Working? You mean witnessing," he reproved mildly.

"Witnessing."

"I have gone over the territory twice already. I expect to cover it four times unless the Society has other plans for me. A complete canvass takes about a year."

Such house-to-house witnessing is the strength of the organization. This fact is common knowledge. From door to door the work is unfolded, published, demonstrated.

As I stood aside and leafed through the *Watchtower*, I wondered if this Witness might let me tag along as he went on his daily doorbell-ringing round. Or would he resent such hitch-hiking on God's highway? What could I learn about the group by being at the rapping, rather than at the receiving end of a visit? What kind of salesmen for salvation were these "only and truly chosen of Jehovah God"? I wanted to know how this Midwestern town of fifteen thousand responded to their message.

As I turned to speak to him, a straight and severe woman of middle age had come up.

"Is this the publication of the Russellites?" she asked tersely.

"They used to call us Russellites," came the well-measured answer.

"*That* is the same as the International Bible Students."

"We use neither of those terms any more. We are Jehovah's Witnesses."

"I'm sure that is what we all want to be." She scraped in her purse for a nickel.

"Yes," cautioned Jehovah's servant, "but we must have the truth. In Isaiah 43:12 Jehovah God says, 'Ye are my witnesses,' but He didn't mean everybody. He meant only those who have the truth."

"Truth, truth," said the woman pettishly. "How do you know you have the truth?"

"We trace the Scriptures right back to their original meaning," explained the Witness. "We prove the Scriptures. And, of course, we have God's headquarters in Brooklyn which aids us in this matter through proper study."

"Oh, well, now," retorted the other, dropping her contribution into the man's hand, "I think I know as much about religion as most of you."

With characteristic passion for pressing home the "truth," the Witness insisted, "That may be, ma'am, but I'm not talking about *religion*. I'm talking about God's word. Now, in 1914 when Jesus came into His kingdom——"

But the good woman was already out of hearing and marching straight on toward Armageddon. Was it the fear of that "great and terrible day" that impelled her to invest in *Consolation?* Or was she preparing a paper for her literary club? To the Witness, it seemed immaterial.

"You bring your message to people the hard way," I observed.

My remark struck the man with great surprise. "Why, it's the way Jehovah God has instructed us. Paul says that we must witness in every city. Acts 20:23."

"About your house-to-house witnessing, do you put in regular hours?"

"I try to. I usually start out about eight or eight-thirty, as soon as people are stirring."

"You've done this for some time?"

"Fifteen years."

"You must learn a great deal about human nature."

"I never thought about that," he said in a preoccupied way. "My only work is to witness."

"I'd like to go with you on some of these trips," I ventured. "I'd like to see what happens and hear how you bring your message to American homes. Would you mind?"

"Not at all. You can come along tomorrow?"

"Tomorrow? That's Sunday."

"That's right."

"You witness on Sunday?"

"Why not?"

"Isn't everyone in church?"

"Are they?" he asked wryly.

"Well, not everyone," I confessed.

"*Watchtower! Consolation!*"

A man in working clothes asked for a copy of *Consolation*. "I've got a *Watchtower*," he explained.

"I know you have," observed the Witness. "I was glad to see you at the meeting last Sunday night. How are you getting along with *The Truth Shall Make You Free?*"

"That's slow reading!" exclaimed the workman.

The Witness' voice was sincere with interest. "I'd be glad to help you understand it."

"I imagine you could do that all right," the other agreed.

"How about this evening?" suggested the Witness.

"Oh, I'd have time this evening. But what is this going to cost?"

"Nothing."

"You mean—you'd sit down with me and go over the book— for nothing?"

"I'll meet with you once a week for nothing," the Witness

JEHOVAH'S WITNESSES 33

promised. "That is part of my work. I thought I made that clear when you got the book."

"Well, maybe you did say something like that. But you know how things go nowadays!"

The Witness got the man's address and made an appointment with him. Then he turned to me. "If you are interested in sitting in on a home study, here's the address. You are welcome to drop around."

"I might do that," I replied, "for I think that is the only kind of meeting I have not attended."

Looking at me with sudden interest, he said, "I don't remember seeing you at our Kingdom Hall."

"I haven't attended locally," I explained, "but I have been an impartial listener-in at a number of meetings."

"Where, may I ask?"

"In this country and in Canada."

"And—you're not a Witness?"

"Well—not yet. In fact, all I've ever heard about your group outside of Kingdom Halls and conventions has been bad."

"Yes?" For the first time he smiled. He seemed amused at the inability of Satan's child to understand him.

"And just about all I've read about your movement has been bad, too," I affirmed. "You are always taking a crack at the Catholic Church or at the Protestant clergy, both of whom I respect. You are nonconformist and nonco-operative in community affairs. You ask for tolerance for yourself, but you are intolerant of others. Your first leader called himself 'Pastor' but there is no evidence that he was ever ordained. And why did he take a title like that if he hated the churches? Judge Rutherford made the prediction that 'millions now living will never die,' but they are dying. And, by the way, I hear that he made a fortune out of the movement. In short, public opinion has put you down as subversive. But if what you believe brings you to this street corner every Saturday and makes you tramp across this town pushing every doorbell at least four times, and if you're willing to sit down with some earnest seeker and study with him for no pay—well, there must be more to all this than meets the eye."

"There is," he said.

"Money?"

He shook his head and, in his remote and ominous tone, repeated the timeworn answer: "Armageddon."

"Scheduled for when?"

"It should come sometime before 1972." He made it sound so commonplace we might have been talking about the weather. And yet, for him, Armageddon would be life's most portentous event.

Reasonably assured that it would not come before the morrow, I said, "I'll see you in the morning?"

"At eight-thirty." He nodded without urging me again to be at the home study that evening. "Shall we meet here on this corner?"

"Fine," I agreed. "Should I bring anything or is there anything I can do to help?"

"Yes, there is," he figured. "I'll let you carry the phonograph."

"By all means! Let me do the heavy work, since I'll only be a witness for a day!"

"Who knows?" he retorted quietly. "The truth may make you free. . . . *Watchtower! Consolation!* Get your copy!"

The sales cry of this spiritual merchant resounded in my ears later that day when I noticed a bold sign on the obscure door of a small office building. Kingdom Hall was located at the top of a flight of narrow, unpainted steps running between whitewashed walls. I went up and peered through the partially open door. It was an unadorned, boxlike room with folding chairs to accommodate about forty. I was somewhat surprised to see a good-sized American flag in a standard at the front of the hall. Spread across the front wall in huge black and red letters was the motto of the year: "BE GLAD, YE NATIONS, WITH HIS PEOPLE." ROM. 15:10, ROTHERHAM.

In an adjoining room I spied another chore boy for Jehovah. He was clearing a space on the large, neat shelves for the latest shipment of books from Brooklyn.

"Mind if I come in?" I called from the doorway.

"Not at all!" His answer was cordial, but he looked up from his work for only a moment. "Make yourself at home. The latest *Watchtower* is on the desk."

The desk was just inside the entrance door. Magazines and pamphlets were spread out in an attractive display, and a row of the Society's books completely lined the back of the table. A contribution box was nailed on the wall above the desk. At the front of the hall stood a small lectern and an old organ.

"You use songs in your services?" I asked.

"Sometimes, but study is more important in these last days," came the confident reply from the bookroom.

I looked around for a hymnal and found a small paper-bound volume published by the Society, *The Kingdom Service Song Book.* Inscribed below this title were the words, "Sing unto Jehovah a *new* song." One glance through the sixty-two pages revealed that this injunction was heeded by all who use the book. I found none of the traditional hymns of Protestantism. It was really a collection of battle songs for Jehovah's regiment of witnessing souls. Below each title, where one usually finds the name of the author, there was a Scripture reference.

"Fear not, O flock of God, the foe
Who madly seeks your overthrow;
Dread not his rage and pow'r;
What though your courage sometimes faints,
His seeming triumph o'er God's saints
Lasts but a little hour.

Jehovah God, O grant our pray'r;
For thy name's sake thine arm make bare,
Let not base men prevail.
A jest thine enemies are grown;
Thou art with us, we are thine own;
Our vict'ry cannot fail."

These words and the music were somewhat different from those I had heard at a United Announcers' Theocratic Assembly:

"Once with confusion my sad heart was filled,
Drinking the cup that *religion* distilled,
Oh, with what gladness and joy it was thrilled,
When thy sweet message I heard!"

Behind the lectern on the front wall was a large chart, showing the month-by-month tabulation of the local Witness work. There were columns for the number of active Witnesses, the number of calls, back calls, and home studies. The comparison of the past year and the present was made outstanding by the use of red and black ink. The chart emphasized the definite semantic distinctions which the Society has adopted in an effort to dissociate itself as much as possible from religious terminology. Local Witnesses constitute not a congregation, but a "company." The place of meeting is not a church; it is a "Kingdom Hall." Leaders of the work may be called ministers—since they are ordained of God—but it is more correct to class them simply as Witnesses. Every Witness is a publisher, for he can become a Witness only by making a covenant with God to "publish" the truth from house to house. Every publisher is expected to devote at least sixty hours a month to the work. A full-time publisher is called a pioneer, for whom the Society has set a minimum service requirement of one hundred fifty hours a month. Emulating the communal life of the Bethel Home Witnesses, the pioneer receives no stated salary. He evaluates his ministry in terms of sacrifice. All contributions that he receives are sent to the Brooklyn headquarters to be credited to his account. In return he has a meager drawing account for living expenses.

The special pioneer assigned to a company by the Society takes charge of all public meetings. On Sunday evenings he conducts a group study, using the current *Watchtower* as a text. Wherever I had sat with Witnesses in their Kingdom Halls, this study had followed the same line of procedure. The leader asks the questions following each paragraph and requests the reading of annotated Scripture texts. After a brief discussion, an assistant reads the paragraph in its entirety. The meeting opens and closes with a short prayer.

I found more variety, however, in the Thursday night meetings, which aim at self-improvement of the publishers. Emphasis centers on the development of a deeper understanding of basic beliefs, but problems faced by the Witnesses during the past week are also discussed. The pioneer gives individual instruction in effective speaking and in meeting the public.

I had once heard a youthful Witness present, as part of an assignment, an extemporaneous talk on "Religion Is Doomed."

"The reason we use the name Jehovah God instead of just God is because there are two Gods. One is Jehovah God and one is a mimic god whose name is Satan the Devil. Long, long ago Satan the Devil told Jehovah God that he could win men over to himself. Jehovah God could have killed the mimic god right then, but He didn't. He wanted people to have a chance to make their own choice. So you know what Satan the Devil did? He went about organizing churches. Satan the Devil invented religion. He started up Catholic churches and Protestant churches and all the hundreds of other kinds of churches and religions. All of them have interpreted the Bible to suit their own taste. They agree on only one great truth and that is 'In the beginning God created heaven and earth.' Yet people believe that religion is the work of Jehovah God. It never was the work of Jehovah God. It is just a trick of the mimic god. It is terrible how many people have been fooled. And because Jehovah God has served notice on Satan the Devil that his time is short, that is why the churches and religion are staging all sorts of campaigns and drives and raising money to get the people 'saved.' They are really saving them for Satan the Devil and not for Jehovah God. That is why religion is doomed."

That evening I crossed the tracks to the address given me

for the home study. An old car was parked in front of a small trailerlike shack. I walked up the dirt path. Framed in a single narrow window was a scene that might have been taken from circuit-rider days. Jehovah's Witness sat on a box with an open Bible in his hands. On the floor beside him was his leather book satchel. Little imagination was needed to convert it into a saddlebag. Books, pamphlets, and a Bible peeped out of it and another Bible lay open on top. Leaning forward in a kitchen chair was the student, still in working clothes. He held a small blue pamphlet and his lips were moving. Beside him, on a table where supper dishes still stood, lay his Bible. He read a moment, then picked up the Bible to verify a Scripture text. No doubt in settings much like this American faith was born, and the foundations of new beliefs were laid.

I rapped at the door.

"Come in!" called the workman.

He offered me the only other chair in the room. The Witness handed me a Bible and a copy of *The Truth Shall Make You Free.*

"Here are the study questions," he said, giving me one of the small blue pamphlets. "We are starting at the beginning."

"That's right—" our host nodded—"but to me the most interesting part of the book is where it tells about 1914."

The Witness smiled patiently. He was ready to continue the study "from the beginning," but the student had discovered a great revelation on page 239! That is where he insisted I turn. He tried eagerly to explain how, by an ingenious bit of divine computation, the author had determined that in 1914 Jesus had entered into His kingdom and set up His Theocratic government.

"The wonderful thing about this," exclaimed the man, "is

that Charles Taze Russell predicted way back in 1880 that Jesus *would* enter His kingdom in 1914—and now, you see, He *did* on exactly that date!"

Our instructor again suggested that we should begin on page one.

"But isn't it wonderful?" the student insisted.

"Sure it is," I agreed. "But how do you know Jesus entered His kingdom—?"

"It says so right here!"

He interrupted so emphatically that I knew he accepted for truth whatever the Watchtower Bible and Tract Society published.

And he was a new disciple!

"According to the Scriptures," explained the Witness, "the time of the Gentiles began in 606 B.C. Jesus referred to this in Luke 21:24. 606 B.C. is the date when Nebuchadnezzar overthrew God's Theocracy. When would it be restored? After seven times had passed over. Read Daniel 4:10-17. That is a symbolic picture of God's rule of the world. What does seven times mean? In Revelation 12:6-14—1,260 days are referred to as a time, and times, and half a time. That means three and a half. A time is one, times means two, and a half makes three and a half."

I was lost, but he went on without me.

"So, seven times would be twice one thousand two hundred sixty or two thousand five hundred twenty days. Now, a month in Scripture means thirty days. You can check this with Genesis 7:11-24, and chapter 8:3-4. Therefore, two thousand five hundred twenty days would equal eighty-four months or seven years. But now Ezekiel, speaking for Jehovah God in Chapter

4, verse 6, says, 'I have appointed thee each day for a year.' Hence, the time of the Gentiles is really two thousand five hundred twenty *years*. All we need to do now is to count from 606 B.C. forward two thousand five hundred twenty years and we arrive at A.D. 1914. Jehovah God is an accurate timekeeper. He said that was to be the year in which the new Theocracy should be set up, and that is the year it was. Jesus came into His kingdom."

"But," I protested, "it seems to me that 1914 was the year that the Devil came into his kingdom!"

"Exactly!" declared the workman with great enthusiasm. "That is just what happened! Jesus came into His invisible *heavenly* kingdom and threw Satan the Devil down to earth. Up until that time Satan the Devil had free run of the whole *universe*. Now he and his demon hordes are restricted to this earth. That's why all the trouble! That's why he's working day and night stirring up the people!"

"Let's go back to Chapter One," directed the Witness. "We were at question twenty in the study: 'The promise of the Four Freedoms by the nations is proof of what fact?' The reference is Luke 21:26 and 27."

The Four Freedoms? That gave the study a contemporary ring, but what did Luke have to do with it? I should not have been surprised. Wherever I had met Witnesses or sat in on their meetings, the jigsaw of current happenings was always pieced together according to the Theocratic pattern. Everything that happens in the world has already been charted in their "Living Book!" God is running the universe and nothing that man can do will aid or hinder the ultimate destiny. That is why the Witnesses are more interested in God's will for the world than in God's will for their lives. They are not individuals; they are symbols in the eternal scheme.

The Witness asked me to read the answer to our question from *The Truth Shall Make You Free*.

I did.

"The very fact that, in the 1940's, politicians of 'Christendom' publish a statement to the world guaranteeing the so-called 'Four Freedoms' is a blank admission that the peoples and nations are not free. Nevertheless, 'Christendom' which, according to her profession of the name 'Christian,' ought to be free, claims to have continued in the word of Jesus and to be His disciple indeed. The facts belie her claim. Instead of knowing the truth, 'Christendom' is a confusion of religions, Catholic, Protestant, and Jewish, and pagan, and a confusion of political systems, democratic and totalitarian. All are now fearfully groping in darkness for some interreligious and international arrangement whereby they can all survive and get along together."

The ardent disciple was ready with the Scripture references as soon as I had finished.

"Luke 21:26 and 27 has this to say in this connection," he began: "'Men's hearts failing them for fear, and for looking after those things which are coming on the earth: for the powers of heaven shall be shaken. And then shall they see the Son of man coming in a cloud with power and great glory.' Now, isn't that wonderful! That sure all fits in!" he ended impetuously.

The longer I listened, the more I felt myself caught in the narrow spiritual defile between the instructor's conviction and his pupil's credence. Here in a lowly domestic dwelling, I was asked to believe that a street-corner vendor and a workingman were custodians of divine prerogatives that had entirely escaped the educated clerics of traditional Christianity! Their truth was at the bottom of everything. They were right; others were wrong. They were the *personae gratae* of the Ruler and Maker of the world. Wherever Witnesses sat together that night—in home study, in Kingdom Hall, in Bethel Home—all who had committed themselves to this truth were those for whom God had made the earth. This, of course, seemed unspeakably impudent until one set it up against the bold facts of religious history. The thought I had about the early circuit riders was forced back until it touched the very beginning of the Christian faith. I had to admit there had always been men like these— "witnesses" whose convictions were biased according to conventional standards, whose words were heretical, but who had the animation of something strangely akin to a triumphant spirit.

Rutherford played a master stroke when, in 1931, he gave his people the name Jehovah's Witnesses. This title linked them with the Biblical heroes. It gave them blood relationship to Abraham, who prepared to slay his own son in order to testify that he was a faithful witness. It likened them to Noah, Moses, David, Daniel, Isaiah. Wherever the word "witness" appears in the Bible, there the Witnesses of today see their prototypes. Nowhere, however, do they find so rich a lineage as with the men whom Jesus called. The Master's disciples were ridiculed and ignored because they were "in the world and not of it." They, too, considered themselves the rightful heirs to a new world and subjects of an invisible King. Were they in the favor of earthly rulers? Were they militaristic? Did they aspire to the things of men? Never, say the Witnesses. These men—their forebears, their kindred—went about warning and pleading, seeking the lost, reaching the hearts of those who would heed prophecy's fulfillment. They, too, went from house to house carrying neither scrip nor purse. They preached in the streets. They were thrown to lions, stoned, crucified.

Rutherford further maintained that the succession of saints bridging the years from the first Christian church to the headquarters in Brooklyn were all Jehovah's Witnesses. In league with these, the instructor who sat on the box before me represented the continuity of the Christian faith in all its original and primitive aspects.

The Witness drove me home.

"Where do you live?" I asked.

He replied in his usual remote manner, "Since my wife and I came to town two years ago, we have lived in a trailer."

"Do you have any children?"

His answer was sincere but impersonal. "No, we haven't. We think it is better to wait until after Armageddon."

This was a new one in my experiences among the "little-knowns"! A young married couple, dead sure that Jesus was coming to set up a perfect kingdom, was postponing the matter of a family until that great day!

"Is this a belief among the Witnesses," I asked, "or is it just your idea?"

"The Society feels that since the time of the end is so near, people can witness more effectively if they do not have too many responsibilities."

"Do you think some of the workers are even waiting to get married until after Armageddon?"

"I imagine so," he answered seriously. "Wouldn't you wait, if you knew the world was going to be so much better then?"

"And it will be possible to get married after Jesus comes?"

"Of course. Life will go on in much the same way, only there will be no sin."

"What about death after Armageddon?"

"There will be none. Everyone will grow to a reasonable age and remain that way."

"But couldn't you be mistaken? Did you ever think about that?"

"There is a chance that some of the more minor details may have certain variations. But basically it will all have to come to pass as we believe."

"Why?"

"Because it is God's truth. And Jehovah God neither lies nor makes mistakes."

Against this backdrop of startling infallibility, I set out with Jehovah's Witness on the following morning. It was a raw, cold January day. The Witness and his wife were waiting in the only car parked at yesterday's busy corner. After a casual introduction, he explained that she was a pioneer and would work an adjoining territory. While the church bells called to early worshipers, we drove to a modest residential section. The Witness took a small plat from his pocket and indicated the blocks he expected to cover before noon. We left the car, armed with a good-sized box, a large pouch full of books, and the portable phonograph.

"Is the machine wound?" asked my partner.

It wasn't. I awkwardly cranked it as we started up the walk to a neat, middle-class home.

In answer to our rap the door was opened wide by a buxom lady in house dress and apron.

"Good morning," began my friend. "I am one of Jehovah's Witnesses——"

"*Ach, Himmel!*" interrupted the woman with a strong German accent. "I am too sick today to buy anything or to listen to anybody!"

She slammed the door before I could open the phonograph.

"Well," smiled the Witness fatefully, "she was quick about it."

"Do most of your days begin like this?" I asked, unwilling to take the incident seriously.

"I don't keep track," he answered, heading stoically toward the big white house next door. "According to Acts 9 that's the way it was with Paul, though."

As we stood shivering on the rambling porch, the door opened stingily.

"Good morning," began my confrere. "I am one of Jehovah's Witnesses and have a timely and important message for you. For convenience' sake, this message has been recorded and I would like you to hear it."

This was my cue. Before the woman had time to object, I set the needle down on the whirling record.

"His faithful disciples," came Rutherford's voice from the phonograph, "propounded to Jesus this question: 'What shall be the proof of the end of the world?' The question did not refer to the end of the earth because, as these disciples knew, the earth abides forever and will never end. . . ."

I remembered Rutherford as I had seen him at a convention during his heyday. His stance at the microphone was as stolid as his message. He was a large man, over six feet, and his studied judgelike bearing always emphasized an undeniable power of leadership. In September 1938 he engaged radio and telephone facilities for a hookup between Royal Albert Hall in London and twenty-three cities in the United States, ten in Canada, ten in Australia, and four in New Zealand. It was the first time that a transoceanic broadcast had exceeded fifteen minutes. For an hour a hundred thousand listened to *Face the Facts*. I wondered how many times that number had refused him a hearing since. Our present listener peeped belligerently through the half-open door. Her Midwestern ears were closed against the Harvard accent of the Judge. She had no idea what he meant by Theocracy and Armageddon.

Why did the Brooklyn headquarters ever permit such an approach to be instigated? Here stood two able-bodied men, perfectly competent to speak out any prescribed message and capable of memorizing any sales approach. Instead, I stood in the cold, a console for Judge Rutherford! And despite his heavy play upon the fact that the sand in time's hourglass was running thin, his recording was endlessly long.

It didn't matter to the Witness. He stood there as if hearing the transcription for the first time. When it finally ended, he asked with eager restraint, "What did you think of that?"

"It sounds like religion," came the banal reply.

"It is a message of truth," my friend corrected, while I closed the phonograph and stood aside to give him the floor. "We believe that these are the last days and that Jehovah God is gathering His chosen people out of the nations."

His experienced hands selected a book from the satchel as he continued. He held it up so that she could read the title for herself, but, to make doubly sure, he said, "This book tells us that *The Kingdom Is at Hand.* Have you ever seen it before?"

"Oh," said the woman as if suddenly catching on, "you're book salesmen!"

"No, ma'am," my friend assured her. "I want to leave this book with you so that you can use it as an aid in studying the Scriptures. You have a Bible?"

"Of course I have a Bible."

"This book will help you understand the Bible in the light of today's happenings. Now here on page 321 . . ." He opened the book deftly to a picture of the Horsemen of the Apocalypse breaking through a calendar page marked OCTOBER, 1914. "This shows that 1914 was the beginning of the end of the age. And here on page 177 is the story of the rise and fall of Satan's kingdom. This explains how we who are living today fit into God's plan and how the Theocracy has again been established."

"I'm not interested in books."

"It is more than a book, ma'am; it's a guide to salvation. I want you to have it. If you contribute as little as a quarter, I will leave it with you."

He held out the book to her. "Wouldn't you like it?" he asked again.

"No. I go to church. I've got a Bible. I read it sometimes. Thank you just the same."

She withdrew defensively.

"Just a moment," said the Witness, digging into his cold, leather satchel. "I have a little pamphlet here I want to give you. It is free. It is called, as you see, *A Commander to the Peoples.* You know how the nations are trying to create a league for peace. You may have heard of the United Nations Organization. This little booklet explains how all of that was prophesied in the Bible and it tells whether it is going to work or not."

"Oh, well," the woman sighed. "But I'm not one for taking things just because they are free."

"That's all right," replied the Witness, putting the pamphlet into her hands. "Please read it. Maybe you will want to learn more about these things or about Jehovah's Witnesses some other time. Good day and thank you."

"Your salesmanship!" I deplored as we moved on. "You could have sold her easily."

"We don't sell," he protested.

"But you do want to place books. And this transcription is entirely too long for a cold morning. Your own presentation would be much better."

"You think so? Well, I don't know. The Society suggests this method and, no doubt, it is the way God would have us do it."

But the next visit supported my argument. The doorbell was answered by a bombastic "Come in!" shouted above the blare of a radio. Eager to soak up some warmth, we hurried in. Our host made no effort to change his comfortable sprawl amid the scattered sections of the Sunday edition. Peeping at us from over the comics, he asked, "What's cookin', boys?"

"I am one of Jehovah's Witnesses and have a timely and important message for you——" began my friend in his usual resolute manner.

"Jehovah's Witnesses!" guffawed the man. "Sorry, fellows, the wife's already gone to church with the whole family."

"Well, now," persisted my partner, "if you'll give us a few minutes of your time, I think I can show you that this concerns you personally. We have the message here on a recording and if you will turn down the radio——"

Again he was interrupted; again I was convinced the Society's prescribed approach should be improved. But I was learning that it was contrary to Witness policy to show any interest in personal inclinations or to play up to the idiosyncracies of the prospects. We left our host content in his own interpretation of "the Sabbath was made for man."

The next man thought I was trying to sell him the phonograph. The Witness hastened to correct the misconception, but he was interrupted with "Oh, you just want to sell me the record! Well, we don't have a phonograph, so we don't have no way to play it!"

At several places my colleague's opening line brought the door shut with a bang. He took it all in stride, and I, like a faithful votary, stooged along.

Once, when no one answered the front door, my friend said he was sure someone was stirring, and we went around to the back. He was not in the habit of casing the house, but this time we did. Our pounding on the storm door sounded malicious. It really wasn't. It was just the rumble of Armageddon. It interrupted a young woman's shampooing, and she came to the door, wrapping a towel around her head.

"I'm not in the market for anything," she warned.

"I am one of Jehovah's Witnesses——" began my companion.

"Is that so! Well, I'm a Catholic!" and the storm door shook the house.

I detected something akin to pain in the Witness' face as we walked away. But immediately he bolstered up his convictions with gleanings from the Theocratic mill.

"Since the time of Abel, religionists have persecuted those who obey God's commandments. This proves that religion is of the Devil. Religionists killed Jesus. I think the worst thing in the world is a political-religious organization."

"Isn't it possible to be a member in good standing in a Protestant or a Catholic church and also be a Jehovah's Witness?" I asked.

"No, a person who is a Jehovah's Witness is not one who has joined an organization, but one who has made a contract with God to carry out His will. If a person is to be a real Witness, he must separate himself from the rest of the world and preach to the people about Jehovah God."

"Must a person be a Jehovah's Witness in order to inherit the earth and enjoy eternal life after the end of the age?"

"That is the way I would put it," my friend nodded. "The fruits of the kingdom are reserved for the true Witnesses of Jehovah."

"Do you mean one must be a Witness according to the Watchtower Bible and Tract Society?"

"According to the belief and teaching of the Society, yes. The Society itself is merely the legal instrument of Jehovah's Witnesses. That will be dissolved, perhaps, after Armageddon. Or," he added thoughtfully, "Jehovah God may want it to continue to print His truth. According to Revelation 20, at the end of the thousand years, Satan will be released for a final test before he and all those on his side will be annihilated. After that the earth will be given over to God."

There was no breaking through the stronghold of Scripture

in which he stood encased. There was no possibility of discouraging him as we continued our cold, unwelcome trek from door to door.

"All a person can do in this work is to find those whose hearts Jehovah God has already touched," he said, as if to himself.

That was it. That is what impelled him to go to every door. That is why he could never be discouraged. He saw life as a cosmic drama which Jehovah God had written and staged. In these closing scenes, he, the Witness, was the protagonist, and in this denouement everything was proceeding in keeping with the script.

Unwilling to believe that no one was concerned enough about Armageddon to invest a quarter, I asked if I might do the talking at the next place.

The house was a small, salt-box type with a broken-down porch. The storm door hung by a loose hinge. When the young, poorly dressed woman opened it, she steadied it with one hand while the other kept a dirty youngster of five from running into the cold.

"Good morning!" I began. "We are ministers and if you will let us come in for a moment——"

She stood aside invitingly. But as we entered, she asked, "What kind of ministers?"

"Jehovah's Witnesses," my friend acknowledged.

For a moment the woman stood with her back against the door. "You don't even believe in saluting the flag, do you?" she accused.

"That's right," nodded the Witness. "We don't."

"Why not?" she asked without moving.

An almost imperceptible shift of her eyes drew my attention to a photograph set on a shelf near the oil-burning stove. It was the picture of a man in uniform. Behind it were stuck the dried palm branches typical of Catholic homes. A black ribbon hung alongside.

"We consider the flag a symbol," Jehovah's Witness was saying. "We consider it an image of what it represents. We are taught in Exodus 20 not to bow down to images or worship them. Saluting the flag is a ceremony which to us would be the same as worship."

"So you don't love the flag?" the woman retorted in an even tone.

"We respect it," answered the Witness. "We have it in most of our Kingdom Halls."

"I didn't know that," she said. "I thought you hated the government."

"I wouldn't say that," he went on in his confident way. "We simply love Jehovah God's government more. We do not believe that any government on earth is doing Jehovah's will."

"But you don't help protect the United States even though it is always protecting you."

"We ask nothing of the United States. All the rights we enjoy are those given us under God's Theocracy. Jehovah's Witnesses do not vote because that would be taking part in the affairs of a worldly government. We will have no part in war because wars among worldly governments can settle nothing. We believe there will always be wars until Armageddon. We will fight in that battle for Jehovah God. But we go to prison rather than take part where men of this world are fighting for power."

The young mother sat down in a straight-backed chair and lifted her son to her lap. "I heard that you don't believe in helping the government in its drive for the poor people of Europe."

"That's right," the Witness admitted without shame. "We have our own representatives in Europe through whom we work. We do not trust worldly governments, but we trust those who belong to the Theocracy."

He was again stating the inviolable beliefs of the Society. It reminded me of the confident, absolute way of priests in the Roman Catholic Church. Perhaps the unshakable testimony of the Witness impressed this woman because of its likeness to the authority of her parochial background.

"We have a record we would like you to hear," my comrade went on, forgetting that he had agreed that I should do the talking.

The woman made room for the phonograph on the table, and I put the needle down on Judge Rutherford. She listened calmly, yet with a seemingly intense desire to extract a personal message from the confusing onrush of ideas.

"I don't understand all of it," she admitted in reply to the stock inquiry at the end of the record, "but he said one thing that really struck me."

"What was that?" I asked.

"He said the world would never get any better, and that is the way it looks unless something unusual happens," she reviewed thoughtfully. "I don't know what it will be, but people can't go on giving everything they have—and then seeing things just as bad as they always were. Everybody says that religion is the answer, but which religion do they mean?"

Her words justified the place that Jehovah's Witnesses hold in the social sweep of American religions. They called up a multitude of overcast souls that I had encountered along many religious bypaths. Caught in the futility of social systems that consistently fall short of idyllic goals, they are still doggedly looking for "the way." Suddenly the phonographic approach which I had condemned, the door-to-door canvass that I had checked off as wasted time, the stereotyped Witness himself, took on significance.

"This will help you to understand contemporary happenings in the light of prophecy," he was saying as he again presented *The Kingdom Is at Hand*. For the first time that morning the book changed hands.

"You have a Bible?" he asked.

"Yes."

"Do you read it?"

"I have lately," she said, paging through the book.

"There is only one true way to read it," said the stolid salesman of Jehovah's goods, "and that is with the help of Watchtower publications——"

She quietly interrupted by handing him a dollar bill. He gave her back seventy-five cents.

"Thank you for your contribution," he acknowledged. "If you find anything that is not perfectly clear, I will be glad to come back."

"I was just thinking," she reflected quietly, her eyes wandering over to the photograph. "What do you teach about the dead?"

"The righteous dead will be resurrected to enjoy the perfect earth. We believe that some of the true Witnesses will return to earth before Armageddon. In order to prove to this unbelieving generation that there are people in the world who look for the return of these faithful men, the Society maintains a mansion, Beth-Sarim, to which the heroes of Jehovah God may come whenever they return to earth. Beth-Sarim is located at San Diego. The deed is made out to such true Witnesses as Abel, Noah, and Abraham. The wicked dead will be resurrected for righteous judgment after the millennium."

With this irrevocable pronouncement the Witness was ready for his exit. He had enacted his part sincerely and the rest was in "the hands of Jehovah God."

After a few more stops, we made our way to a small tearoom. The Sunday crowds were just leaving, but the wife of the Witness was waiting for us at a table in the corner.

"Did you have a good morning?" I asked.

"A very good morning," she admitted in a tired manner. Turning to her husband, she went on, "I placed two books and made arrangements for a home study."

"Did you run into any bad receptions?" I asked.

She smiled bravely. "People meet us as they really are. Because we're Jehovah's Witnesses they seem to have no regard for our feelings."

I caught a glimpse of something amazingly human behind the confident stronghold of Witness conviction. Her husband, also sensing her moment of faltering, was ready with a Scripture text. He touched her hand awkwardly, with a reassuring caress. " 'Fear not, little flock,' " he quoted; " 'for it is your Father's good pleasure——' "

" 'To give you the Kingdom,' " she finished.

CHAPTER III

THE FOURSQUARE GOSPEL

📖

I HAD seen Angelus Temple filled to capacity many times: at Wednesday night prayer meetings and tarrying services, Thursday night baptizings, Saturday night healing services, Sunday night shows—sensational services that people said provided the best entertainment in Los Angeles. Naturally, such a religious powerhouse was more than an ordinary flag stop on my itinerary. In fact, my stopovers at the Temple had been remarkably consistent. But I had never seen and would never again see a service like today's. Five thousand five hundred people sat around me, jam-packed into auditoriums that strained to hold Foursquaredom's record attendance. Five to ten thousand more ranged the streets, flooded Echo Park, blocked traffic, covered the roofs of neighborhood houses, leaned out of office windows, sat in cars that barricaded streets. From the radio towers above the Temple, KFSG was carrying the service to other thousands beyond the physical range of human voice. It was Sister's most colossal audience. Cameramen and reporters commanded the scenes. For a little while a world at war was forgotten. America's boom city, America's Hollywood, together with America's crossroads, paused to listen. And, oddly, at this greatest of all Angelus Temple services Sister would not speak.

The great organ was playing. Someone near me whispered, "It's a song *she* wrote. Sister. It's 'Why Are They Whipping My Jesus?'" Around me people touched kerchiefs to their eyes. The hundred choir members gripped their hymnals. In typical Foursquare fashion they sat in a V-shape, flanking an improvised grotto. Above it was a gigantic cross and corpus with the three Marys, lonely and forsaken, standing near by. Within the cavernous grotto opening I could see a huge ansate cross of fresh-cut roses, perhaps thirty feet high. Touching this was a shield of white roses on which red roses spelled *Our Commander.* An open Bible of white carnations—floral gates ajar, large enough for a person to walk through—a vacant chair of white asters—a clock of flowers with the hands pointing to 11:15—a globe of white chrysanthemums— horseshoes, wheels, anchors, hearts, harps, a replica of the Foursquare Temple, carpets, flags, lighthouses—all of flowers —a hundred thousand dollars' worth of flowers. My imagination staggered under this compound of wonders encircling the auditorium and covering part of the balconies overhead. Yet neither the beauty nor the fragrance of this memorial pageantry—nor the policemen standing at subdued attention— nor the orchestra in its pit—nor "Why Are They Whipping My Jesus?" could for long lure my gaze from the impressive open casket in front of the grotto.

There Sister lay, half concealed from where I sat. Suddenly a fierce thought swept my mind. What about the well-affirmed nexus that existed between Sister and everything dramatic? Was this just another dramatized sermon? What if Sister Mc-

Pherson plans to—? It was a ghastly yet half-hopeful thought, and with it came a vivid remembrance of the first sermon I had heard within these walls.

That night Sister gave us "The Green Light Is On." The opening remarks were the deafening roar of a motorcycle speeding down the ramp with the cutout open. The world's greatest evangelist sat in the saddle dressed as a speed cop. She rode expertly. No flowers then to bar her way. No sad-eyed, sobbing worshipers that night. It was Sister's heyday. She drove recklessly to the front of the auditorium, slammed on the brakes, blew a screech on a police whistle, raised a white-gloved hand to the congregation, and shouted: "Stop! You're speeding to hell!"

With the cutout open—that is how Sister went through life. Into these somber settings of her funeral, the spell of her sensational ministry crept in from everywhere. There where the roses stood—there where Sister lay—many a theatrical thriller had brought its message to the ears and hearts of a hurrying world.

Gradually I became insensitive to the pulsating sorrow that surrounded me. The floral tributes diffused into a carrousel. The organ music faded into the lively discordant honking of a calliophone. I saw this same auditorium draped in canvas like a circus tent, and I heard the hoarse cries of a barker. It was Sister Aimee preaching her sermon, "The Merry-Go-Round Broke Down." The merry-go-round was civilization. Every once in a while it broke down and all the riders tumbled off. This happened at the beginning of the Christian era. To get things started, Jesus came. But civilization stripped its gears again in the sixteenth century, and Luther appeared as the *deus ex machina.* And when the good old merry-go-round of life crashed for the last time in the roaring twenties, who should enter as the mechanic and fixer-upper but Sister herself?

The next Sunday the circus moved out and a gridiron was set up. Sister, in football togs, carried the ball of the Foursquare Gospel for a touchdown. Jesus ran interference.

Who else around me was thinking back on these theatricals—wondering, analyzing, evaluating? I was ready to admit that great acting had always been a counterpart of great preaching. Was Sister's method so different from that employed by other illustrious spiritual giants? Luther, disguised as a knight, went about the countryside finding out what people were thinking about him. He threw inkwells at the Devil and dramatically burned the Pope's edict in the courtyard square. Wesley's fervid preaching once inspired a placid Quaker to leap to his feet and cry, "Thou art the Son of the living God." Whitefield wept when he preached and his audience wept with him. Under the power of Moody's message, listeners fell prostrate to the ground. But the clerics of the traditional churches had never extended their histrionic enterprising as far as Sister carried hers. She capitalized on what had already taken hold of the American mind. She kept her finger on the public pulse. She took the popular trappings of the secular world and draped them around the cross. To some this was disgusting. They called it exhibitionism and burlesque. To others it was redemptive. For them, power lingered behind the vaudevillian performances—the merry-go-round and the motorcycle were a part of the renowned and classical technique of this great religious leader of our time.

A voice broke into my reverie. An elderly man, half hidden by the wall of flowers, was saying, "We are here to commemorate the stepping up of a country girl into God's hall of fame. Along with Huss, Wycliffe, Savonarola, Luther, Wesley, Whitefield, Knox, and Moody, Aimee Semple McPherson rightfully takes her place with the greatest of spiritual leaders!"

He paused for a response of amens and trembling cries of "Oh, Sister!" and "Oh, Jesus!"

"In Ingersoll, Ontario, Canada," the speaker continued, "a young, spirited high-school girl——"

We were already filling in the details . . . the Kennedy farm . . . Aimee, pretty, vivacious, glowing with a healthy passion and zest for life, heart set on a stage career. Ma Kennedy thought it was wonderful how her daughter could play-act both on and off the stage. She had a rare ability for personalizing every event, and a lively eloquence gave to everything she said embroidery and high coloring. These girlhood propensities were the blueprint for Sister's future technique, the recognized symptoms of her charm and human appeal.

Was it her love for the romantic—the charm of the dramatic—that took her to her first evangelistic meeting? She had always said that she went for a lark. But when the handsome, six-foot apostle of the good tidings opened the Bible, when he preached on the text, "Repent and be baptized," she listened intently. Robert Semple spoke with deep conviction. Aimee watched him with a youthful critical sense. Mr. Semple was also an actor, but his was not a studied role. He was "coached and directed by the Spirit." The drama in which he was the protagonist was the greatest to be enacted on any stage—it was man meeting God.

That night revival fires lighted up the countryside. Believers "prayed through" to the spiritual baptism that Mr. Semple preached. Aimee, huddled in the family sleigh on the way home, was silent and thoughtful. Semple's exhortations ran counter to the worldly allurement of the theater. For days she "struggled against conviction." At night she lay looking up at the dark ceiling of her room, seeing the young evangelist, hearing him again through the vivid impression of that first sermon, wondering if she could "believe and be baptized."

A few days later she drove home from school alone. As the old horse plodded through Ingersoll's winter, Aimee was thinking, arguing, praying in an awkward kind of way. Finally, far out on the country road, with nothing between her thoughts and God but snow-blanketed fields and winter skies, she suddenly dropped the reins, threw up her hands and cried, "God be merciful to me a sinner!"

That sleigh-ride conversion was followed by a greater experience, the "baptism of the Holy Spirit." One morning at the home of a friend she rose early "to tarry for the blessing." An hour later the household was awakened by hysterical laughing and weeping. Aimee was "receiving the Spirit." They knew because they had seen the same light on the faces of other converts. Somehow, it burned brighter as this young girl testified ecstatically of an onrush of heavenly rapture and a feeling of destiny.

A few months later, more startling news about Aimee Kennedy was noised about among the enthusiastic religionists of Ingersoll. One night she was helping a friend whose children were seriously ill. Robert Semple came to pray for them. Under the calm, confident sound of his voice as he prayed, the children fell asleep. He led Aimee into an adjoining room. A geography book lay on a table. Robert opened it. He put his finger on Hong Kong.

"Here," he said, "is where the Lord is calling me."

In the lamplight their eyes met.

"Since that day in the sleigh," she said, "I, too, have felt the call of God. Many times I have found myself singing, 'I'll go where you want me to go, dear Lord, over mountain or plain or sea——' "

Robert was laughing. He took her arms.

"Will you go? Will you marry me, Aimee?"

Around me in Angelus Temple, the listeners nodded understandingly. The elderly man, reciting Sister's memoirs, was saying, "She married the one who led her to Christ and accompanied him as a missionary to China." For the faithful, the story was as familiar and as much a part of their belief as Scripture. They had often heard it in Aimee's characteristically romantic style.

"Life began for me when I headed for China with Robert Semple. It was tremendously thrilling when we stepped aboard that ship in Toronto. The first ground swell set us rocking so furiously that I thought the world would turn completely over. Up, up, up we went! Then down, down, down! I would not have been surprised if we had gone straight down to Davy Jones's locker. But a special Providence watched and guided and cared. I realized this more than ever as we passed through the Holy Land. Oh, the footprints of faith on those Judean sands! Footprints of Jesus! Footprints of His faithful followers! And Robert said they were just plain folks like us."

But Sister McPherson spent only one year with Robert Semple before his death on the mission field. Sentimentalists in the auditorium must have remembered how Sister had recalled 'and described this tragic event. "Coolies came and laid him on a litter. They put the poles on their shoulders and swung rhythmically along the long trail that wound up the hill to the sanitarium. I followed, praying. But God in His infinite wisdom called him. I will never forget that night. A storm burst upon us from the yellow waste of the China Sea. The foamy waters clawed at the high gray crags. The wind wailed, the rain beat madly against the windows. All the elements were struggling with me in the anguish of that dark night when Robert died. I was like an ivy vine which had clung to a good stout wall. Now the wall was gone and I was just a crumpled heap on the ground."

When Robert's child was born a month after his death, Mrs. Semple named her Roberta Star, because "God had given a star of hope in the night of dark despair."

"Her unswerving devotion," the speaker continued, "caused her to evangelize throughout this entire country, enduring incredible hardships and misunderstandings, yet tenaciously persevering, until she packed the greatest tents and auditoriums in the country——"

His words spun scenes from Sister's career as graphically as though the grotto's flower-filled proscenium were a movie screen. Mrs. Semple returned from China with nothing in the world but a babe in arms. She preached on shipboard and a freewill offering from the passengers enabled her to get back east. Her parents tried in vain to persuade her that Robert's passing meant the end of her ministry. Then the scene changed to a battered old car with a megaphone in the back seat. There were streamers on the side that said, "I'm on my way to the revival service! R. U.?" Sister was at the wheel. She preached wherever people would listen or wherever a street corner could be converted into a pulpit. Her following grew. Soon she had a tent of her own—a big tent and good benches.

One night a windstorm beat against the tent, threatening to break up the meeting. Men looked up helplessly. Women screamed as a furious blast ripped at the canvas. Sister sprang to the platform, raised a commanding hand, lifted her voice above the roar of the storm and shouted to the reeling tent, "Stay where you are in the name of Jesus!" It stayed—caught on a nail.

Often during these services, Mrs. Semple would rush from the pulpit to see if little Roberta were all right, then dash back to "call the lost to penance" and to "pray them through to victory." She was driving toward the heights as America's greatest evangelist when suddenly the battered old car came to an abrupt stop in Florida. Sister was lonely and she married Harold McPherson, a groceryman. An understandable proviso went with the nuptials: if ever she felt the "call of the Spirit" she must be permitted to resume her evangelistic work.

Varying scenes now flashed across my imaginary screen. Mrs. McPherson grew ill, restless under the domesticity of this second marriage. A son, Rolf, was born. Sister had great affection for him, but he seemed only to draw her back to all that Robert Semple had meant to her. Again the "command to preach" came as a persistent, deafening call. Mr. McPherson balked. What was this talk about "going where the Spirit willed, seeking the lost the wide world over, leaving all to follow the Lord?" In the spiritual struggle that followed, Mrs. McPherson's health broke. She was hurried to the hospital where doctors consigned her to what she called the "death room."

"It was there that I came straight up against complete service to God or the grave," she had always avowed. "But when I cried to the Lord and said, 'I'll go where You want me to go,' I walked from that death room with victory."

Never again would anyone or anything come between her and her high destiny!

Twenty-two thousand Americans believe that that destiny was the triumphal march of the Foursquare Gospel. Sister landed in Los Angeles in 1920 at the end of a "transcontinental gospel auto tour." When the largest halls became too small for the mammoth crowds, she began gazing longingly at a weedy lot looking out upon Echo Park. She knelt down beside the FOR SALE sign and talked it over with Jesus. She rose from that prayer, jerked down the sign and started clearing away the weeds with her own hands.

Mrs. McPherson called the next three years sublime because of the constant feeling of achievement they held for her. She was "like a homing pigeon that brings twigs for the home nest one by one and weaves them in, then speeds away to get another." She told Foursquare friends in San Diego and Sydney, in Wichita and Winnipeg, London and Los Angeles about "the staccato song of the riveting hammers, welding steel to steel; the clatter of the hungry open-mouthed cement mixers whirring round to make the walls." She told how the construction elevators were carrying their burdens ever nearer the sky. She made them see the broad arches through which the whole lost world might enter to find Jesus.

The result: money poured in from every country and city that Sister had visited in her evangelistic barnstorming—one and a half million dollars before the job was finished.

On January 1, 1923, a thousand-voice choir sang "Open the Gates of the Temple" and Angelus Temple flung open its crystal-glass doors. The converted high-school actress had reached stardom in the service of the King. From now on, she would sweep gracefully to her pulpit stage in a white costume covered by a blue and gold cloak. When she greeted the crowd she flung out her arms, and the sheer white material that draped her shapely body made the sign of the cross. She always carried her white Bible and had a habit of hugging it to her breast. Her words and manners were unpredictable, but the famous McPherson smile was always there.

Little did the public realize how hard this beautiful woman worked. She personally organized and managed her congregation as if it were a great business enterprise. Usually she preached six days a week, often twice a day, catapulting every phrase with tremendous force. Songs, articles, books, and religious operas appeared under her name. Whenever the curtain opened upon the grassy banks of the baptismal pool with its palms and flowers, Sister stood waist-deep in the rippling waters. Disregarding convention, she sometimes immersed her candidates two and three at a time. At healing and tarrying services her invincible energies were again exhibited. Sometimes her prayer would be a loud, fierce cry; sometimes a whisper low and emotional, as though she were enticing the

Spirit to do her will. Sometimes she would clasp a weeping convert in her arms.

And now the eulogist was concluding, "Many will rise up to call her blessed." But if I were to be a faithful investigator of faiths, I knew that I must also consider the thousands who would say, "She was a clever girl."

While the vast religious empire which she had founded continues to generate spiritual and emotional current for "full-gospel" followers, the scandals surrounding her name will become legends to be told and retold.

There was a hasty marriage in 1931 to David L. Hutton, a baritone in the Angelus choir, that ended in a divorce in less than four months. There was a report of "quite an exhibition" at a marathon dance. Sister was accused of tossing money onto the dance floor and booing the couples when they began sagging on their feet. There was a lawsuit with her associate pastor, Rheba Crawford Splivalo, who charged that Sister had called her a "Jezebel." Sister's name was linked with that of Homer Rodeheaver, former song leader for the late Billy Sunday. There was a lawsuit with Ma Kennedy, who claimed that her daughter struck her.

But, because of the publicity given it, the kidnaping incident caused more people to doubt Sister's fidelity than any other event. It occurred May 18, 1926, on the beach at Ocean Park. Sister disappeared while her secretary was making a phone call. Soon the frantic world of Angelus Temple gathered at the scene. While sirens screeched and policemen struggled to keep the crowds in hand, Foursquare followers staged a prayer meeting. Divers sounded the deep ocean drop-offs. The faithful dug their knees into the sands. Two men lost their lives dragging for Sister's body. Supplicants expected to see her walking in on the waves.

For four weeks American and European newspapers head-lined the mysterious disappearance of the world's leading evan-gelist. Then a story filtered down from Carmel-by-the-Sea. It was a bizarre account of how a clandestine couple had occu-pied a love nest there for some days. Someone said the woman was Mrs. McPherson and the man Kenneth C. Ormiston, radio operator of KFSG. Those who took the story for true said it would be the death blow to Sister and her Foursquare faith. But at Angelus Temple the faithful remained earnest in prayer. They resolutely closed their ears and their hearts to any such "newspaper talk," and continued to batter God's gates for her return. They vowed she would come back and tell them the truth about all that had happened. She did.

At Agua Prieta, Mexico, Sister announced to the world that she had been kidnaped while relaxing on Ocean Park beach. A man and woman had approached her. The woman was in tears; her child was dying. Wouldn't Sister come and pray? Wouldn't Sister call down the power of Jesus the Great Phy-sician? Sister went with this couple to their car. They opened the rear door saying that the sick child was there. Suddenly the evangelist was pushed from behind and landed helpless and struggling on the floor. The man's hand went to her face and something wet and sticky was pressed against her. Slowly she lost consciousness. Then there was a shack in the desert, torture with a burning cigar, a darkened room, a cheap iron bed on which she slept bound hand and foot, a tussle with strong men, a matching of wits with an old hag, and finally her escape by sawing off her shackles on the ragged edge of a large tin can!

Unbelievers said it was a hoax. How about the Carmel incident, they wanted to know? They said that Sister's story had all the features of a Hollywood quickie and the thrills of an old-time Western. But faithful followers took their stand with Sister. Events only strengthened their faith. All great religious leaders, they recalled, had been maligned and persecuted and misunderstood. Why should Sister expect less from the Devil's advocates? When a man finds the truth, they contended, he must expect ridicule and temptation. But what about the woman at Carmel? That was the Devil's work. Somebody masqueraded as Sister.

But scandal persisted. In 1933 Mrs. McPherson left for a year's cruise to recover from harassing months divided between court battles and sickbed. Know-alls predicted that she would "never rule her throne again." However, when here and there a faint heart lamented that Sister had "lost her power with God," a cloud of witnesses arose to defend her. She was sick. The Devil had given her a nasty round. Somehow all that was questionable was purified, and the tradition was gradually immortalized that she was ordained of God to found the International Church of the Foursquare Gospel.

Many of the worst critics reluctantly admitted that she embodied more than mere human pyrotechnics. The desperate, the lost, the sick, the neurotic, the spiritual gypsies found an answer to their religious groping in the person of this woman who had marvelously extricated herself from the "Devil's machinations." Hollywood stars were numbered among her converts. A judge in Rochester said, "I want to commend the ministry of this noble woman who is following closer in the footsteps of that Holiest One than anyone I know." Ministers across the country were impressed. A Presbyterian cleric testified that Denver had been shaken until thousands appeared to be in a haze of wonderment. An Episcopal rector in Berkeley admitted that "my life and ministry were stimulated and blessed for the service of the Master by the McPherson revival in Oakland." A Baptist minister in Chicago compared the throngs of hungry church members flocking to hear Sister with the multitudes who sought truth from the Master and His disciples. Whenever she returned from a missionary tour, crowds mobbed her at the Los Angeles station. Generous admirers carpeted her path with flowers. Their veneration for her was as strong as that of any primitive tribe passionately devoted to their harvest queen.

Thousands who now sat at Sister's funeral in reverent silence had found voluble expression for their grief when the news of her death fell like a thunderclap on Angelus Temple. Throughout the vast church, sorrow and bewilderment touched every worshiper and employee. They sang. They shouted. They prayed. Classes in the L.I.F.E Bible School Building were halted for mourning. In offices, in the Prayer Tower, in the commissary—everywhere people hovered, weeping quietly. One woman committed her grief in a broken cry but said, "He raised Lazarus and He'll raise Sister, too!" "Jesus, Jesus, Jesus," wailed another, "bring her back!" Outside the Temple mobs of curious began to gather, and crowds of believers hurried inside to join the growing multitude that came to mourn and pray or to sit in confused fashion. Sister was dead. She had flown to

Oakland, California, on September 26, 1944, for a series of revival services. Always the showman, she rode from her hotel to the auditorium in a horse-drawn carriage. Ten thousand people were waiting to greet her, waiting to hear her relate "The Story of My Life."

The last chapter in that spectacular story was concluded at 11:15 the following morning. Her son Rolf found her in her hotel room at 10:30 unconscious and breathing heavily. Scattered about the floor were empty sleeping capsules. Doctors reported that they believed death was caused by a heart attack, but added that the evangelist might also have taken too much of the sleeping compound. Followers explained that Sister "had not been well for three years; she had worn herself out for God."

The body had lain in state until today, October 9, 1944, Sister's fifty-fourth birthday. For nearly a week a thousand people had passed by her bier every hour.

Now the service was ending and Rolf McPherson arose to speak. "I feel I have the greatest heritage in all the world," he said quietly, "in having the mother I did. As you know she has asked that I carry on her work. I want to pledge my life in a greater way than ever before to the Lord. I want you to join today in a consecration service. Mother has expressed she would like a consecration service at the close of her funeral; that people would stand for God who had never stood before, and that those who have stood once will stand again. Will you all join with me, pledging your lives to God in a greater way?"

Around me the great throng in Angelus Temple came to its feet to stand in silent prayer. Then, in a ground swell of feeling that lifted and shook Angelus with the strength of a new revival, they sang "When the Roll Is Called Up Yonder."

Dr. Watson B. Teaford of the Angelus staff stepped forward. "In a sermon preached on December 1, 1941," he told us in his strong way, "Sister said, 'If God should call me home before Jesus comes, I don't want anyone to be sad or weeping. I want them to be rejoicing, for it will be my coronation day. And I want the choir and the band to sing and play "When the Saints Go Marching In." What a glorious day that will be when the saints go marching in!' "

The choirs, the thousands within and outside the Temple sang this song. The band and the great organ played it. They sang it as Mrs. McPherson had never heard it sung, and there were those who believed that at this very moment she must be meeting Jesus.

> "When the saints go marching in,
> When the saints go marching in,
> Oh, Lord, I want to be in that number,
> When the saints go marching in."

I stood outside Angelus Temple where the procession was forming. The cordon of motorcycle police broke through the tightly packed crowds. The sun shone down on Echo Park. A line of nearly a thousand cars accompanied the body of Aimee Semple McPherson to Forest Lawn. Here, where many a movie great had been laid to rest, where Hollywood interments were a commonplace, nothing like the burial of Sister had ever been seen. The papers would report that the bronze casket weighed twelve hundred pounds. They would say that it took the twelve pallbearers twenty minutes to move it four hundred yards. The acres of flowers were photographed from every angle and a picture of the six-hundred-foot cross of flowers was taken from the air. There were processional arches of American flags and columns of flags of the Foursquare faith. Honor guards were composed of military figures and lowly uniformed workers of Angelus Temple. Roberta, who had married an orchestra director, flew in from New York. Ma Kennedy was at the grave. Rheba Splivalo had returned to say that there was never a greater worker for God than Sister. A thousand ministers of the Foursquare Gospel paid their tearful tribute. The curious stood by impressed. The poor who had always been fed at Angelus were there, the lost who had been spirit-filled, the healed, the faithful—here they were eager to immortalize the Ontario farm girl who loved the Lord. Here they laid the body of Sister Aimee to rest in the marble sarcophagus guarded by two great angels on Sunrise slope.

I turned away with the crowd, feeling the sincere and awful aloneness of Sister's followers. But I was fully convinced that those who had set their hearts on the Angelus highway were surer than ever that theirs was the right road to glory. Sister, like a faithful pilot, had gone before. She, who had given them the Foursquare Gospel, would also prepare a place for them in the Foursquare City.

Across the nation skeptics were predicting that the work would suffer now that the superdramatist of Angelus was gone. No one expected the dignified and reserved son, Rolf, to command the crowds and hold the organization intact. But those who had been backstage ventured a different opinion.

A Sunday evening performance fails to reveal the full scope of the International Church of the Foursquare Gospel. With adept organizational abilities, Aimee Semple McPherson had divided the United States into six districts and placed a field supervisor over each. Four hundred branch churches and sixty foreign mission stations serve as "Lighthouses of International Foursquare Evangelism." This little-known denomination boasts twenty-two thousand members and twelve hundred active ordained ministers. The substantial character of the work is best evidenced in the organizational plan of the mother church, Angelus Temple. Sister McPherson as pastor of this congregation supervised sixty-three departments. In this well-organized religious corporation everything necessary to produce tangible spiritual results was provided. If anyone was by-passed by the Foursquare technique it was definitely not for want of departmentalization. There were jail workers, bedside ministers, and city sisters.

Roaming Angelus Temple, I found a commissary with stores of food and clothing for the needy. In conjunction with it, the salvage department collected and reprocessed articles obtained by donations and outright purchases. A relief kitchen combated the hunger of depression-ridden Los Angeles in the early thirties. An employment service was also set up to meet the emergency. Policemen throughout the city directed destitutes to the Angelus storehouse of material blessings. Staff workers tramped from house to house, dispensing food, clothing, money, and "the Word." World War II saw the Temple equipped with a service center that furnished free food, beds, shaves, shines, and showers to five thousand GI's each month.

As early as 1924 the radio station went up—KFSG—Kall Four Square Gospel. A new complaint reached the Los Angeles Chamber of Commerce, "Aimee is always on the air." The next year a college was founded to train men and women to fill

Foursquare pulpits. It was christened L.I.F.E., a name coined from Lighthouse of International Foursquare Evangelism. Sister held the first class in the Five Hundred Room, but these quarters were inadequate. In 1927 a special building was erected to accommodate the average enrollment of over a thousand. Youth has its opportunity to serve at Angelus in numerous choirs, orchestras, and bands. The international youth organization is the Crusaders' Club with a chapter in each local church. It sponsors about twenty summer camps each year.

Yet more impressive than the organizational pattern was the people's phenomenal devotion to duty. From the corps of altar workers to the quilting department, they knew what was expected of them and accepted the job as a personal responsibility. Sister McPherson's influence was obvious enough, and yet I was sure there must be a higher motivation. Wherever I asked the question—in the sewing room, the bookshop, the administrative office, the classroom—the answer was always the same:

"When Sister built Angelus Temple she built a Prayer Tower. Fourteen thousand prayers go up from it each month. We pray in two-hour shifts twenty-four hours a day."

In the Prayer Tower I found a book containing fifty thousand recorded answers to prayer evoked by the ever-persistent "in Jesus' name." I was to learn that this Name unquestionably went far beyond Foursquaredom's devotion to "our dear Sister." The movement was really not built around Aimee Semple McPherson but around Jesus Christ—Saviour, Baptizer, Healer, Coming King! These are the cornerstones in the Gospel Foursquare. Sister quarried them out of "Ezekiel." It happened one night when she was preaching on the prophet's vision. "Ezekiel saw the face of a man, a lion, an ox, and an eagle." Sister said, "The man is Christ, our Saviour; the lion— why, that's the power of His baptism with the Holy Ghost; the ox, that's Jesus as our Burden Bearer and Healer; the eagle, that's the glorious symbol of His second coming!" Then in a moment of high inspiration, she cried, "Why, folks, it's the Foursquare Gospel!"

And for many it became the end of the search for meaning in religion, the compensation for the indifference of the church at large, engendered fire for the spiritual obsolescence of old faiths grown cold.

Jesus Christ—the Savior. This first tenet in the Foursquare faith conjures up sawdust trails and flapping canvas, the old wooden cross propped against an evangelistic altar, worn-out hymnals, a folding organ, and the creaking planks of an improvised chancel. But souls were also "saved" in the million-dollar Angelus Temple and in municipal auditoriums throughout America. Sister was at her best during altar calls. I watched her in action "on the road" many times. Believing in her, one saw a Pentecostal fire; doubting, one saw a designing actress playing to the gallery. But whether a man doubted or believed he could never deny that she was pre-eminently equipped with personality, energy and spirit.

Frequently, after introducing prominent city officials who were greeted with applause, she would say, "Now, I want you to meet my good friend Jesus! He's my Saviour, folks! Come and make Him yours!" Stirred by a huge choir singing, "Jesus Is Calling" or "Just As I Am" or a livelier gospel hymn, the crowds were softened for the pleading, dramatically earnest altar service. Crying to the lost, calling the penitent, begging cajoling, she dared the worst sinner in the house to "come up and meet Jesus!" I saw them jam the aisles, the hesitant shoved along by the eager, the saved urging the unsaved, the baptized shouting to the seekers. The crowds surging toward the altar often became too large to be counted. More benches were moved in. The lost filled the orchestra pits and overflowed the platforms. Altar workers, local ministers, Foursquare assistants swelled the murmuring, chattering, groaning groups which knelt over the benches, crying, "Save me, Jesus!" "Lord, be merciful!" "God forgive me!" Mrs. McPherson, a white-robed sister of mercy, would catch a penitent in her arms, laughing joyously at his hysterical confession, then kneel down to hug a weeping convert and exclaim, "Pray, brother, pray!" Back on her feet, she would call to the crowd that there was still room. Sometimes she would sing a line with the choir or answer the shriek of a convulsing soul. It was Sister, the reaper for Jesus, bringing in the sheaves!

She set a precedent for her people when she said, "When I go home, I am determined to have such a long comet of souls saved, coming after me, that it will strike like a meteor across the sky!"

Jesus Christ, the Baptizer with the Holy Ghost. It is this second cornerstone that makes the faith of these people dynamic. Sister maintained that without this a church was dead; an individual was powerless. She said it was through the Holy Ghost that the Christian Church started at Jerusalem on the day of Pentecost, and she referred scoffers to the second chapter of the Book of Acts. Her quarrel with the traditional churches of Christendom was that they had become "lifeless," "dead moons shining on," "spiritual cripples," "shackled giants." They had grieved and lost and turned their backs upon the only true and living power of faith: Jesus Christ the Baptizer.

Once at a "Holy Ghost meeting" I saw a well-dressed, businesslike man "receive the Spirit." He was sitting just a few seats from me. Suddenly violent trembling seized him. His muscles contracted. He flung his hands into the air, crying, "God! God!" His convulsed shouting reached Sister, who stood on the platform in her white gown, Bible in hand.

"That's right, brother!" she called. "It *is* God! You can depend on that!"

Her voice was warm and generous. An understanding lilt of laughter seemed to say, "Bless you, brother, I've seen cases like yours all my life and it's always thrilling and wonderful!" Then she ordered, "Let yourself go! You're receiving the baptism of the Holy Spirit!"

Others in the auditorium shouted encouragement: "Go through, brother—let God have His way!"

"God *will* have His way!" Sister corrected. At the sound of her voice, the man's body shook as though he had touched a live wire. He rose to his feet. "Glory!" he shouted. "Glory!" His hands fluttered high in the air. He cried, unabated, but to the initiated it was the sign of victory. Some of the worshipers laughed aloud as the man started his groping, trancelike movement toward the aisle.

"The altar is this way, brother!" Sister called and she extended her hands in a generous invitation. Her voice rose expansively, volubly, but her mastery of this man and hundreds of other shouting converts marked her as a leader of experience and strength.

Temple workers tried to assist the man, but he shook them off. As he moved on, he seemed impelled by an intoxicating freedom from restraint. In a rhythmic, abandoned sort of way he turned his head to the right and left and cried, "Glory! Wonderful! Jesus!"

Then with swift suddenness he began "speaking in tongues," an ecstatical, rapturous chatter "not of this earth." To the believing it is heaven's language, the evidence of the Holy Ghost baptism. An awed hush gripped the congregation. Then Sister took on the role of interpreter, translating the musical chant into English in the cadence and pattern used by "the Spirit." The manifestation was an antiphonal act and continued for perhaps three or four minutes. Exclamations of praise and wonder broke from the listeners when the man finally sank to the floor at the evangelist's feet and lay still.

But only to the believing is this baptism meaningful. To the skeptic it is insane emotionalism, and "speaking in tongues" is stupid gibbering. In spite of these criticisms, I had to admit that such "power-filled" apostles were the actual strength behind the Foursquare movement. One night in Wichita I was riding a streetcar. It was late, after midnight. I was the only passenger. The motorman stood at his controls looking absently ahead at the dark line of tracks. Suddenly I realized that he was singing, had been singing for some time:

> "What shall save us from our sins?
> Nothing but the blood of Jesus!
> What shall make us pure within?
> Nothing but the blood of Jesus!"

I walked up front.

"Pardon me," I said. "Do you go to the Foursquare Church?"

"How did you guess it?" he exclaimed.

"Thought I recognized the Pentecostal spirit," I told him.

"Praise the Lord!" He laughed, suddenly letting the car run itself. "Have you had the baptism?" Then he shook his head. "No. You haven't. I can tell by looking at you." He sighed as he put his hands back on the wheel.

As I left the car he called to me, "There's a revival on now. Better come over, brother!"

Sister's showmanship was overshadowed by the faithful work of the men and women who believed that they had received power for service through Jesus Christ, the Baptizer.

Jesus Christ, the Great Healer. Faith healing had caused many a sufferer to keep his hopeful tryst with Sister. It had made Foursquare services occasions of mystery and blessing. It had filled the corridors of Angelus Temple with the sick and the maimed. Mrs. McPherson's first miracle took place at an evangelistic meeting in a suburb of New York. A young woman, body twisted and limbs crippled with rheumatoid arthritis, walked to the altar on crutches. Sister called upon God. "I had the habit even then of thanking God that what I asked for was already accomplished. I reminded Him of His promises. The prayer of faith *shall* save the sick. I prayed for this girl and left it to the Lord. He didn't fail. He has never failed. I told her to drop the crutches. She looked at me as if to say, 'Dare I?' 'Drop the crutches! God's standing there with you!' She let them fall. Her hand reached out for the chancel rail. 'Walk!' She took a step. Two steps. Her hands clung to the railing. Now she let go. Her body straightened. Her head lifted. She raised her hands and cried, 'Thank God, thank God!'"

This was the beginning of a trail of healing miracles that crisscrossed the nation. Sister McPherson said there was no need preaching Jesus Christ as the Great Healer if it could not be practiced. Her only admonition to those who looked to her for help was, "Where faith is, God is." And where faith was wanting, Sister had it to spare. In Jacksonville, Florida, a man's broken arm was instantly healed. In Iowa a woman arose from her wheel chair and walked away. In San Diego a middle-aged invalid, paralyzed since childhood, stood up and walked. In Los Angeles, a blind girl received her sight.

Healing—miraculous, instantaneous healing—became ineffably linked with the name of Aimee Semple McPherson. In Angelus offices the cures were recorded, but there were many people who discounted the most conclusive demonstrations of divine aid. They said that Sister aroused "hidden energies" in imaginary invalids, used "good psychology," and that her healings were deliberately staged. A Hollywood maid told me that Sister paid her twenty-five dollars to "play the cripple," hobble to the altar on crutches, and then "play cured." However, I encountered too many who testified that they had "been healed" for me to check them all off as frauds, neurotics, or victims of paranoia. They answered my queries with questions of their own. "Has not every true religion had its miracles?" "Shouldn't a person expect and demand miracles of religious leaders?" "Isn't healing what everyone is seeking?"

These devotees, indifferent to all the vicious rumors about

Sister's miracle technique, were confident that it was "healing as in the days of the disciples." If Sister's manner of duplicating the apostles' power was often spectacular, this could also be explained. In a modern age it was necessary to be sensational in order to catch the interest of a speedy world. I was consistently reminded of Mrs. McPherson's classic statement, "I am not the healer. Jesus is. He does the work. He's the Boss. I am only the office girl who opens the door and says, 'Come in. The Great Healer is waiting.'"

Jesus Christ, the Coming King. Sermons on this final cornerstone had always filled Angelus Temple with a chorus of amens, pulsing like an echo from wall to wall. And many times the firm, clear voice of a singer would intone Sister McPherson's musical interpretation:

"Perhaps in the morning, His face I shall see,
   The Redeemer and Saviour of men!
And lo, what a glorious day that will be;
   He's coming! He's coming again!

I know when He's coming 'twill be as a King,
   Forever and ever to reign;
Though watching and waiting for Him I will be;
   He's coming! He's coming again!"

Once I had asked her, "Do you believe in a personal return of Jesus—the sound of the trumpet—the breaking of the skies—clouds of glory and all that?"

"If you don't believe that, brother, you don't believe your Bible!" was the answer. "Someday soon He'll split the eastern skies and catch away His own in the bursting clouds of glory." She looked up at the dome of the Temple where fleecy clouds unfolded against a canopy of blue skies. "That is a constant reminder that He *will* come again!" she concluded with finality.

With the passing of Aimee Semple McPherson, Angelus was removed from sensational headlines and gossip columns, but through these four cornerstones and the superbly integrated organization, her abiding influence remained. They proved impregnable whenever the gospel ranks were jolted. In them Foursquaredom was perpetually sustained. They defied the pessimistic voices that had predicted, "When Aimee goes, the Foursquare movement is done for." On the first anniversary of her death, the administrative office announced a high-powered campaign built around the catchy phrase, "A Medal for Sister." Accompanying the story was the artist's conception of a million-dollar Aimee Semple McPherson Memorial Building designed to front on Glendale Boulevard near Angelus Temple. Stretching backward to Lemoyne Street, it will embrace thirty-two thousand, four hundred square feet within its seven stories. The publicity, with its magnificent descriptive flourishes, mingled practical plans with a Hollywood touch: housing facilities for four hundred students—"relax in California sunshine in the eleven-thousand-dollar patio"; gymnasium and recreational center—"play in a Christian environment"; a cafeteria, library, conservatory of music, and a new home for KFSG. Nothing, apparently, is overlooked in these plans to bring the Foursquare gospel straight into the fold of the major American faiths and to equip it for a new world service. An odd note in the modern and model establishment is a pharmacy, an intrusion into the realm of healing by faith. The announcement also provides a convenient pledge card, and the challenge to join the 100 Club. The names of the first hundred persons to contribute one thousand dollars or more will be engraved on a bronze plaque in the main lobby.

This was in keeping with the McPherson method of money raising which always vexed the leaders of conservative Christendom and charmed the public. The first time I saw the great evangelist at a Kansas City revival, I was amused by the command she gave the corps of strapping ushers who marched up heroically for the collection plates: "Boys, do your stuff!" At Angelus Temple I saw the ingenious innovation called the clothesline collections. Spectators with nothing but loose change felt ill at ease that night because Sister had instructed, "We'll just pin our offerings on for the Lord!" The ushers passed a rope equipped with clothespins over the heads of the worshipers. The frequent announcement, "Put bills into the plates, folks; the jingle of silver makes me nervous," always brought a hearty laugh from her coterie. But these were elementary devices compared to big-time drives for special funds. "Wait till she turns on her personality!" they used to warn. When she turned it on in Denver, a convert wanted to build her a temple there. Detroit meetings saw her moving back and forth across the platform, buoyant as a danseuse, "raising money for God and making Him glad." Calling upon those to stand who would pledge a thousand dollars, she ran down the scale to a single dollar, then passed the plates for the silver so that all could have "a chance in building up the heavenly treasury." Angelus offerings frequently averaged seven thousand dollars a month, special funds skyrocketed to almost any figure Sister named. A Los Angeles story told of a woman who gave thirty thousand dollars because, after her baptism, oil was miraculously discovered on her little plot near Signal Hill. Some said that the more you gave to God via Angelus Temple the more you would receive, but a minister who left the Foursquare staff raised a malicious voice of accusation and called his boss, "A Gospel Gold Digger."

But statistics say Foursquaredom is carrying on. There is a marked increase in fieldworkers, finances, and faith. Average Sunday school attendance in the California district alone is over fifteen thousand. In the year following their leader's death, Foursquare fieldworkers established forty-three new churches. The McPherson extension fund, which was a special account to meet the cost of Aimee's campaigns, has now become a Memorial Extension Fund to build new churches and to open new fields as ministers are ordained. Fifteen hundred of them are actively engaged in the slow, laborious process of changing the common man according to a modified ministry of evangelism. They are ready to admit that there is not one among them who can wield the personal appeal of Sister. There was always a special providence for her, and, for years to come, she will stand above them as the morning star of their faith. For them she was the symbol of a vital religion that brought about the phenomenon of the Christian church. Enlarged photographs, "the living proof of Sister's power," adorn their vestibules and prayer-meeting walls:

STRETCHER DAY AT REVIVAL, MUNICIPAL AUDITORIUM, DENVER.

THOUSANDS BEAT ON DOORS TRYING TO GET INTO ROCHESTER
CONVENTION HALL.

SISTER WINS THE GYPSIES FOR JESUS.

ST. LOUIS COLOSSEUM OVERFLOWS WITH THE GREAT CROWDS.

FIREMEN AND POLICE HOLD BACK CROWDS AT MEMORIAL
HALL, DAYTON.

SISTER BATTLES FOR JESUS IN DALLAS.

SISTER WINS HARD BATTLE IN OLYMPIC THEATRE,
MELBOURNE, AUSTRALIA.

THOUSANDS TURNED AWAY AT FAIRFIELD, IOWA.

The McPherson ministry will prosper and grow even though the last truly great evangelist of the old-time religion is gone. While she lived, her followers were willing to make their lives the filter for all her moods and genius. As one of the district superintendents said in memoriam, "We have lighted our torches from yours and by the grace of God we will carry on faithfully." When all is said and done, that has been the mission of believing people since the start of time.

CHAPTER IV

SPIRITUALISM

STAY away from puppet shows and mediums. Both are of the Devil." This was a major premise in the platform of maternal advice impressed upon me as a child in my strict Christian home. But wherever I went I heard the magic words, "spirits," "voices," "taps," "table lifting." Spiritualism was such an interesting subject in every nook and cranny of society that I ventured clandestine jaunts to spiritualistic circles and made hopeful visits to clairvoyants. All ended in confusion and disgust.

Yet, as my detour off the traditional religious highway led me on, I collided with the fact that 131,105 Americans profess spiritualism as their religion. To me, this was shocking. I had set out to give every man his right of way on the roads that lead to God, but did spiritualism actually lead to God? The early conclusions forced upon me even after I began a serious objective study were negative. After each experience, I was more inclined to accept my mother's sage admonition as common sense if not divine revelation.

I wondered what she would say if she could see me now, standing ready to assist a medium in a spiritualist service in Hollywood! I had entered the church with a party of four just as the Reverend Madam Medium was explaining how she had been accused of trickery the previous Sunday evening because her son had assisted her. Tonight she wanted a stranger from the audience. As I started to sit down, George Storm, the other fellow in my party, propped me up as if to say, "Here's just the man for you, lady." The medium accepted my apparent willingness to stooge for her while I stood glaring at George.

"Go on and help the spirits!" he bantered, again betraying his typically blasé attitude about my sincere research. George was a practical man.

As I walked up the aisle, the situation suddenly took on a providential twist. Wasn't this an opportunity for me to test the veridicality of mental phenomena? Perhaps my interest had always been too impersonal.

I stepped to the platform.

"You'll make a good assistant," beamed the medium, taking my hand.

She then announced that the meeting would be devoted to reading sealed messages. What—no spirits? Patience, gypsy, patience!

Cards and envelopes were distributed to the hundred or more curious souls in the audience. They were instructed to write questions on the cards and put them into the envelopes, seal, and initial in one corner. This done, the ushers collected them and the minister asked me to blindfold her. I did—with the black cloth she provided. I was sure she could not see. She couldn't; so she asked me to remove the blindfold. She wanted to put a square of cloth over each eye so "no one will possibly doubt my fidelity."

Disillusioned once more, I blindfolded her so she *could* see and stepped back defeatedly. Just another parlor trick. The squares permitted her to see objects close to her body—unless the blindfold were tied completely under her nose, and there must be a law against that, even in California!

Cloth squares! According to "spiritualism," to make sure she couldn't see; according to any book on amateur magic, to make doubly sure she could!

So she read the messages and called the meeting a church service, which is one way of getting around the fortunetelling tax regulation.

Fortunetelling is what it was, and respectable spirits would have no part in it.

The act wore on. Between yawns, I mechanically counted the envelopes still to be read. Suddenly I spied a sprawling "G.S." under the medium's hand. Here was my chance for retribution!

"The name is George Storm," I whispered.

She caught on quickly.

"The name," she said loudly and confidently, "is George Storm!"

You should have seen George! He came up stiff and straight in his chair, glued his eyes on the woman, and listened entranced while she gave him his reading. When the meeting was over, he was among the first to come up and shake her hand.

As we were leaving, I said, "Well, what do you think?"

"Terrific!" he exclaimed. "Terrific! I made an appointment with her for a private reading tomorrow. She's wonderful! I even heard voices!"

When I told him what had actually happened, he gave me an angry glance.

"That's what you say!" he flared. "I know she got the information from the spirits!"

Again I was persuaded that an unscrupulous medium and a credulous gentleman are a fearful and wonderful combination!

Did spiritualism actually lead to God? The question persisted, not because of what I had seen and not seen, but because of the preponderance of great names connected with psychic phenomena and research: James Fenimore Cooper, William Cullen Bryant, Robert Dale Owen, Daniel Webster, Harriet Beecher Stowe, Elizabeth Barrett Browning, Horace Greeley, Elisha Kane.

There were also names of contemporary interest: Sir Oliver Lodge, English physicist and author; E. Lee Howard, D.D., former pastor of historic Congregational Church at Painesville, Ohio; Dr. Ozora S. Davis, president of Chicago Theological Seminary; Sherwood Eddy, world traveler and writer.

The late A. Conan Doyle made the statement that he had approached the subject as a skeptic and emerged a disciple. Hamlin Garland contended that no explanation other than interworld communication would confirm the facts uncovered by his forty years of psychical investigation.

Sir William Crookes, with degrees from at least five English universities, inventor of the Crookes' tube and discoverer of thallium, reported that he had seen manifestations of levitation, had heard accordions play without being touched by human hands, had seen a luminous hand write upon the wall and a medium handle live coals with bare hands. All this he had subjected to scientific tests that proved there were forces at work which could not be explained by any known physical law.

And there was Miller Reese Hutchinson, an associate of Thomas A. Edison, who claimed that when Edison died he knew about it instantly by mental perception and spirit aid. Edison's picture flew from its place on the piano and landed at Hutchinson's feet at the very moment of Edison's death. I was with Hutchinson one summer in the Berkshires when he was trying to get Edison's voice by means of electrical devices.

This impressive "Who's Who" was paralleled by official statistical data. Scattered through urban America were five hundred churches affiliated with eighteen spiritualist bodies. Four of the leading groups were: National Spiritualist Association, Progressive Spiritual Church, General Assembly of Spiritualists, and National Spiritual Alliance of the United States of America. I discovered that the form of worship and the organizational plans in these churches were set in the conventional pattern.

There were sacraments, ceremonies, and confessions of faith. Sunday schools operated along accepted Protestant plans. It was the basic tenet embraced by each denomination that was startling and radical: "Jesus Christ was a medium!" I also heard that every true religion is a result of the "flow of the psychic stream," that spiritual revelation comes only through mediums and that the only interaction between earth and heaven is psychic phenomena. Yet, in none of the churches I visited had I found the psychic demonstrations to validate these claims.

Out of this conflict of interest and hapless search, I took the long step to Lily Dale, New York. Here stood a spiritualistic shrine, the Fox Cottage, which had been moved from Hydesville. Within these lowly, innocent-appearing rooms, American spiritualism had its birth. Here, where worn old boards now feel only the tread of the believing and the curious, there were heard, a hundred years ago, footfalls of the unseen and raps and rumblings not made with human hands. So says spiritualist history.

It attests that on March 31, 1848, Mr. and Mrs. John D. Fox heard uncanny noises and stirrings in these rooms. Sometimes the sounds issued from upstairs, sometimes from the cellar, always they were mysterious. A few nights later, neighbors were called in to verify these inexplicable goings-on. They, too, heard the noises. Former tenants admitted that they had been aware of such sounds but had said nothing because of fear of ridicule. A former maid confessed that she had heard running feet in the buttery. The neighbors continued to meet and listen. Finally the noises were localized in an upstairs room where slept the two Fox daughters, Margaret, fifteen, and Katie, twelve.

This upper room had its veil of mystery which nearly a hundred years had not fully rent in twain. Mr. and Mrs. Fox and Hydesville townsfolk sat in this room and heard the raps obey the commands of the young Fox sisters. When the girls were moved into their parents' bedroom, the raps followed them. Wherever they went the phenomena of noises were their companions. Neither time nor travel could alter this state of things.

In Rochester where the girls went to live with their sister Leah Fox Underhill, the raps were in attendance. At public meetings in Buffalo, Boston, and New York, and on tour through Cleveland, Cincinnati, and St. Louis, Katie and Margaret induced raps, gave messages, stirred up poltergeists; in short, manifested such strong mediumistic talent that they started the fad, science, philosophy, or religion of spiritualism—depending upon your point of view.

The girls were subjected to many tests. In Buffalo their demonstrations were investigated by a self-appointed committee of three doctors—Flint, Lee, Coventry—professors in the Buffalo Medical School. They claimed that when the ankles of the Fox sisters were securely clutched in the sure grip of a scientific fist there were no raps because "the raps were made by the deliberate snapping of the toe joints."

Spiritualistic science maintained that the delicate ebb and flow of psychic power could not be properly judged under such "adverse and trumped-up" conditions. In a test sponsored by the *Boston Courier*, a committee of "the foremost scientists of the time," headed by Professor Benjamin Pierce, attended séances for three consecutive days. The promised final report was never made.

The famous Seybert investigation sponsored by the University of Pennsylvania decided against the reliability of psychical demonstration. "To teach a good Christian lesson," the staff of the Harvard Divinity School expelled student Frederick Willis after submitting him to tests which showed that he had mediumistic tendencies.

Despite these refutations, interest increased and competent people were numbered among a rapidly growing coterie. The first long communication purportedly received from the spirit plane was widely publicized and accepted as the groundwork for a new faith: "Dear friends, you must proclaim these truths to the world. This is the dawning of a new era, and you must not try to conceal it any longer. When you do your duty, God will protect you; and good Spirits will watch over you."

Good spirits or the divination of an unlettered "Poughkeepsie seer" helped fan the spiritistic spark into a conflagration. In 1856, Andrew Jackson Davis analyzed, compiled, and published voluminous findings (thirty-three volumes) that gave weight and dignity to the new revelation. He claimed that *Penetralia*, a catechetical treatment probing the various departments of human existence, was written with spirit aid; it was the direct result of automatic writing and clairaudient perception.

Under this impetus there appeared, within twenty years, six hundred practicing mediums in Cincinnati and a thousand in New York. Spiritualists claim that Abraham Lincoln was a convert, and that a message through a medium moved him to emancipate the slaves.

On October 21, 1888, Margaret threw spiritualistic realms into confusion when she suddenly became a convert to Roman Catholicism and published a personal exposé in the *New York World*. She asserted that spiritualism was a hoax, that she had been deceiving the public and that the raps had indeed been made by snapping the toe joints. She heightened the story by saying that Katie and she had also fooled the Hydesville folk by thumping an apple against the floor under their bed! Although I remembered the credulity of my friend, George Storm, this explanation made the American public appear more gullible than even I wished to admit.

Could a few hundred thousand Americans be fooled by the childish halloweening of two farm girls? If this were true it out-Barnumed Barnum. But that is what Margaret avowed and her statement was called the death blow to spiritualism. Before she died, however, she made another confession on matters spiritistic. She now insisted that an undefiled communication with the spirits was and would ever be the only explanation for what she and Katie and other mediums had demonstrated. The drama behind this story, if not the claim of something beyond the depths of physical forces, certainly justified the preservation of the Fox home at Lily Dale.

When I came from the cottage, Ralph G. Pressing, editor of the *Psychic Observer,* was waiting for me in his office. He had the keen, decisive characteristics of the successful American businessman, and there was an air of confidence and security about everything he did and said. He immediately wanted to know what my general interest in spiritualism was.

"First, its philosophy," I told him, "and second, a hope of seeing demonstrations of psychic phenomena." Then I asked him the question that people were always asking me, "Is spiritualism a religion?"

"Spiritualism a religion?" Pressing echoed in amazement. "Heavens, yes! Why not? If it isn't a religion, what is it?"

I could have said a superstition or something in the realm of magic or a special field of psychic science, but Pressing gave me no opportunity. He was an enthusiast of the type one finds among the disciples of vital faiths everywhere. Didn't I know that the psychic flow had given rise to every great spiritual movement? Had no one ever explained how the true relationship and contact of man with God is through the etheric channels?

"Spiritualism a religion? Say, rather, that every religion is based upon spiritualism! In fact, spiritualism *is* religion, not in

the sense of communication with the dead only, not in believing in raps and table lifting and levitation, but in the true revelation of God through the psychic channel!"

Pressing was telling me that the underlying questions of
man's eternal search were answered in this philosophy. Through
the psychic and medium, we discover the silver cord that binds
us to the creative forces of the universe. Without it we live
estranged from God—orphans, wanderers, lost souls. Man is
etheric as well as physical. He lives in a spectral world and
through spiritualism there is an interplay between this shadowy
realm and man, an interplay which is intelligible, forceful, and
comforting, immense in implication. There were words which
sought to describe this interpenetration of etheric man and the
imponderable source of his being, expressions like "tuning in,"
"contact," "getting the vibrations," "tapping the psychic
stream," "communication," "intimacy with the cosmos."
Through it all ran the conviction that man's ultimate destiny
is oneness with the Spirit who has created him. In short,
spiritualism is man's relation to God, and this has ever been
the primary function and meaning of religion. A common de-
nominator of all great religions is that God is Spirit and they
who worship Him must worship Him in *spirit!*

"So much for the philosophy of the movement," I agreed.
"But what about psychic phenomena?"

Pressing looked at me a moment. "There's an assembly
going on at Chesterfield, Indiana," he said knowingly, and
then went on to assure me that there sincere and scientific development of all phases of mediumistic phenomena in the realm of
truth was being demonstrated.

"You mean," I queried, "fraud is eliminated?"

Pressing was emphatically brief. "Definitely!"

"But, Mr. Pressing," I objected, "I have witnessed so much hocus-pocus and have seen so much cantrip passed off as the real thing——"

"Naturally," Pressing interrupted. "There is fraudulent phenomenon in spiritualism. There are also records of misconduct associated with other religions, and in most professions."

"But you think it is eliminated at Chesterfield? How?"

"In the first place, mediums come to Chesterfield to serve only after an invitation from the official board," he began. "The secretary must already have good reports from the cities in which they have worked. All mediums are on probation; that is, they cannot work on the grounds for the public until they have submitted to the tests of the Examining Committee. This is a committee of five or more competent psychical researchers familiar with the techniques of all phases of mediumship. Test conditions are exacting and varied. Mediums never know what to expect. But they must agree to whatever conditions the Examining Committee proposes, and they must submit to its findings. In some instances, the medium's hands and feet are held. His movements at all times are guarded. The committee must be convinced that he does nothing by normal or mechanical means. The test covers everything. When it comes to the actual levitation part of the psychical demonstration, it is even more thorough. In direct-voice mediumship, each spirit voice is questioned as to its identity, must know its name in full and must be able to carry on an intelligent and convincing conversation. Furthermore, spirit guides are interrogated on many subjects pertaining to the requirements of mediumship and the philosophy of spiritualism."

"What are the tests for materialization?" I asked.

"The medium enters the room clothed in a plain robe. He must submit to an examination of his person. The doors are always locked and all entrances are kept under the closest surveillance. When the spirits appear, they are also questioned. After the Examining Committee has completed its investigation, the medium must go through what is called a 'testing period.' Even though he does pass the tests, he must spend at least one season at the camp so that officials can be assured that he will serve the public satisfactorily. In the final analysis, the public tests the medium."

"How about a date, Mr. Pressing—at Chesterfield!"

"Can you make it on the twenty-sixth? Some of the best mediums in the United States will be there. If you can stay a week, I believe all your questions about our philosophy will be answered and your desire for demonstrations will be satisfied."

On August 26 I drove into Chesterfield, Indiana, and proceeded immediately to the spiritualist camp adjoining the town. It is called a city of peace, a New Jerusalem, a Great Mecca. Expecting a morbid cloister for communication with the dead, I found to my surprise a bucolic vacationland. Two large hotels and twenty cottages look out upon a grass-carpeted amphitheater and a grotto in a "garden of prayer."

Symbolizing the unbroken tradition of spiritualism, there is a "Trail of Religions." Spiritualists say there is nothing like it in the world. Life-sized busts of Abraham, Buddha, Zoroaster, Mohammed, Lao-tse, Confucius, Vardhamana, Zeus, Osiris, and Jesus suggest that spiritualism is universal in appeal and application. Overlooking the scene, an Indian stands with face uplifted to the invisible heavens of the spirit world.

I registered at the *Sunflower Hotel* and found myself sur-rounded by an astonishing assortment of about two hundred students of spiritualistic science. Young and old, all had some distinctive quality that told me they were not scaled to the pat-tern of the mediums I had met before. The Chesterfield enthu-siasts did not have the gleam of the cults in their eyes. Neither were they the shifty, evasive type which I had found behind curtained rooms in office buildings and homes in metropolitan areas. The hefty double-chinned medium with bulging bosom and a dab of rouge on her sagging cheeks was conspicuously absent. The students at Camp Chesterfield could have passed as delegates at any professional convention.

One whom I met informally at the hotel had been a school superintendent in a suburb of Milwaukee. She was a direct-voice medium, receiving messages through the perception of spirit voices, but her chief interest was in the theology of spiritu-alism. She said she felt that people were losing the deeper meaning and truths of the science because of the spectacular aspect of the phenomena.

"It is the relation of spiritualism to Christianity and the Bible that seems so wonderful to me," she said.

This challenging statement demanded an explanation. The medium eagerly launched into a seemingly endless disquisition pegged on specific Biblical texts quoted with dexterity from Genesis to Revelation.

"How about Matthew 3:16-17?" she insisted with a captious burst of enthusiasm. " 'Lo a voice from heaven, saying, This is my beloved Son, in whom I am well pleased.' Of course, that was a spirit voice. We hear the voices all the time. You will hear them in the séances. Samuel heard them. So did Abraham and the prophets and Mary and many women of the Bible. Proof of clairvoyant perception runs through the entire Scriptures. Daniel was a medium. He interpreted the dream of Nebuchadnezzar after the fraudulent magicians failed. That's Daniel 4:4-28. Of course, Jesus was the greatest medium of all. He was clairvoyant, clairaudient, and materializing. If He wasn't clairvoyant how could He have predicted what the disciples would find when they went into Jerusalem during that first Holy Week? He said, 'You will find a colt tied there.' He said, 'You will meet a man with a pitcher; follow him. He will take you to the house.' Along with being clairvoyant, Jesus was also telepathic. In John 4:17-19, a woman told Him she had no husband. Jesus said, 'You had five husbands and the man you are living with now is not your husband at all!' He was a materializing medium. The synoptic gospels tell how He materialized Moses and Elias and they stood beside Him. Read Luke 9:28-30. And, of course, you know how often Jesus materialized and appeared to His disciples and to others after His death. You will see materialization here in Chesterfield. It is all the same. When you understand spiritualism the Bible becomes alive and wonderful—until you relate it to spiritualism it is a mystery and even dull reading!"

Pressing interrupted this defense of faith to announce that it was time for our first séance.

As we walked across the grounds, he explained that Clifford Bias, with whom we had our appointment, was a specialist in direct-voice mediumship.

"If it is a successful séance, you will hear the voices of Mr.

Bias' spirit collaborators," Pressing promised. "These voices will become audible to you through the use of aluminum trumpets."

I knew that in the scale of mediumistic progression such a voice demonstration was surpassed only by materialization. I had come a long way since my experiments with mediums of planchettes and ouija boards, automatic writing, and psychometry.

Clifford Bias, a slightly built man in his early thirties, was sitting on the porch of his cottage smoking a cigarette. He was a bit on the nervous side, yet thoughtful in expression and quiet in speech. Introductions were informal, and conventional questions about my first impressions of Camp Chesterfield followed. Then Bias casually suggested that we go in for the séance. The number of people admitted to a séance is variable, usually from seven to twelve. Today, Pressing and I were to have the privilege of a private séance with trumpet-medium Bias.

There was nothing unusual about the front room of the cottage. It was about ten by sixteen; there was a rug on the floor and Venetian blinds on the two windows. With Bias' consent, I examined the surroundings. There were no furnishings except a small table and a few folding chairs. Both the door through which we had entered and the door leading to other parts of the house were now locked. Pressing and I sat at one end of the room facing a chair which had been set out for the medium. Set upright in the space between were two trumpets painted with luminous bands. They were really aluminum tubes that flanged out into a bell-shaped end. The larger was about three feet long and sectional; the other, a foot in length, was constructed in one piece.

Closing the Venetian blinds, Bias said, "I will turn off the lights, take my place, and allow myself to be entranced. If voices speak, ask any questions of them you wish. I will appreciate it if you will continue in a spirit of devotion and co-operation. Is there anything I should explain?"

I wanted to know why he needed to turn off the lights.

"Spirit chemists collaborate with all physical mediums. These chemists must build psychic structures from ectoplasm drawn from the medium and sitters. Light rays disintegrate ectoplasm in the same way that light ruins photographic negatives. Aside from this fact, it is easier to rid one's mind of the things of the world and maintain a proper attitude toward the service," he explained. "In the light you would be tempted to watch the medium. This would distract you from the phenomena. The disciples met at night for séances. You remember how they selected a remote place, like the upper room? They, too, wanted to be free from the disturbing influences of the world."

Here was another suggestion that spiritualism was a component part of Christian history. Here, in startling contrast to Mrs. McPherson's interpretation of Pentecost, was the hint that the "rushing wind," the "cloven tongues as of fire," the "speaking in tongues," were psychical phenomena! A remembered line from the book of Acts intruded into my thinking, "They spake as the *Spirit* gave them utterance."

Clifford Bias snapped off the lights. I nodded wisely in the dark. There was a trick behind all of this, a trick of hypnotism. Clever Mr. Bias had played upon my mental susceptibilities, expecting me to be taken in. I was confident he would be disappointed.

It was now very dark and very quiet in the room. Before us the narrow luminous bands on the trumpets became brighter and more shimmering. From outside came an occasional sound of people walking on the graveled paths across Chesterfield's grounds. I heard Bias breathe heavily; each breath was a slight groan.

The moments passed. My eyes became accustomed to the dark and I could make out the vague outline of Pressing next to me. He leaned over and whispered somberly, "Well, when's something going to happen?"

Before I could answer——

"How do you do, Dr. Bach! How do you do, Mr. Pressing!" came to us out of the darkness. It was a tantalizing, childish voice with a slightly roguish touch. It might have been a winsome little prodigy stepping out in debut. It might have been a tiny actress in a puppet show.

"Good afternoon," responded Mr. Pressing.

"Who are you?" I asked.

With a friendly lilt the answer came, "I'm Sylvia."

I had to admit that this voice, for some reason, carried with it more convincing qualities than any "spirit voice" that I had heard before. Its identity did not seem to be related even remotely to Mr. Bias. But mere refinement of voice would not change my reaction. The medium, I hastily concluded, was a ventriloquist. If Bergen could do his amazing stunts with Charlie, why couldn't Clifford Bias do as well with Sylvia? I yawned.

Sylvia must have had mental perception. "We are glad you

are here, Dr. Bach," she said with a neat curtsy in her voice. "This is going to be a good séance. There are good vibrations. Look!"

The small trumpet was slowly rising from the floor. It stopped slightly above the larger one and hovered uncertainly.

"What do you think of that?" asked Sylvia.

"It's a good trick," I confessed stubbornly.

"Trick?" Sylvia laughed, unoffended.

"Who is doing that?" Pressing asked.

"I am," said Sylvia. "I am Clifford's guide."

"What's a guide?" I wanted to know.

"Well, you see," the girl's voice said in a mature, thoughtful way, "Clifford is in trance. His spirit is out of the body. I can see it but you can't. It is very close. I use his vocal cords to speak with."

"But who are you?" I insisted.

"Sylvia!" said the voice emphatically. "Didn't I tell you I am Sylvia? Clifford's guide—Sylvia. I can get other spirits for you, if you want me to."

"How?" I demanded. "With millions of spirits in the spirit world, how do you get them? Call Bob Whitehand for me."

"Bob Whitehand?" The voice seemed to drift from us for a moment. "Bob Whitehand?" it returned reflectively. "I'll try. It is done by vibrations. Like sending vibrations through a funnel, a big funnel leading to the spirit world. Each spirit has its vibrations. I'll try to get Bob Whitehand afterwhile. But look at the trumpet now, Dr. Bach!"

It had risen to five or six feet above the floor and was slowly floating in space.

"That's pretty high for you to reach," I suggested.

"Where would you like the trumpet to go?" asked Sylvia.

"Bring it close to me," I told her.

Outlined by the luminous bands, the trumpet floated toward me. It stopped close to my right ear.

"Put it in my hands, Sylvia," I said.

"Hold them out!"

I extended my hands and the trumpet came to rest in them. Now, I thought, here's my chance to find those strings. Balancing the feather-light tube in my left hand, I passed my right hand completely around it. No strings.

"Put your hands on each end of the trumpet," Sylvia directed.

I did, holding the trumpet about elbow's length from my body.

"Now I'll talk to you from inside the trumpet."

A whispered voice—Sylvia's—came from within the trumpet. I put it to my right ear—the voice was there; to my left ear—Sylvia speaking.

"Well," I admitted, "that's interesting." Then I withdrew both hands quickly. Unaided, the trumpet remained fixed in space.

A conversation between Sylvia and Pressing was lost in my amazement upon seeing the other trumpet begin a slow take-off. Without stopping, it ascended to a point near the ceiling. It hung there, then started a slow swinging motion, round and round, like the retarded movement of a helicopter. Then the deep-throated voice of a man issued forth.

"How do you do, Dr. Bach! How do you do, Mr. Pressing! This is Dr. William James! When I was on the earth plane I, too, was interested in what people believe. Had I but known what I have since learned! Do you have any questions?"

The voice, speaking so apparently from the void, was authoritative, convincing. And I had many questions: what is a spirit? What is the first sensation after death? What is life like on the spirit plane? Do material things exist in the spirit world as Sir Oliver Lodge mentioned in *Raymond?*

The replies came deliberately in deep, full tones. "Spirit is energy, the highest form of energy. . . . The sensation after death is one of waking, as from a confused sleep; there is a time of adjustment, bewilderment; gradually the mind, intelligence, consciousness, the aurelian personage comes into a fuller stature. . . . Life here is filled with inexpressible possibilities, related to the highest conscious order of the universe. . . . Sir Oliver meant that in whatever way you interpret material things, so we must describe through the inadequacy of language conditions in the ethereal world."

The message went on—ten minutes, fifteen, perhaps twenty, judging from the over-all duration of the séance. The longer it continued the more uncanny it became, the more it seemed that this *was* a voice from the spirit world. The trumpet continued its circular motion.

Once, Pressing leaned over and whispered, "Very good, don't you think?"

Yes, I was compelled to confess, it was good. So good that I wished then, as now, that I had been able to record every word. But I kept telling myself that it could, of course, be Clifford Bias, good ventriloquist that he very likely was. It might all be memorized copy from James's *Varieties of Religious Experience.* Sometimes it sounded like it.

The voice, now near, now far, was constant and clear until

"Dr. James" said, "I can stay no longer. Good-by, Dr. Bach. Good-by, Mr. Pressing. Come again."

With this farewell, the trumpet hung poised for a moment, the large aperture pointed in my direction, very much in the direction of my head, I thought. It came toward me, not swiftly, but with certainty until it was within two feet of me. Then it swerved upward, took on as much speed as the distance allowed, and crashed with a bang against the wall behind me. There it telescoped and clattered to the floor.

"What the devil was that?" Pressing asked.

Sylvia's impish laugh was the answer. "I wanted to show you how poltergeists work! Well, that's the way!" The room was quiet for a few moments. Nothing could be seen save the luminous bands of the small trumpet. Then Sylvia's voice said, "I think I have Bob Whitehand for you."

"Good!" I said, in a tone of co-operation. "Bob? Bob? Can you hear me?"

A luminous head appeared levitated about four feet from the floor. It was not materialized in the way that materialization is usually described. It simply appeared out of nothingness. It was like a blurred flashlight reflected on a human face. I made out the unmistakable features of my friend who had been killed in France. This apparition hovered in the room for only a few seconds and then blacked out. How should I explain it? If it were actually a human face illuminated by a flashlight, it must have been shrouded in a curtain in the center of the room. But I knew there had been no curtain. Besides, why would the flashlight diffuse over no other single part of the room, curtain, or apparatus—if apparatus were used? And if it were someone impersonating Bob Whitehand, how could he make up such a marked resemblance of Bob, inasmuch as no one knew that I would request Bob's appearance? It was an inexplicable happening and remained the most vivid of the afternoon's demonstration.

Sylvia was now bidding us good-by. The little trumpet returned to its original position. Clifford Bias moved restlessly in his chair. He sighed heavily. In his natural voice, he called, "Pressing? Bach?"

"Are you okay?" Pressing asked.

Bias switched on the lights. He looked tired. "Let's go on out," he said as he unlocked the door and led the way to the porch. "Tell me everything that happened."

He lighted a cigarette.

I gave him a quick glance. Didn't he really know? My skepticism had been shaken and my confidence heightened by the events of the past two hours. I was anxious for further investigation—more systematic investigation than this trumpet séance had been. Pressing suggested that we attend a message séance which was scheduled for the public in the auditorium.

Sealed messages—in envelopes—with the initials on the front? Of this I had seen plenty! But Pressing wisely advised that here would be an opportunity to compare Chesterfield methods and results with those "of the world."

The man on the large auditorium stage was Homer Watkins of Detroit. He opened the meeting with Scripture and a prayer. Then the audience of two hundred sang a few gospel hymns. It might have been a Christian service anywhere, but the sermon was sharply punctuated with spiritistic phrases. During another song, slips of paper were passed to the audience. Almost everyone wrote a question. I did, too: "To which pub-

lisher should I submit a manuscript on which I'm working?"
We initialed the questions and folded them any way we wished.
No envelopes were used. So far, it seemed even more obvious
than Hollywood.

This thought persisted as the questions were dumped on the
table behind which Watkins stood blindfolded. He faced the
audience stolidly and with a sweeping movement of his hands
thoroughly mixed up the questions. Snatching first one and
then another, he whipped them past his ears with a rhythmic
motion as though listening for vibrations. Now he cast them
back on the table and snapped up two more. In the midst of
all this action, the readings were given in sharp staccato tones.
"This question is from John. John Day. Yes, John, I can hear
your cousin. It is your second cousin. His name is Charles
Wright. Not White. Wright. He married Julia Stafford. You
ask about the farm. You mean your farm on which the Austin
family is living. It is Harlan Austin and he has three children.
You want to ask Charles Wright what you should do about the
farm. Charles says——"

He spoke with the infallibility of a well-trained artist. Maybe
he was. But as I listened I had the feeling that Watkins was
but the mouthpiece. The unerring recital of involved names,
places, and family relationships, the rapid and inexhaustible
flow of instruction and counsel left me agasp. From the auditorium the questioners gave satisfied endorsement of the demonstration: "That's right! Exactly right! Thank you!"

The conclusiveness of the demonstrator recalled Pressing's
standard for a true medium: "He never needs to ask a question.
He doesn't throw out bait. He doesn't need leads. He knows
and he tells you."

"Marcus—Marcus Bach!" the authoritative voice of the medium came challenging through my thoughts. "You wanted to know about a manuscript—where to send a new manuscript——"

I leaned over to Pressing. "The man can see!"

"There will be a leaping dog on the jacket," the medium was saying.

Pressing jumped to his feet. "Just a moment!" he interrupted. "Here's a man who wants to examine the blindfold!"

The medium's hands stopped their fanning motion, letting the slips of paper drop to the table. Pressing led me to the platform.

I examined the blindfold. No cloth squares! I retied it myself. I am convinced that the man could not see and yet, immediately, the threshing movement of his hands was resumed, the messages issued forth again, casting a spell like the solemn murmur of an incantation.

The same mood, with further intensity, prevailed under the mediumship of Fanchion Harwood during a materializing séance early the next evening. There were seven of us in the circle: a medical doctor from Texas, Ralph G. Pressing, Mrs. Belle Daiches of Evanston, Illinois, who has written for the *Psychic Observer,* two other women and a man from Louisiana who were studying to become mediums. Mrs. Harwood's assistant received us.

Pressing told her that I wanted to examine the room. I did. It was located in the basement. We had entered by the outside cellar stairs. I thumped the walls. They were solid. There was a door in one corner of the room that led into another part of the basement. I asked that it be locked. The assistant obliged. As I continued around the room, I found nothing suspicious save a velvet curtain suspended in cyclorama fashion from one of the walls. It was somewhat higher than a man's head and projected out into the room to form an enclosure about three by four feet.

"What is the purpose of this curtain?" I wanted to know.

"That," said the assistant, "is the cabinet. Look it over."

I pulled aside the curtain and went in. There was a chair against the solid basement wall. Nothing more.

"What is this cabinet for?"

The assistant explained that it was behind the enclosure that the medium sits entranced.

"Why must she be concealed?"

"The reason for concealing the medium," I was informed, "is because a red light is used during a materialization séance. Even a dim light interferes with the generation of the ecto-plasm necessary in building spirit forms. The cabinet shields the medium during the time this force is being assembled and then, when complete, the form can stand the light rays long enough to be seen outside the cabinet by the sitters—from thirty seconds to three or four minutes. The medium entranced is also sometimes disturbing to the spectators. It is not a pleasingly aesthetic sight—especially not during a materialization, for ectoplasm exudes from her mouth and body in the nature of a gauzy, foggy, smokelike substance from which figures are formed by the spirit chemists."

Since there was no way for anyone to enter or leave the cabinet without coming through the room, I accepted it as part of the required setting.

"But what about the lights?" I inquired.

"The bright lights will be turned off," we were told. "Ectoplasm, with its quality of luminosity, shows up best in dark or semidarkness. The séance will take place in a red light, which will not detract from the materialized forms. It will be bright enough for you to discern one another all the while and to see me standing near the cabinet."

About this time Mrs. Harwood rapped at the inside door and was admitted. The door was relocked. Mrs. Harwood was diminutive, gentle, and refined. She greeted us in a cordial, forthright manner. But as she stepped inside the cabinet, I reminded myself that "true art is the ability to conceal art."

The assistant took her place beside the cabinet.

"Let us enter the séance reverently," she instructed, and there followed a brief word of prayer. Then she continued: "I have these requests to make. Be sincere. You can assist very much in the success of the séance. Please do not speak among yourselves. If, however, a spirit appears and indicates he wants to speak to you, if he calls you by name or motions to you to come, get up and speak to him. I only ask that you will please not touch the spirits. Are there any questions?"

"Why shouldn't we touch the spirits?" I asked.

"There is a connection between the spirits and the medium," the assistant explained. "When you touch the spirit you are really touching the medium and disturbing the conditions of the trance. Do you remember the words of Jesus when He said to Mary in the garden after His resurrection, 'Touch me not, for I am not yet ascended to my Father'?"

I had further questions but, convinced that the success of the séance depended as much on us who sat in the circle as upon the medium, I put myself in a receptive though not a credulous state of mind. I was determined today to fight against hallucinations or hypnotism or whatever might intrude under the guise of psychical demonstration.

When the assistant turned out the bright lights, the room was illuminated with a deep red glow which came from a spotlight directly over my shoulder. I turned to examine it. It was a theatrical spotlight covered by a thickness of gelatin. In its light I could easily see Pressing at my left and the doctor from Texas at my right. The others in the group, sitting in a half circle on folding chairs, were also always discernible.

After perhaps five minutes of silent waiting, the assistant suggested that we sing a song. Someone started, "I Heard the Voice of Jesus Say." We sang one verse and were about to begin another when a voice spoke.

"How are you, everyone?" It sounded like Sylvia. But I knew that Clifford Bias was at this same hour giving his demonstration of trumpet mediumship.

"I am Twilight," said the voice.

At this everyone responded, "Hello, Twilight. How are you?"

"I'm just fine," said Twilight, "and how are you, Dr. Bach?"

"I'm fine, too," I replied, piqued at having been singled out just because I hadn't chimed in with the others. It struck me that a spirit should think of something more profound in the way of a greeting than the old earth-worn phrases.

Twilight was chatty. "Everybody happy? You happy, Mr. Pressing? You happy, Mrs. Daiches? I think this will be a good séance. Oh, a very good séance, I think for sure. It is a good circle. Oh, it's a good day for a séance. Nice and sunny. Atmospheric conditions have a lot to do with séances. When the atmosphere is heavy, it is hard for the spirits to manifest. Materialization is hard then. Oh, yes, it is. And we must have materializations! We just must have!" This last was said with an ironic twist.

"All religions must have phenomen—how do you say it— phenomena—or phenomenon—or phenomenons! I never can pronounce it." Twilight laughed.

A *good* séance? I wondered.

A light flickered near the floor, close to where the assistant stood. It was a luminous glow, like the quick beam of a flash-light shining up through a cloth. It came suddenly, tarried a moment, and faded reluctantly. Twilight's disconnected talk persisted as the mirage of light loomed again. This time it mounted higher like silver smoke curling around a light bulb. Then the light went out, but the silver smoke continued to hover. I can describe it best as a bright, shimmering vapor, struggling for expression. Slowly it began taking form. Something like shoulders—then a face appeared. It developed into a bodily form and spoke. It called for Mrs. Daiches. She got up, took a few steps, and said, "Yes, Mother?"

"How are you?" the figure asked in a low, hushed whisper.

"I'm fine, Mother. Why didn't you bring Father with you?"

Immediately a man's voice spoke. "She did." And hovering beside the figure of the little old woman was a somewhat larger figure of a man. They had form and masklike features. For a moment I thought they might be two actors dressed in lumines-cent costumes and wearing papier-mâché masks. Where had they come from? How had they entered the room? I felt sure I would know before the séance was over. Houdini once said that he could duplicate any such manifestation.

Then a third figure appeared. Let us say "materialized," for it is the best description. It seemed to come out of the floor—an inchoate mass of ectoplasmic stuff—growing, taking form, speaking. I made out the semblance of a young boy.

"Mother," he said, "do you remember the walks we used to take?"

"I surely do," said the mother.

"Let's take one now!"

He took his mother's arm and they moved back and forth across the room, coming so close to where I sat that I pulled back my feet.

Throughout these doings the whisperings continued—sometimes simultaneously. Twilight was still chatting. And there was spirit laughter, low and pleased. I was seeing the *raison d'être* of spiritualism: demonstration and proof of the continuity of life, coupled with the comforting assurance that that life is good.

Here was the reunion of a family—a son telling his mother that life "over there" was just a continuation of life on earth. There were not two worlds at all; there was but one inter-blended, interrelated world closely interwoven by memory and the love of life. Consciousness could not die. Personality could not be destroyed. The spirit of man was, indeed, eternal.

I drew my attention from the Daicheses' reunion and touched Pressing's arm.

"What do you think?" I asked.

"I have been to many séances," he replied. "This promises to be one of the very best."

I analyzed the possibilities of fraud and deception. The room was sufficiently illuminated that I would have seen holes in the floor or shifting walls. And if it were "done with mirrors" how would one explain three figures speaking at once, gliding across the room, touching "arms," brushing past my feet?

This was the séance. The implausibility injected into the first ten minutes carried through the entire demonstration. For an hour new figures materialized and disappeared. Once Twilight cautioned, "It is getting very bright. Too bright to see. Fix the red light."

"I will, Twilight," said the assistant, coming over to put another thin sheet of gelatin over the spotlight.

I was making minute mental notations of all that was happening—the hovering, swaying motion of the "spirits," the rhythm of life, like the rise and fall of a tide, as many as four speaking simultaneously in whispered voices, excited, hurried, persuasive. Suddenly the galaxy of spirits melted away. For a long still moment nothing happened. Then the swirling ectoplasmic effluvia glowed from the floor and quickly took on the form of a girl. Before the figure was complete, it spoke.

"Marc, dear—Marc, dear—Marc, dear."

Those who know me well call me Marc; those who know me better call me Marc, dear, so I knew this must be a "familiar spirit!" I got up and walked over until there was a space of less than four feet between us. "Yes?" I said. "Who are you?"

The answer was fraught with disappointment. "Don't you know me?"

I did not. I had no idea who this might be. I had really been too absorbed to think very much about personal contact with the spirits. If I had had anyone in mind throughout the séance—if thoughts could have conjured up anyone—surely Bob Whitehand would have appeared. Nor did I propose to offer any hint of whom I thought she *might represent*. No leads, I determined.

"I do not know you. Who are you?"

"Paula," came the answer.

The name and the soft manner in which it was uttered brought the sudden unfolding of a forgotten drama. Twenty years ago my sister Paula had died at the age of twenty-three. Her child Janette had died shortly before. These deaths had been among the deep sorrows in our family, but time and travel reduce the past into forgetfulness. No medium or spirit had plucked this name out of my mind because I wasn't thinking of Paula. I had not thought of her even once during the séance.

I looked at the presence before me closely.

"How do I look?" she asked.

"You look fine," I replied.

"The right height?" she whispered. "Do you think I should be taller?"

"No. You are about the height I remember."

"I wanted to do a good job," she told me earnestly. "Do I look all right?"

"Yes," I assured her, recalling that one theory of materialization is that the spirit "takes" the ectoplasm and fashions according to its memory the human form which clothed it on earth. This is etheric sculpturing, and most spirits ask questions like

Paula's. It seemed gratifying to her to know that consciousness could once more reveal itself in features and form.

Did this form and these features resemble Paula? I must admit they did. Very much. The outline of the figure was recognizable and convincing. It was like a "false front," a flat, two-dimensional body with the semblance of arms clothed in a shadowy gray-white film. The face, though typically masklike, was strikingly reminiscent. There was an illusion of long blond hair. I cannot say whether the voice was Paula's or not. After twenty years I would not remember. Just now, however, it was Paula returned.

But why shouldn't it be? I asked myself as I stood there. The spiritualists at Chesterfield knew I was coming. If, as some people say, they have a well-laid system of espionage they could easily have traced my family and got Paula's description. If this was someone "dressed up," play-acting, if this was a marionette using the voice of a ventriloquist, naturally it would be so constructed as to represent Paula. This thought haunted me more than the presence. I wished I could convince myself someway. The impulse to reach out and touch the figure became stronger. I moved closer. I moved slightly to one side so that the red light would strike the spirit's face more directly. We were about three feet apart now. Paula was talking about life in the spirit world. I was asking hasty questions: Have you seen Jesus? What is heaven like? What about the element of time? Can you be everywhere at once? Are terms like Methodist, Reformed, Presbyterian, Catholic ever used where you are?

Her voice seemed to laugh. She answered, "No, no," to all questions save the one about heaven. It was like speaking to a living person secretly, clandestinely, knowing that time was running out. Her features seemed to become clearer. Perhaps it was my mind playing tricks.

And then a thought came to me. "Paula," I said, "do you remember the catechism we learned at home?"

"Of course!"

"Paula, do you remember the first question in that catechism?"

"I remember."

"What was it?" I asked almost fearfully.

The answer came at once. " 'What is your chief comfort in life and in death?' "

"Go on," I urged.

" 'That I, with body and soul, both in life and in death am not my own——' " She interrupted herself. "Here where we are the words have a greater meaning!"

Then quickly, breathlessly, she told me that serving God means personal development. Life on the spirit plane is an evolvement. Like the breaking of a chrysalis. Like the ascent in a spiral. Like the growth of moral affection to higher and higher "heavens." Several times she interrupted herself with "Do you understand? Is that clear?" as if she felt her message was vital, all-absorbing. Death, she insisted, was not a violent result of sin. It had no sting. It was neither friend nor enemy. It was part of the divine purpose, a purpose without beginning or end.

The whispering grew fainter. "I can stay no longer. I must go now."

"Paula, one more thing. Can you put your arms around me?"

"I'll give you a kiss," she said. "Come closer."

"You come close to me." I wanted her to come nearer the red light. She did. There was now scarcely a foot between us. Her face was luminous, seemingly transparent, and without depth.

I leaned forward and lowered my head. The weblike texture of ectoplasmic arms encircled my neck. Something soft and flaxen brushed my forehead. Then Paula vanished—into the floor, it seemed.

I walked back to my chair and sat down.

"Was that all right?" Twilight was asking. "What do you think?"

I did not reply.

What did I think?

A few minutes later the lights were turned on. The cabinet assistant called to Mrs. Harwood, "Are you all right?" From within the curtain the medium announced that she was.

The séance was ended.

I left the room, overpowered by a strange onrush of comfort about life—and death. If this is all true, I thought, it will be difficult to speak of it without emotion. I had always believed in life after death. The traditional churches believed it, too. Spiritualism went a step farther. It asked us to believe that the spirits were interested and active in human affairs, that they could be reached, seen, communicated with. The sense of surety and comfort lingered. The feeling of genuineness persisted. I walked past the Chesterfield grotto. Someone was praying within the shrine. For those who believe, spiritualism leads to God.

Then, two months later, I visited with the good lady who, long ago, had warned, "Stay away from puppet shows and mediums. Both are of the Devil."

"By the way," I said in a casual manner, "I saw Paula the other day."

Mother looked at me. "Paula—who?" she asked slowly.

"Our Paula."

"What kind of crazy talk is that?" she asked with a characteristic wave of her hands.

I told her the story. To my astonishment she asked for details.

"Did Paula mention Janette? Did she look like Paula? Was she happy?"

My dad sat smoking his cigar, thoughtfully smiling.

"May I ask," he began, turning to Mother with a winsome tone, "do you have even the faintest, remotest idea of taking any stock in this story?"

She made a gesture of almost hopeless submission. With a gentle, enigmatical smile of incredulous wonder, she said, "After radios and the atomic bomb—who knows what can happen in the world?"

CHAPTER V

OXFORD GROUP—MRA

A MERICA MUST RE-ARM MORALLY! WORLD SECURITY LIES IN GOD CONTROL! These were the startling signs along America's superhighways of faith in the late thirties. The Moral Re-Armament caravan had taken over. From seaboard to seaboard outdoor advertising got religion. ONLY GOD-CONTROLLED MEN WILL MAKE GOD-CONTROLLED NATIONS! Shopwindows carried special placards. WHEN MAN LISTENS, GOD SPEAKS! Advertising space in streetcars and buses was utilized. WHERE GOD GUIDES, GOD PROVIDES! Churches, universities, and civic organizations displayed and distributed bulletins by the millions. SIN BLINDS AND SIN BINDS. The message entered home and restaurant via milk-bottle tops. GOD HAS A PLAN FOR EVERY MAN!

A graphic analysis of these messages struck the newsstands of ten countries in December 1937 under the compelling title of *Rising Tide*. The magazine was a glorified *Life* or *Look* with the ambitious idea that nations could be remade through a rising tide of "changed lives." It carried no advertising and its publishers were volunteers working without financial backing and without salaries. Through fifty pages a *montage* of photographic masterpieces told the story vividly: the world, precariously balanced by misdirected energy, enthusiasm and invention for a long time, was now wavering over an abyss of self-destruction! Human wisdom had failed, but God had a plan:

> "Everybody wants to see the other fellow changed,
> Every nation wants to see the other nation changed;
> But everybody is waiting for the other fellow to begin.
> If you want an answer for the world today, the best
> place to start is with yourself."

Through a continuity of action shots, high-lighted by arresting captions, *Rising Tide* showed how this could be done. Depicting a sanctuary swept by enemy fire, one page proclaimed, "The answer to burning churches is the church aflame!" Violent strips of riots and strikes in industry were accompanied by "Workers led by God can lead the world." Below an avalanche of news clippings that told the story of deteriorating home life were the words, "Out of a million homes in touch with God will come a nation's peace."

In Europe where the peace of the nations was threatened, the thunder of the "rising tide of changed lives" was most emphatic. In the Netherlands, in Switzerland, and in the British Isles gigantic mass meetings were held. Government officials in Norway, Sweden, and Denmark admonished their people to accept the challenge of a great Christian revolution. They meant Moral Re-Armament, the dream child prodigy of Frank N. Buchman, an American Lutheran minister. When Chamberlain was flying to Munich for his rendezvous with Hitler, Buchman was addressing a world Moral Re-Armament Assembly of two thousand delegates from forty-five countries at

Interlaken, Switzerland. The keynote of his talk was "Guidance or Guns!" Statesmen of the League of Nations Assembly heard him say, "The voice of God through you will become the will of the people!"

He called upon a Japanese delegate to the interparliamentary congress at the Hague to speak. F. Mitsui arose to declare, "Through Moral Re-Armament you can keep the peace in Europe intact. I will carry this message from the land of William Tell to the land of the Rising Sun!" Bernard Bourdillon, member of the British delegation to the Paris peace conference; Todd Sloan, British labor leader; Baroness Dina Hahn of Latvia; and Sven Stalpe, Swedish labor leader, picked up genius Buchman's phrases and went away saying, "Nationalism can unite a nation. Supernationalism can unite a world. God-controlled supernationalism is the only sure foundation for world peace!"

Hitler struck with his blitzkrieg. The world was being shoved into war, but under the black shadows of such realities, Moral Re-Armament refused to go down. Buchman was still a power, a pilot of souls; God's man for Satan's hour. Conterminously with the preparation for war, England girded herself with a Moral Re-Armament publication, *The Battle for Peace*. It cried for dependence upon God, for direction and guidance. It argued that "minorities are bridges between nations." Refusing to forget Interlaken, it recalled that "God in every heart will put the nations in the heart of God!" *The Battle for Peace* was written by an apostle of the "changed life," Bunny Austin, a former Davis Cup winner. It was endorsed by an army of British spiritual bluebloods who valiantly hoped that Moral Re-Armament would stop the war. Could not their devastating weapon of prayer strike a spiritual blow to halt the enemy? Out of the deluge of slogans with which their leader had fed the "rising tide," they seized one of his most famous for their battle cry, "The Day of Miracles Is Not Over!" Many remembered how he said, "I thank heaven for a man like Adolf Hitler! Think what it would mean to the world if he surrendered to the control of God. Or Mussolini. Or any dictator. Through such a man God could control a nation overnight and solve every last bewildering problem!"

These words re-echoed in America where elusive peace was still masquerading as security. From his England headquarters Buchman flashed a warning. On June 4, 1938, while two thousand of his followers gathered at Stockbridge, Massachusetts, he telephoned from London, "America must re-arm spiritually or all is lost!"

But a transoceanic broadcast was not enough to arouse a people who lay wrapped in a soft and comfortable blanket of indifference about the rest of the world. So the self-appointed steward of the world's crumbling peace came home to America. After extensive preparation, Moral Re-Armament was launched with the kind of ballyhoo that Americans best appreciate and most enthusiastically applaud. On the night of May 15, 1939, fifteen thousand gathered at Madison Square Garden to see pageantry, hear speeches, and listen to transatlantic telephone messages from London believers who said, "Moral Re-Armament is the only hope." Representatives of many nations carried their flags in a stirring procession. Bands played. A Canadian cowboy wearing a ten-gallon hat sang a song about peace. Bunny Austin spoke about the place of God in sports. John Ramsey, CIO leader at the Bethlehem Steel Company, retold how he had been changed from "being a rebel to being a revolutionary in a revolution that builds bridges between classes." George Eastman, a former president of the Los Angeles Chamber of Commerce, related how Moral Re-Armament had changed his life and the lives of his employees. And leader Buchman, in characteristic mastery of quotable lines, said, "There is enough in the world for everyone's need, but not enough for everyone's greed."

The Moral Re-Armament caravan was rolling. For two months I followed its sensational meandering tour from Madison Square Garden to the Hollywood Bowl. Americans who hopped on this religious band wagon actually believed that the world was on its way back to the guidance of God. Some said that MRA was the white horse of the Apocalypse that would save America from destruction. More mundane souls chanted:

> "The spark has caught in the tinder,
> The fire is sweeping the plain,
> A call is rousing the nation,
> Revere is riding again!"

It was the dream of world conquest by way of the spirit, a theocracy through religious awakening. A United States Senator, Harry S. Truman, endorsed the idea; so did Harry H. Woodring, Henry Ford, Richard E. Byrd, Joe DiMaggio, and Fiorello La Guardia. The President of the Federal Council of Churches admitted, "The ice of formalism, foolish pride, selfishness and partisanship is melting in the gulf stream of prayer, penitence, and purposeful living. A revival powerful enough to match the hour seems imminent." William Bankhead testified, "Never in my long experience in Washington have I found anything on which all parties in both Senate and House have so thoroughly agreed as on America's need, and our own need, for this new spirit!"

With these dynamics of political and social backing, the Buchman fleet, a twenty-two car railroad special, hit the coast. A thousand people were in the entourage. On the evening of July 19, four giant pillars of light led thirty thousand volunteers for God's great "army without guns" to Hollywood Bowl. Thousands more stood outside to watch in curiosity and wonder as the "rising tide" came in. Following the dramatic pattern set in New York, the meeting opened with a spectacular international march. Citizens of enemy nations walked hand in hand to the great stage where they stood at attention under the slogan: NEW MEN, NEW NATIONS, A NEW WORLD! Capital and labor stopped their quarrels long enough to permit their representatives to pose for photographs. Political rivals dramatized a brotherhood above partisanship by admitting antagonisms and yielding to "God's plan." A Negro pledged the enlistment of her people. A message was read by Joseph Scott, a Catholic lay leader. "Doctor" Buchman's patent medicine for the invalid world was once more being publicly compounded. Was it the prescription needed for the healing of the nations?

An analysis of the elements inherent in this movement again convinced me that Moral Re-Armament had a glorious heritage in the old Oxford Group. My first knowledge of Frank N. Buchman did not come through a staged politico-religious spectacle, but through the quiet transformation of a friend, Ned Barton. He was the only man I ever knew who contemplated suicide one day and talked about miracles the next! In 1932 when the depression had compelled people to be unusually realistic, such a sudden change-over was astounding. Like many another college graduate's first job, Ned's had lasted only two years. This was no tragedy, for a hopeful philosophy had always carried him over. He lived the way he played the races, doggedly trusting his luck. But as workless days stretched out into years and the horses stubbornly refused to pay off, I detected a sinister undercurrent cutting through his confidence.

One evening I was waiting for Ned in a coffee shop. He rushed in, late, noticeably upset.

"When I left you this afternoon," he began breathlessly, "I was as low as a man can get. I was wondering if the fellows who have taken the easy way out weren't smart. I couldn't get the idea out of my head. Then what do you think happened? I was sitting on the bleachers watching a parade down Euclid. The stranger next to me nudged me with his elbow and blurted out, 'Listen, pal, if you were going to commit suicide what method would you use?' Lord! For a minute I couldn't say a word. Then he asked me again. I said, 'I don't know. Why?' 'I was just wondering.' He shrugged. Then he got up and disappeared in the crowd."

Ned paused and, clutching my arm, went on: "Now on my way up here—you won't believe it—there was a big crowd on Prospect, between Eighth and Ninth. I walked over and asked, 'What's up?' 'A guy just jumped out of a window and killed himself.' I pushed through the crowd. There lay the man who had talked to me on the bleachers! My God! And me thinking of the same thing!"

Before I could comment on this remarkable coincidence, a man sitting at an adjoining table pushed back his chair and came over.

"Pardon me, fellows," he said. "I couldn't help overhearing your story, and maybe it's well that I did."

"Yeah?" Ned's troubled expression deepened as the stranger's eyes sought his discerningly.

"You need help," he went on candidly. "Why don't you come along to the Statler with me? There is someone there tonight who will tell you exactly what you should do."

These words, though cast in a completely new mold, suggested the soul-saving fervor of a city-mission worker. The amazing contrast was in the appearance and manner of the speaker. He was smartly dressed, debonair, and, in spite of a deeply religious sincerity, might have been on his way to a night spot. But, as his affable entreaty continued, it was so appealing that Ned turned to me with a laconic, "What you say we go along?"

We did.

When we arrived at the Statler, our friend, who had said, "Just call me Lew," escorted us to a suite of rooms in which I detected none of the usual atmosphere of a spiritual assembly. He explained that the group in the outer room, about ten young men and women, were waiting for private conferences with a man whom they affectionately called "F.B."

"We'll see him," he promised confidently, "but while we're waiting, let's go in for the party."

The party was Lew's name for a revolutionized religious service, and within the next hour I discovered a "little-known" that seemed to be working entirely through the subconscious.

Twenty-seven worshipers were seated informally about the room. Almost everyone held a pencil poised over an open notebook. Some were writing. Lew whispered to us that this was a "quiet time" in which personal messages from the Unseen were recorded. They called it waiting on God. Interspersing the silence were discussion periods based on the instructions received, with vague allusions to checking the messages against "four absolutes." The new spiritual lingo aroused my curiosity though it was as yet quite meaningless to me.

"You'll catch on." Lew laughed, but I was still in a maze when he led the way to "F.B.'s" room half an hour later.

As we walked across the room to where this "surgeon of souls" sat at his desk, I was reminded of the times I had reluctantly made my way to confess college sins to the dean of men. F.B. was a thin-nosed, bespectacled gentleman of about fifty years. There was nothing particularly striking about him except an almost arrogant confidence that seemed to contradict the hopeful predictions which had drawn us here. Without the formality of introductions, Lew plunged into Ned's story.

Almost immediately F.B. silenced the eager disciple with a somewhat impatient wave of his hand and, turning abruptly in his chair, said, "Tell your own story, Ned. Tell me everything."

His words carried a mysterious power of persuasion which drew from Ned a confession so detailed and so serious that it astonished me. After relating the strange experiences of the day, he talked on, attempting to justify his desperate intentions by enumerating a series of bad breaks. I had the feeling that long before Ned had finished, F.B. had stopped listening. This man, whom I had considered definitely unprepossessing, began to take on the stature of a psychic. By some process of spiritual diagnosis, he seemed always far ahead of the story. He sat there, boring through the penitent with an omniscient gaze that seemed to put the words of confession into his mouth. Suddenly he rose to his feet and, pointing a long forefinger at Ned, interrupted sharply.

"You've told me your side of the story. I'll tell you God's. Bad breaks didn't drag you down. You're a dirty gambler. Every bookie in town knows you for a sap!"

The words rent the veil of Ned's life. Amazed, I looked at him. His stunned expression told me he would never forget this moment. F.B. was laying his soul "bare as the judgment day" and telling him what to do to save it. Ned made futile attempts to interrupt but was consistently suppressed. Though unquestionably sincere, the diviner's rapid-fire exorcism seemed wholly without sympathy and warmth. Poor Ned, I thought. He came for help and would leave chastened. But the orders were direct: "Find God in a quiet time. Right your wrongs. Purge your soul by sharing, by confessing your sins. Then live under divine guidance."

As we walked home, Ned grudgingly admitted, "The fellow was right. He knows what I need." Then, with a flash of un-mistakable conviction, he added, "And I'm going to get it!"

This sudden turn in the road confused me even more than what I had witnessed at the Statler. I knew that Ned had heard this type of thing, in somewhat other terminology, since he was a youngster, but conventional religious procedure had left him untouched. Local ministers had frequently seen him in their congregations without suspecting that he was in any great danger. Had this chance meeting with F.B. simply found him ripe for the acceptance of a new moral faith? Or had he really met a master technician who was dispensing power that had already produced results in his own life? Who was this man who dared walk into people's lives and claw at their past? By what divine right did he demand "changed lives" of strangers?

There was no mystery about him. Frank Nathan Daniel Buchman was born in Pennsburg, Pennsylvania, in 1878, the son of the local hotelkeeper. He grew up in a Lutheran home under the discipline of a deeply religious mother. He went to Muhlenberg College in Allentown and to Mt. Airy Lutheran Theological Seminary in Philadelphia. After accepting a pastorate in a little parish in Overbrook, he realized he had come to grips only with historic religion. His experiences had revolved comfortably in a geographical orbit of less than a hundred miles. At the end of a featureless year, he shook off clerical duties with the heroic pronouncement that he was setting out to do something constructive. In Philadelphia he distinguished himself by building the first Lutheran settlement house. He would very likely have carved out a place for himself as a social leader had it not been for a tiff with his board of trustees. Stung by their rejection of his ideas, he started an aimless pilgrimage that took him to England.

The Buchman canonization began in a little wayside church in Keswick, England, on a Sunday afternoon in 1905. The preacher, a woman, spoke about the "miracle of the cross" and its "power to save." These were words from his own ministry, but, in the intimacy of this chapel, he had his first real spiritual experience. He described it as an explosion in his soul. It was actually something so imperceptible that none of the other worshipers were conscious that a man's life had been completely changed. Frank sat there analyzing himself, taking an inventory of his iniquities, tugging away at his sins until he "came clean." He decided that it was pride, selfishness, and ill will that stood in the way of self-realization. Dragging these covert sins into the light of honest examination, he "waited upon God" for guidance.

That night he wrote each of the board members back in Philadelphia a letter: "I've borne you ill will. I've been headstrong and sinful. I ask your forgiveness and I'm ready to make restitution."

He received no reply. But that did not matter. Confession of sin and an attempt to right the wrong carried its own reward—a "changed life," a sense of complete adjustment to God and man.

No longer the parish pastor who had drifted into obscurity at Overbrook and into hostility in Philadelphia, Buchman was "guided" to Penn State College and the job of "Y" secretary. Here his new principles of faith made their debut on the wild stage of student affairs. He approached campus capers just as he had dealt with the renegade trio that had been rooted out of his own life in Keswick Chapel. One of his first official announcements was that students were more interested in sex than in the spiritual life and more concerned about money than an education. Why not drag such indignities into the "light of the cross" and take a look at them? As part of his developing technique, he had introduced a "morning watch," an "hour with God." It was working wonders. He urged students to come to him, and he would show them this better way. He promised emancipation from secret sins. He was not a great speaker or an outstanding educator. He insisted on constructive action, not eloquent theories.

Surprisingly little resulted from the efforts of seven years. Then "Y" Secretary Buchman hit on an idea. With a talent for organization, he regimented the entire campus for a Student Christian Movement. A "Macedonian call" went out to religious leaders of other colleges and brought to Penn State such men as John R. Mott, Robert E. Speer, Henry B. Wright, and Sherwood Eddy. Though this was an exciting inning for student religion, the permeating revival swept most remarkably over Buchman himself. Fired by the spirit of this revivalistic campaign and feeling the narrow limits of Penn State too confining, he joined Sherwood Eddy's world evangelistic tour. It was during this period that his uncanny talent for ferreting out the sins of others reached its fruition. At an evening meeting a heckler confounded the revival leaders with the demand, "I'm an atheist. Prove to me there is a God." When the enthusiastic arguments wore themselves out against the man's rank unbelief, Buchman took over. Fastening his diagnostic gaze on the man, he charged, "It's not unbelief that keeps you from God. You're an adulterer! Let's clean that up first and then we'll get around to the God business."

An atheist was miraculously numbered among the converts at that Sherwood Eddy meeting.

It was not long until Christendom heard of Frank N. Buchman on the campus of Oxford University. He was conducting a one-man revival, introducing workable techniques, "changing lives" with remarkable success. His converts banded themselves into an energetic, soul-winning organization and, given advantage of the classical title and tradition of their institution, were called the Oxford Group or, simply, the "Fellowship." Soon reports reaching America told of missionary teams spearheading for Buchman around the globe. It was no longer a campus campaign; the college-tested ideas were now invading entire cities. Another spiritual metamorphosis was under way. The "Y" secretary was becoming a world religious figure. He returned to the States to fit the Oxford technique into the religious pattern of the American campus. At Yale, Harvard, and Princeton young men and women began talking about "guidance" and "changed lives." At the University of Iowa a Catholic professor joined the movement. In Chicago an instructor said that teaching Oxford Groupers was like holding classes in heaven.

"Statler scenes" such as I had witnessed dated back through more than a decade. In the early 'thirties Ned was but one in an estimated fifty thousand who had been brought to this spiritual architect to receive a divine blueprint for a new life. I doubted if the transformation in Ned would be as complete as some I had heard about. His destination had always pointed the other way, but I was compelled to revise my judgment when I saw him again.

Even before he spoke, I detected the light in his eyes which, years later, I was to identify as the gleam of the cults. In the days of the depression it was an enviable hint of glory, as if a man had suddenly found something to take the place of money.

"It's a system! And I don't mean for the horses," he exclaimed in an onrush of enthusiasm. "They're out! It's living under guidance. It's tuning in. I've contacted God and everything's changed! I've been starting each day with a quiet time. You remember, Frank explained it as a fifteen-minute period early in the morning in which a fellow gives God a chance to say hello!"

"Now just a minute!" I broke in. "You've come a long way, so how about bringing me up to date by picking up where we left off three weeks ago?"

"Well, it all works just as Frank said it would. First, you make up your mind that you want to be God-guided. That means playing fair all around. But you can't do this without the Oxford Group technique. The quiet time is the first step."

"That quiet time—it sounds like spiritualism to me," I protested.

"No connection! It's really scientific praying. The trouble with most prayers is that people have their say to high heaven and don't give God a chance to answer. Our quiet time sets up a two-way circuit. Every morning before I leave my room, I just sit quietly in a chair or kneel alongside the bed and wait on God. You don't talk to Him; He talks to you."

"How?"

"That's what the pencil and paper are for. When you wait on God, thoughts and inspirations come through, and you write them down."

"You mean, anybody can get messages by just sitting quietly and—waiting on God?"

"No. You must be in tune. For the first week I didn't get anything, but now I get messages fine. That's what I came to tell you about. Yesterday morning the pencil wrote, 'See Arnold Nelson for a job in the storage house.' I had met Arnold at a party the night before. And when I went down to see him, he said he needed a man part time on a moving van. I got the job," he ended with a grin.

"Did you tell Arnold how you got a line on this job?"

"Sure," affirmed Ned, anxious to give God-guidance all the credit.

"Well," I admitted, "it sounds as exciting as playing the horses. Do you think it will eventually produce tangible results at the races?"

"I'm not expecting that!" He laughed, then added seriously, "The messages are a day-by-day guide for good living. We Groupers call them orders. They give advice, suggestions, and instructions."

"But how can you be sure the messages always come from God?"

"Frank's worked that all out as part of our technique. We call it checking for guidance. Each message must stand the test of the four absolutes: absolute honesty, absolute purity, absolute unselfishness, and absolute love. These are our touchstones. If a message measures up to them, who can doubt that it's of God? Of course, there are borderline messages. These are checked against the judgment of others in the group. I got a borderline message last week. I was flat broke and my quiet time said, 'Talk to Lew about it.' I was afraid the message didn't reflect absolute honesty and I told Lew exactly how I felt. Lew said there was certainly nothing dishonest about it and let me have five bucks to prove it!"

It was evident that indoctrination had gone deep. Whatever the magic of the Oxford Group or whatever its power, the spiritual aid which Ned had received was neither diffused nor fragmentary. It was giving strength and relevance to his whole life. He was working this technique just the way he used to play his systems for the races. But this had to do with his own running, and he was off to a remarkably good start. Frank had lifted him out of his suicidal moods and the results were prodigious. He was no longer seen with the bookies. He regained his former confidence and became conscious of personal possibilities. The storage company trusted him with an office job. Other religious leaders seemed mild and anemic alongside the man who had made him one of the God-guided in the courageous cavalcade of twice-born men.

"That's the most wonderful thing about it," he told me enthusiastically some months later. "You have no idea how many outstanding men have been changed. An Oxford Group roll call would sound like a *Who's Who*. I'm meeting prominent businessmen, well-known artists and scholars. In England, where the movement is strongest, they say that most of the leaders are of the nobility. C. J. Hambro, the president of the Norwegian Parliament, testified that his life had been changed. It's sweeping like fire through Norway and Denmark. And have you heard about Samuel M. Shoemaker? He's the rector of Calvary Church in New York City and Frank has no better disciple. When a prominent minister like that admits that he needs the Oxford Group, it just proves that we have something the churches can't give!"

"Isn't that the claim of every new religious movement?"

"I suppose it is. But most of them have failed exactly where the churches themselves have failed. The individual is always lost in the organization. I never hear any talk about organization in the Oxford Group. We don't even have a membership roll. Frank is out to save the individual, not to start a church. He works according to the Jesus-way—save the man and you save the masses. Why, I knew a publisher right here in town who went over his books and started paying higher wages after Frank got hold of him."

Ned was a well-seasoned Grouper when he asked me to be his guest at a "house party." When I questioned him about an invitation from the hostess, he assured me that this was not necessary.

"It isn't that kind of house party," he explained. "It's really a part of the Buchman technique. Every Grouper brings a guest. Woo, win, warn, is the motto. I agree with Frank—a person isn't completely changed until he changes someone else. You'll probably call the party a socialized prayer meeting!"

And that is what it was.

We drove into the palatial Rocky River estate through a winding road cut through a lovely arboretum. When we came in sight of the old brownstone mansion, I was confronted by a scene that I had never before associated with religion. The hilarious sounds that reached us suggested all the fun of a country club. Swimmers dolphined in the blue waters of a large pool. On the near-by tennis court, balls volleyed back and forth with rhythmic rapidity. There were also a croquet game and archery and tables for bridge.

"You'll find our worshipers jolly," Ned chuckled, completely at home. "And we have a right to be."

Small groups dotted the lawn; some were relaxing on blankets. One fellow shaded his eyes with a book as he lay reading it in the sun. More cars drove in. The atmosphere was gay and refreshing. A comradely feeling hung like an aura over Groupers and guests. First names were always used, and a sense of emotional exhilaration pervaded the conversation. Occasional sharp, almost fanatical exclamations, typically Buchmanesque, identified the gathering.

From the apparently serious group at a card table came, "My spiritual thermometer was running high that night."

From a couple returning from a walk in the woods, I heard, "That's the first time they've ever come faster than I could write them down."

"Frank Buchman brought religion home to me and that's more than my mossy old parson ever did," came from a flippant teen-ager.

"That's a big order," was the skeptical response of a guest after listening to a sixty-second discourse on the four absolutes.

"It works." The Grouper grinned.

It was religious gravity decked out in modern robes of gaiety, fervent faith conveniently adjusted to the unrestrained temperament of a pleasure-craving generation.

Ned was consistently greeted with "Get anything good lately?" (They meant messages.)

"Never get anything bad," he would always answer. "But I can use some help." (He must have had a "checking" problem.)

I had been presented to almost every member of the "congregation" when the hostess, a plump, impetuous woman, made her dramatic appearance. In the ordinary social situation she would very likely have had little time for such a multifarious group. Today she played her role of "just one of the Groupers" with noble restraint. She moved through the crowd and, to the accompaniment of a fluttering small kerchief, announced invitingly: "There are easy chairs in the drawing room."

This was the official "call to worship." Leisurely, the Groupers crawled from the pool and made their way to the dressing room. Cards were put away; croquet and tennis were called off. Ned and I walked to the house with the hostess.

"I'm expecting a good old-fashioned washing out," she remarked while we settled ourselves comfortably in the pretentious setting of the drawing room. As others came in I caught these lines:

"If you can't be good, be honest." (She meant that if you sinned you ought to confess.)

"Did you hear about her infidelity? It was wonderful!" (He meant that her confession was wonderful.)

"So you've cleared up the back tracks." (He meant that restitution had been made.)

"The better the laundry, the cleaner the linen." (He meant the better the house party, the more effective the regeneration.)

The mood was suddenly changed when, unannounced and informally, someone started singing:

> "When I survey the wondrous cross
> On which the Prince of glory died,
> My richest gain I count but loss,
> And pour contempt on all my pride."

Silence, rehearsed silence, unmistakably a part of their worship, followed. Instinctively, I felt that this was a motivated device which moved at the very heart of the Buchman technique. Through the extended silence came the challenge, not of reason, but of the basic principles of human relations—honesty, purity, unselfishness, love. In this setting one was ready to admit that these four absolutes were the basis for a sound religious philosophy. In this moment of divine quiet, rationalizations were dissolved in the glowing warmth of an inner light. Was this why each Grouper had brought an "unchanged" guest? Ned had already made it clear to me that persuasive argument could not change a man. In Buchmanite phraseology he had put it this way: "It is a waste of time to argue with a man who is not downright honest. It is fruitless to talk about God to a man whose heart is impure. No logical reasoning can knock selfishness out of a man if he is not willing. Without love a man is nothing in the most absolute sense of the word."

So the "hopeless sinner" was caught in the mood and mechanics of the movement at a house party!

A low murmur intruded inoffensively into the silence. An older man, very ministerial in appearance, was talking to a young girl near the fireplace. As his voice rose, the periphery of attention widened, and he became more and more the cynosure of an attentive, listening audience. He was telling the girl how his life had been marvelously changed at a party such as this on the Oxford campus.

"I was a godless, atheistic, morally perverted college student, selfish as the devil. You don't have a sinful thought that I didn't have. But—" he began fitting an emphatic gesture to every word—"at that party, a great hope sprang up within me. After my public confession, I began following truth as fast as I could find it. Don't worry about your guidance. Take the first step. A man's true creed is what he believes in enough to do."

Ned whispered to me that this man had been on Oxford Group teams with Buchman. Perhaps that accounted for the professional manner in which he proceeded to "change" a life. With consummate skill he followed scientific steps which the Groupers designate as the five "C's": Confidence, Confession,

Conviction, Conversion, and Continuance. By sharing his sins with the girl, he gained her "Confidence." Others assisted by enumerating major sins which they had whipped out. In the ferment thus created a tension was built up around the girl which evoked the next step.

"Guess I've got so many sins I don't know where to begin." She was off to her "Confession" with a nervous laugh. "I quarrel with George whenever we're together. I want to be loved all the time, but he doesn't want to do that. I laugh at him and he gets mad. To make him snap out of it I drink, and this only makes him madder. I smoke too much. Look at my fingers. I'm a slave, as you say, and I'm dragging my chains around with me! All I've ever thought about is myself. I spend all my money on clothes. I try to outdo the other girls at the office in order to impress the boss."

"Go to him and confess just that," said her prompter. "See what a difference that will make. If you really want to make an impression, come clean!"

"Make restitution!" cried another, enthusiastically.

Such suggestions from everywhere in the room constituted a "bearing-down" action which spun the confession from the girl in rather complete detail. Fervent appeals were made for the acceptance of the "better life." In the parlance of the Groupers this would produce "Conviction." It did.

"I'm completely washed out!" This rapturous cry from the penitent was the cue that another changed life was being processed. "What's next?"

"We'll have a little prayer," said her adviser and without a change in his tone put the case straight up to God. Soon she was praying, too, and her voice told us that "Conversion" had been effected. When the prayer ended, a friendly torrent of congratulations fell upon the postulant. It was somewhat disappointing to me because I had heard lurid tales of the emotional exhibition that accompanied an actual "change." Ned was elated. "She'll work out the fifth C, 'Continuance,' just the way I did," he maintained confidently.

For two days the Rocky River estate was the scene of a spiritual clinic. Other lives were "changed" during the prolonged periods of "sin-sharing." And yet, in none of them did I hear any of the obscene accounts about sin and sex of which the Buchmanites had often been accused. It was, rather, intimate reporting on the value of living under the four absolutes. People came and went with refreshing informality. There were quiet times for those who wanted them, walks along the trails for those who needed special checking, seminars devoted to the Bible and the Buchman technique. A message of good will from Frank was relayed by our hostess at the Sunday tea. This reading inspired a hesitant "convert" to make his final decision. Standing with teacup still in hand, he burst out:

"Folks, I'm entering the ministry! And I'll preach the four absolutes! I'll play the whole field for Frank! Men are sinners; men can be changed. The changed soul has direct access to God. The age of miracles is not over. Those who are changed, change others. But no matter how many dirty sinners I change, there never was a dirtier one than the one you folks changed when you changed me! And if it happened to me, it can happen to every last sinner in the world!"

The teatime group received this announcement with the same enthusiasm they demonstrated for the winner on the tennis court. Restitution testimonies brought a similar response.

When Ned told how he had paid up debts accumulated by his early weakness for the horses and how he had remunerated fellows who had no record of having helped him, he stood for a time in the spotlight of Oxford Group approval. The consensus in every activity seemed to be the same: give us a chance and we can save the world.

I had no intention of posing as a spiritual saboteur, but when Ned and a young English friend, Aylmer, talked me into going with them on a "guidance walk," I took along the explosives that had been accumulating in my mind since I first heard of Frank N. Buchman.

In response to their exaggerated praise of the man, I contended that his genius lay in the appropriation of other men's ideas. "Your four absolutes," I recounted, "came from Henry B. Wright, who got them from Robert E. Speer, who got them from Henry Drummond, who very likely got them from someone else."

Aylmer responded to my mention of these men with "Never heard of them!"

I was in the awkward position of an outside informant enlightening the neophytes. They did not know that the workable technique which Buchman had popularized had been tested in the laboratory of a Yale professor's life. At the time of his death in 1923, Henry B. Wright was collaborating with Buchman on a treatise devoted to personal religion. Wright's earlier publication, *The Will of God and a Man's Life Work*, was Buchman's text. Before Buchman became famous, he confessed that much of the best in his message had come from Henry B. Wright. It was Wright who made Buchman "system-conscious"; it was Wright who taught him the first words of his spiritual lingo.

Neither of my companions on this morning walk was impressed or disturbed by my exposé of their leader. Aylmer, with a gesture of unconcern, said, "All that may be true, but don't we always ascribe originality to the man who makes a thing memorable? And you'll have to admit that F. B. has certainly sold the Oxford Group idea to the world."

"But I must protest against the use of that name," I retorted. "There was an Oxford Group long before Buchman ever set foot in your country, Aylmer. It was initiated in 1833 and was intended to clarify the position of the Anglican Church in the light of its higher function. I've often heard the charge that Buchman was never averse to capitalizing on the prestige this name afforded. It slyly put him into the company of men like John Henry Newman and John Keble and tied him to a great tradition in a way that was downright misleading."

"Oh," said Aylmer deprecatingly, "let's not quibble about that."

But my supply of critical bombs was not exhausted. What about Frank's personal life? Would it endanger the admirable faith of these believers if I retold the rumors that persistently drifted in from Princeton and Oxford campuses? When I brought up the matter, Aylmer dismissed it with a wave of his hand, but Ned demanded an explanation.

"It's an established fact," I supplied, "that Buchman was ordered out of Princeton by President John Grier Hibben in 1924 for saying that sex ruled the campus roosts."

"Well, maybe he was right!" Aylmer retorted.

"Maybe. But there were charges that the confessions prerequisite to change turned out to be orgiastic demonstrations. Some say the washing-out is as satisfying to the listeners as the original sin was to the confessors."

"Lies like that are characteristic of Christian persecution," countered Aylmer valiantly. "It's the same thing they said about Moody and Wesley. Why do men try to vilify the movement? Because our message is a challenge to their whole philosophy of life. There's not a better moral character in the world today than F. B. You can add Oxford itself to the schools that haven't understood what it's all about. There the editor of *Isis,* the undergraduate publication, said the Groupers were psychopathic. You didn't see any psychopathic cases running around here at this house party, did you?"

"And you don't find them anywhere," Ned added in disgust.

He was sure that my warped evaluation of the work would never permit me to balance the Buchman ledger. Was I overlooking the thousands indifferent to their own fate until they met Buchman? Was I forgetting that squads of full-time workers, serving without salary, had revitalized religion in many American cities? How could I doubt that the Oxford Group was executing a divine commission in a distracted world?

I stopped with Ned at many another spiritual caravansary along the Buchman road. In the summer of 1936, it was the first national assembly of the movement at Stockbridge, Massachusetts. Here I was confronted by a strange dualism. In some quarters Groupers were observing a quiet time. Elsewhere others loudly applauded a patchwork parade of American Legionnaires, Oxford Groupers, flag-bearers, and Uhm-Pa-

Tuth, an Indian chief. Airplanes droned overhead unfurling streamers against the clear Berkshire skies: AMERICA AWAKE. This was the new Buchmanism. In a rousing open-air meeting five thousand Groupers heard Frank say:

"Civilization is tottering on the brink of collapse. Only the God-controlled process can save the world from sin, war, poverty, and all other current evils."

The prediction was that out of this assembly would come a "world conversion" as real as the experience that shook his soul in the Keswick church. His latest aphorisms were:

> "When man listens, God speaks.
> When man obeys, God acts.
> When men change, nations change."

For ten days at this exaggerated house party the hodgepodge of celebrities and the great multitude of the unknown stood by for the miracle. A tabulation revealed eighteen hundred members of evangelistic teams and regular disciples of the cause. Hotel registers bristled with such names as Mrs. Henry Ford, Mrs. Harry Guggenheim, Emily Newell Blair, Cleveland Dodge, Baroness de Watteville Berckheim, Carl Vrooman, Sir Philip Dundas, Mrs. Henry Noble McCracken, and Lord Addington.

The transition in emphasis became more obvious each day. Groupers discussed it on their walks. Some were bewildered. Sin and confession were being played down; good works and Americanism were being played up. At one of the meetings Buchman went so far as to say that whatever an individual found compatible with the divine program could be justified. To many of the Groupers this sounded like philosophical chatter. Did the man who had changed their lives mean that the natural liberty of will could now be made the criterion for conduct? They felt that even though a man had been relieved from the tyranny of sin, he should "lean not on his own understanding." Yet F. B.'s interpretation became public domain: "So long as the desire for good exists, nothing can be genuinely bad." The orthodox sensed that if these ideas persisted, the movement would become a religious fraternity for those with only a superficial understanding of what constituted a God-guided life. Remembering how Frank had always said, "Your guidance is as good as mine," they continued to "wait upon God" in the familiar premises of the "morning watch."

Other Groupers were encouraged and strengthened by the Stockbridge meeting. They argued that the shift in favor of the commonweal was the logical development of the "workable technique." It was expansion for greater output. Having tested his ideas on a small scale, Buchman had now courageously gone out for the redemption of the masses. To those overawed by the sudden influx of the elite, the liberals retorted pleasantly that all names look alike on heaven's social register. Moreover, the "big" sinners and keymen were joint tenants whose prestige and money were indispensable. These arguments upheld Frank's "higher guidance." For most of his followers he would always be the center of unity.

Ned took his stand with the sequacious. Sincerely heaven-bent before he went to Stockbridge, Ned returned with his head brushing the stars. But, like a cool scientist, he worked his "silent time," "checked for guidance," and believed in Frank as the world's greatest religious leader. He sent contributions to the movement, expecting nothing in return and seeming to receive everything in the way of practical success.

One day he emerged from his "quiet time" with a message that stretched the four absolutes to a breaking point. It said, "Put a small stake on Carmel Queen to place in third race."

At first Ned felt it was not even necessary to check such an atrocious message against the four absolutes. It was an impish twist of the subconscious. But throughout the morning the heavenly tip-off persisted, and underlining it was Frank's Stockbridge edict. The refrain was tantalizing: there are no taboos for the godly. At noon, Ned dialed a half-remembered number not listed in the directory. In midafternoon the number called back. "Welcome home, Ned. You caught Carmel Queen straight on the nose!"

I saw in this humorous and perverted appropriation of the morning watch an ominous sign of what was happening throughout the Buchman empire. From Stockbridge, Oxford teams had moved across the country to raise their battlecry: "Every last man in America, in every last place in America, in every last situation in America, guided by God." And Buchman had returned to Europe to fire the opening salvo in a campaign for the conversion of nations. The world felt the faint reverberations of a twentieth-century Pentecost. Wherever practical religion was talked about, the name Frank N. Buchman was heard. Some hailed him as a contemporary prophet and a genius in modern methods of evangelization and social reform; others dismissed him as a "canting cheat" pulling together a colossal front to "hide his scandals." But I recognized in his newest venture a superstructure that obscured the tragic turn made at Stockbridge. Buchmanism could no longer be interpreted as the surrender of the individual to the will of God; the will of the nations had become more important. The *élan vital* of a great movement was being crushed out by the grandiloquent ambition of its leader. Out of the disintegrating Oxford Group, Moral Re-Armament arose. In the Hollywood Bowl on July 19, 1939, the sententious boss of the imposing show announced to thirty thousand spectators, "Tonight you are witnessing the preview of a new world order."

For a time this looked like honest prophecy. On July 23, a "world assembly" opened at Del Monte, California. It was Interlaken, U. S. A. Every day a new Buchman slogan reached the press.

July 23: "THE PLUS OF THE CHARACTER IS THE PLUS THAT WILL CHANGE THE WORLD."

July 24: "THE QUALITY OF THE INDIVIDUAL IS THE QUALITY OF THE NATION."

July 25: "YOUTH TODAY IS FACED WITH THE ALTERNATIVE OF BEING FODDER FOR WAR OR THE FABRIC OF A NEW WORLD ORDER."

July 26: "MRA MEANS REVOLUTION IN ALL POLITICS."

July 27: "WE MUST GIVE OURSELVES FOR PEACE OR WE WILL AUTOMATICALLY GIVE OURSELVES FOR WAR."

July 28: "MRA, SCIENTIFIC MEDICINE FOR THE MORAL ILLS OF THE WORLD."

July 29: "GOD HAS BOUND US TOGETHER TO RECONCILE THIS FIGHTING WORLD."

July 30: "AN ENGLISHMAN CALMLY STATED: 'I LOVE IRELAND. THAT IS WHAT MRA HAS DONE FOR ME.' "

The final act of the Del Monte World Assembly was set on Treasure Island at the Golden Gate International Exposition.

Buchman, in the leading role, read messages from King George VI and Queen Elizabeth, from premiers of every nation where MRA banners were waving, and from governors of thirty-three American states. President Roosevelt's Washington message was heard again:

"The underlying strength of the world must consist in the moral fiber of her citizens. A program of Moral Re-Armament for the world cannot fail, therefore, to lessen the danger of armed conflict. Such Moral Re-Armament to be most effective must receive support on a world-wide basis."

Before the final curtain fell, a radio hookup carried MRA's warning message to the far corners of the world: "The choice is between a vortex of fear and a pageant of triumph. MRA is the essential foundation for world settlement. The next step is for men and women in every nation to enlist in the world war for peace!" Buchman's challenging quota was: "One hundred million mobilized in all countries by December first to listen to God!"

It was a race with time to remake the world, and Buchman lost. Wherever MRA was strong, war's threat was stronger. Before December first, peace was broken in England where MRA had been a morale-builder, a fostering mother in the years of crisis. MRA's idealistic dream of "bridges between nations" was being swept away. The strategist for souls saw Europe breaking in his hands, while vicious rumors arose to taunt him. Chamberlain, who had believed in MRA, was disgraced. He had trusted Hitler too much. Out of the failure of the tragi-comic Munich appeasement, Buchman's words bounced back. What did he mean when he said, "I thank God for a man like Hitler"? Secessions from the group reached landslide proportions. Was he a Nazi sympathizer? He had said, "Systems don't matter, whether capitalism, Fascism, communism. The worst system will not work if the people are lost in selfishness and sin. The worst system will work if God guides it."

Stories that had been discounted in the days of peace were now subjected to brutal investigation. A member of the Goebbels gang was said to be one of the changed lives of MRA, getting guidance, but continuing as a worker in the propaganda mills of the National Socialists. What had happened to the message that the Jap had taken "from the land of William Tell to the land of the Rising Sun," now that Japan was marching into China? For once Buchman dodged correspondents. No public statement came from MRA headquarters.

To find out what was really happening, I called at the MRA Los Angeles office. In painful contrast to my expectations, I found an unimposing three-room suite on Hill Street. Through an open door I caught sight of the man who had dreamed the dream of salvation for the world. He slumped over an empty desk half-listening while a young man gave what sounded like an inconsequential office report.

In the quick impact of this moment, I felt the untold tragedy of a shrinking spiritual giant. I saw him again at the impressive confession in the Statler room. I pictured him at Interlaken, Stockbridge, Madison Square Garden, Washington, the Del Monte World Assembly . . . now Hill Street, Los Angeles. Was it possible that this solver of other people's problems could not solve his own? I had come to stir up the mud in his life as he had stirred it up in others. But when I saw him sitting there in the afterglow of glory, I seemed to see about him the procession of souls, men and women of many nations, to whom he had made life more meaningful and God more real. Against the backdrop of fleeting global acclaim, the loneliness in which he sat was his *Götterdämmerung*.

I experienced a sense of relief when I saw the young worker come quickly from the room and close the door. Dr. Buchman, he informed me, was seeing no one today. Was there anything he could do? Was it literature I wanted?

In the adjoining room two men were running multigraph machines. The papers, fed through by hands that seemed eager to work, were headed, "You-Can-Defend-America Campaign for Total Defense." An addressograph stood ready and the tables held pamphlets prepared for mailing. All this was further indication of the compression of a great leader's spiritual system. It was a radical change in the old Buchmanite plan of superinternationalism, but I saw in it an anodyne for the world's rejection of MRA.

It was more than that. It was Buchman doggedly fighting back, substituting patriotism for brotherhood, and preaching preparedness under the symbol of the four absolutes. These touchstones were never to be scrapped. In 1941, the You-Can-Defend-America Campaign diffused into the School for Home Defense in Maine. In 1942 it became the Midwestern Industrial Morale-Building Campaign. These activities drew little attention from the press. The ranks of MRA had thinned; prominent names had disappeared; the beloved disciple, Samuel M. Shoemaker, had forsaken his master. The New York rector had been attracted to the movement because of its emphasis on vitalized personal religion. But after charging that the Buchmanites were listening to the voice of Frank rather than to the voice of God, he requested that they vacate the parish house

near Gramercy Park that had long served as national headquarters.

The homeless remnants of the Oxford Group-Moral Re-
Armament were gathered up by Buchman's guiding genius on
Mackinac Island in the summer of 1942. For whatever reason
this unique resort spot may have been chosen, the fact remains
that it was a masterful selection. The island looms like a turtle's
back in Mackinac Straits, four miles from the Michigan main-
land. Old-fashioned surreys are the only means of transporta-
tion, and Mackinac has always been a symbol of the simplicity
of America's yesterdays. The Buchmanites took over with their
old crusading spirit. They came singing:

> "Out beyond our knowing
> Are these bridges going,
> Spanning need,
> Hate and greed,
> Far-flung highways growing.
> The call rings clear and plain:
> Work as one with but one aim
> And build together
> What none shall sever—
> Bridges from man to man,
> The whole round earth to span."

The Island House, the Murray Hotel, villas and private
homes yielded to the dynamic invasion. The religionists were
so consciously diffused with the regular tourists that it looked
like a big comeback, conveying to the public that a great
many famous personalities were involved. The project
was the Summer Training Center for Sound Homes,
Industrial Teamwork and National Unity. The aim was to

provide the necessary foundation for sound education and Christian leadership during the terrible years of war. The approach could hardly be aligned with the renowned and world-famous "sharing" process. The unpredictable Buchman! Play production was the chief activity here. Hollywood names, not too well known, figured in the production of *You Can Defend America.* This patriotic revue was taken on tour for a number of grand "world premières." Original musical numbers had a painfully childish appeal. One of these, cheaply planographed for distribution, carried the sketch of a short-horned critter, "Junior the Steer."

> "There once was a handsome young steer.
>   He's the hero of this little song;
>   With his Mom and his Dada
>   He lived in Nevada,
>   And he played in the hills all day long.
>   Woo hoo! Woo hee!
>   What's the future to be?
>   There's a two-fisted meat packer waiting for me!"

Through ten limerick verses Junior shied away from his fate, then finally came to the conclusion that, since everyone needed to sacrifice to win the war, he would do his bit by going off willingly to the slaughterhouse. His "girl friend" went to the depot to see him off.

> "There's a moral attached to my song,
>   That to every true patriot applies:
>   If you're feeling that you
>   Have done all you can do,
>   Think of Junior and his sacrifice!"

The divine mandate of Buchmanism was plummeting a good deal lower than tin-pan alley, but Mackinac became a fashionable spiritual retreat and the summer school an annual affair. In 1944, *The Forgotten Factor,* an industrial drama for national teamwork, was on the boards under the auspices of citizens' committees in many American towns. In Washington the co-chairmen were Harry S. Truman and James W. Wadsworth.

In 1945 the Mackinac project was rechristened the MRA World Assembly. Although the comparison with Interlaken and Del Monte scarcely went beyond the name, I recognized once more an honest effort toward helping people discover a source of power outside themselves. At times one felt one was again moving among the old Oxford Group. Each day was begun with a "morning watch." There were walks, house parties, discussions and lectures for the "two thousand delegates from twenty nations."

World figures at this assembly were eclipsed by the rising tide of a new Buchmanism personnel. The spiritual rays now centered on youth. There were high-school and college students who had "revolted against the drift and disunity in their gangs and in their countries." There were vets of World War II and young men still in uniform. This youthful crop, moving in the glamorous light of first love, found in F. B. and his method an absorbing power. Typical was a brilliant young lieutenant of a college professor's family. He had given up his study of law for Oxford Group-MRA.

These young people were being sent out, not to start a new movement, but "to spearhead a revolution which will make America think straight and live great." With the old motto-making technique the newcomers set out. The touring playlet, popularized during the war, was still considered the best vehicle for gaining recruits. *Drugstore Revolution* hit the road. Chatty dialogue and a flimsy plot tackled the problems of the American home. Buchmanites claimed that lives were changed after each performance. Skeptics saw in it another means for distributing literature and for circulating the current periodical, *New World News*. This eight-page tabloid issued from its Washington office each month glittering with big names and extravagant claims:

"MRA—The One Hope of the World," says Head of UNO Security Council.

"The Force and Framework for a New World," Stoyan Gavrilovic, undersecretary of state for foreign affairs of Yugoslavia.

"My Philosophy of World Revolution," Generalissimo Chiang Kai-shek.

"An Answer from Okinawa"; Infantryman, killed in battle for Japanese island, writes blueprint for America's future greatness.

"More Potent than the Atom Bomb," says Herbert Turnbull, British scientist.

Were these men MRA-ers? No one knew. No one was clear about the strength of the movement. In the summer of 1946 I spoke to earnest followers at the Island House on Mackinac. "The Movement is stronger now than at any time in its history," I was told. The teeming grounds, the crowded dining room, young, clear-eyed Oxford Groupers working co-operatively, writing and rehearsing new plays, seemed to bear out the statement. "Dr. Buchman is in Europe with a team of a hundred followers—the time is ripe for the world's acceptance of

the MRA ideals and the application of the four absolutes in
every life." In Redlands, California, juvenile delinquency was
stopped short by the presentation of *Drugstore Revolution*.
Teen-agers confessed their sins and began working with, rather
than against, the city officials. In Britain, members of Parliament were once more talking about living by Buchman standards and building a better world on the "Jesus Way." It was all
very great and confusing. But what about the original Oxford
Groupers, those who had withdrawn into the "morning watch"
when Buchman announced the beginning of his world revival
at Stockbridge?

As I had watched the great wings of MRA spread to lift the
whole universe into heavenly places, I had often wondered
about Ned and other old-timers. Had they been the happy
victims of a human machination that had failed, leaving nothing but disillusionment behind? Somehow they reminded me
of lowly converts in the high liturgical churches, watching from
afar, craning their necks to catch the glimpse of a red biretta or
the shimmer of a cardinal's ring. In the dark vault of some
mysterious cathedral poor worshipers crawl on their knees
down cold stone aisles to kiss the fringe of an altar cloth or to
light a candle humbly. But who can tell how tremendous these
acts are for the faithful? Could it be the same in Oxford Group-
MRA? Were those who had learned to live by guidance still
receiving divine directives?

I looked up Ned and put these questions to him. He prefaced
his opinions with a confession.

"Carmel Queen," he laughed, "was my old self bobbing up.
I came out of that quick. Even though she paid off, I never
tried it again. I knew it wouldn't check against the four abso-

lutes. The thing that made the Oxford Group great was changed lives; nothing else but the sheer fact of the spirit of God saying to the spirit of self, 'Move on out!' It went deep. Mind you, I'm not sure, but it doesn't seem to go deep any more. Stage shows can never take the place of the old-time washing-out. I went to Mackinac to see what was really going on. I wanted to see Frank. A talk with him would have meant a lot. Did I see him? Once. He was second in a reception line at a tea. He was supporting himself on an ivory-handled cane. You know, he's a sick man. Maybe that's why things have gone as they have. Or couldn't he stand success? I'm ready to admit that a religion, no matter how great, no matter how popular, is no stronger than the life of its leader. Did things really go to his head? I can't believe it. He's Frank Buchman! Some left him when he said that about Hitler. I didn't. I knew what he meant. Everyone knows now. It's common knowledge that the Oxford Group was persecuted in Germany. Many others left him when the war broke. They said his ideas had failed. It was the world that failed when people refused to answer his call for one hundred million listening to God. But despite all of this, he lighted a fire in many of us that will never die down."

From what I had considered the crumbling walls of the Oxford Group-MRA, Ned's faith was still shining. He was one of Buchman's "interesting sinners" transformed into a "compelling saint." For him it was advantageous that America has a way of faith for every seeker.

CHAPTER VI

THE KINGDOMS OF FATHER DIVINE

I MET "God" in Philadelphia. He was wonderful. We bowled together and sat through part of a movie and ate fried chicken. He was humble and wise and generous and he had a sense of humor. He was an American kind of God. He did things in a big way. He drove a big car. He ordered big meals. And the people who followed him were lowly people of great faith.

The fact that he was black was incidental. I forgot about color while I was with Father Divine. Sitting at a meeting in one of his kingdoms, I was surrounded by people, black and white, who had found in him a remarkably potent and human messiah and were receiving from him dramatic guidance for their lives. Their enthusiasm was powerful. They shouted, "Peace, it's wonderful!" and "Praise Father!" They testified about "changed lives" and the wonders of being "reborn." They sang original songs and let themselves go. It was like a political convention. The spell increased until it become volcanic. Then a gentle old Presbyterian minister from Florida was asked to speak. He was sitting with me, just an outside observer. But that crowd of three hundred reborn souls got hold of him. When he said something that they agreed with, they let him know it. They shouted their approval from the pews, until he was saying things that were definitely not in the script. He began talking "as the Spirit moved him" and presently he was swinging his arms and shouting: "I appeal to you, Father Divine! I send forth a Macedonian call: Come down to Florida and give us the influence of your Divine kingdom! Presbyterianism is dying! Help us! *Help us!* HELP US! We want what you have here tonight!"

Was this minister merely caught in the Divine tail winds or had his tour of the kingdom disclosed a higher motivation not apparent to the casual visitor? Intermittent stops at the Peace Mission Movement had suggested that one should not sell Father Divine short. I had heard him say many times that he had come to give himself unselfishly to all races and all faiths for the sole mission of leading lost humanity up the dazzling landscape of the glory road. I had asked his followers about confessions of faith, articles of belief, catechisms and sacraments. They always answered, "There's God!"

"Where is He?"

"He's here—He's Father! He's working, giving, changing lives! Showing us the way! Going on ahead!"

A young, intelligent Negro boy told me, "It's wonderful to see God in the flesh! That's what I had been looking for all my life! Now I've seen Him. It's wonderful to be able to go to a telephone day or night and get God on the line!"

"I believe that Father Divine is God absolutely and *impartially*," another of the newly reborn testified. "There was some chairs to move one time in the Mission and I says to myself,

'Let him move his own chairs. If he's God that ought to be easy—to move chairs.' Listen, brother, listen! Next day I had a pain across my back like the pain of fire. It wouldn't let up till I went and moved the chairs the way I should have done right at the start. Here's how I got it figured out: if he can help you to *bad,* he can help you to *good* in the same way. That's the secret and the mystery of Father God M. J. Divine!"

Traditional religionists steadfastly refused to take any hand in this burgeoning business, observing stiffly that such audacious claims were blasphemous. Others, winking at the maelstrom of idolatry, saw that it was good. They were ready to applaud the rare spectacle of made-over lives. Oblivious of the pros and cons of pedantic lookers-on, all of "God's children" kept saying, "He's here and here to stay!"

Moving in the midst of this apotheosis, I slowly unraveled the Divine epic. There is reasonable evidence that the Reverend M. J. Divine was born, but there is no record of his birth, and his age is a heavenly secret. All this is like God, say the followers. In the early days of his spectacular ministry, when his smart repartee frequently put him into the headlines, he explained it with "I wasn't born. I combusted on the corner of Forty-second Street and Lennox!" The best evidence available is that he was born George Baker on a rice plantation on Hutchinson Island in the Savannah River about 1880.

Today he is a commanding little man, strongly built and dignified. His bald head accentuates the rounded features of a pleasant chocolate-brown face and thoughtful, prophetic, almond-shaped eyes. He dresses well, but not extravagantly. He conducts himself with refinement. When he talks he does so without any particular gestures and expresses himself in a shower of coined words and aphorisms the like of which has never invaded the American pulpit.

His presence is hypnotic. He works his "miracles" by way of the subconscious. He continually thinks out and materializes the God-presence. To use his classical phrase, "I visibilate God!" "Visibilation" is the keynote of his success and is best expressed in his major principle of operation: "The Spirit of the Consciousness of the Presence of God is the Source of all Supply and it will satisfy every Good Desire." Add to the workability of this tenet a shrewd business sense, a conscious desire to help the underdog, a few lucky breaks, and you have the formula that has made him the Dean of the Universe for at least a million followers, some say twenty million.

And how did this son of ex-slaves get to be "the True and Living God"?

It all started back in Nassau County, New York, down Hempstead way in 1932. The man who calls himself Father Divine had been preaching for about twenty years, all the way from Georgia to New York. In Nassau County he was arrested for disturbing the peace. This was to be expected, because frequently celestial fires ignited the services and the worshipers shouted lustily when somebody crashed through the golden gates to victory. Then some sleepy neighbor, roused abruptly from his slumber, notified the police. So the judge sentenced Father to jail.

Judge Smith was a hale and hearty man, and he was not superstitious. But five days after he sent this man Divine to prison, His Honor died of a heart attack. "That," said Divine's followers, "is what a man gets for fooling around with God!" And Father, in his jail cell, shook his head sadly and shyly confessed, "I hated to do it."

Shortly thereafter, Divine was a free man. His step was more ethereal, his halo more perceptible, and it was no longer a secret that there were angels hoverin' round. Then stories began to tumble over one another. Folks told how Father sent his messengers of peace down to see Huey Long, and how they were refused a hearing. Subsequently Mr. Long met an untimely death. No fault of Father's, understand—it was God working. Will Rogers had a take-off on Father. Father said, "Stop it!" Will saw nothing offensive in his act and kept on. There was a plane crash. God was visibilating. One of Father's angels, Faithful Mary, said that Divine was immoral. She threatened to expose him. On the way to a radio broadcast, Faithful Mary was accidentally struck by a car. Lying on her hospital bed, she had to admit that Father was God, and she returned to the kingdom penitent. The "Lord" was getting personal.

In a sermon on September 11, 1938, Father said: "You might not be amused, but you may be surprised to know, just one year ago when we opened the Divine Greenkill Park in Ulster County, near Kingston, a boy was drowned in the pool. The coroner came and was very antagonistic and very malicious to me, even tried to personally stop my car and tried to take the key out of the car, and spoke of what he would do. I gave him to know he did not know who he was fooling with. Thursday I saw an article in the paper where he had been killed instantly. They said he was driving his car, he and his brother. Without a collision, colliding with any other car, the car just merely left the road and smashed into a tree and was cut in two. Both he and his brother—the two men—were killed instantly, and many other such things have happened with those who maliciously make attacks upon the FUNDAMENTAL."

Along the rugged course toward deification, Divine never called himself God. Some have compared him with Jesus who never called Himself the Christ. With subtle finesse, he extemporizes: "If God dwells in me, my body is His body. . . . God is your great emancipator. With or without a body, I came to do it. . . . I carry the weight of the masses, for I have harnessed their mentality and I have harnessed their energy and by it I have brought out many inventions. . . . I am ruling and reigning and having my way. God dwells in the midst of men. . . . Mankind must recognize God as He is, as I am."

Divine is convincing. For twenty years his followers have told him in songs and testimonies what a great God he is. They affectionately call him Condescending Saviour, King of Kings, King of the Universe, Father God Almighty.

My introduction to the bearer of these lavish titles took place in his office on the corner of Broad and Catherine Streets in Philadelphia. I was ushered into the Divine presence by a white girl, or, as they say in the Peace Mission Movement, a girl "of the lighter complexion." Father rose from his swivel chair, unhurried and divinely at ease. A corps of twelve stenographers began taking down our conversation from the moment I said, "How do you do?" and Father said, "Peace." They caught every precious word that fell from his lips and the less precious ones that dropped from mine. I asked him how he rated so many secretaries. With characteristic calm he smiled. "I apologize. Half my staff is on vacation."

After a general discussion of the philosophy and history of

the Peace Mission Movement, I inquired about the extent of membership.

"I have no idea," he answered simply. "I do not keep a record. There have been all sorts of estimations. We have people who are following the doctrine in Europe, Asia, Australia, and Africa and all over."

"How did you arrive at your particular calling?" I ventured.

He touched the tips of his fingers together thoughtfully. "Well, it is something like Biblical history. Of course, the Bible does not give the history of God, neither of creation. Life, as I see it, is not confined to a person, neither to personality. I see life without the beginning of days and without the end of life—eternal—therefore, I cannot justifiably give a legible answer to that question because I do not see myself as one that has begun at some certain time. I see the impersonal and yet personifiable, and I believe, as life goes on, it will evolve and take on and shape and form itself in many different expressions of its creation. It is wonderful!"

"Tell me, Father, are you grooming anyone to take your place?"

"Well," he smiled mysteriously, "not through mortality. I do not observe to be perpetuated by knowledge, neither by the mortal version, but yet it is impersonal and it is personifiable; it is reincarnatable and reproducible. Mentally and spiritually, in our daily conversations, we reimpregnate our thoughts in the hearts and minds of others and they, too, will eventually, as they give vent to the Spirit of Truth within, develop them and bring them to fruition even as we believe we have!"

It was in this idiomatic style, replete with coined words and impassioned phrases, that I followed the Reverend Mr. Divine through three hours of "harmonization by the unity of the spirit." During it all, he maintained a gracious self-confidence. It was impossible to find a rift in his armor of perfect integration.

When I asked if he was satisfied with the progress of his work, he answered, "I am. Of course, I know it will take time to universalize it as I intend to do, but of recent years I find that we are coming closer to a democracy than we have been a few years ago. According to my often rehearsed saying: by the unity of the spirit, of mind, of aim, and of purpose, we unify."

"How about the reaction of the churches?" I wanted to know. "Have you found them to be quite sympathetic with your work or have you met with opposition?"

"Years ago I used to find them quite opposed to it," he admitted. He turned in his chair and became introspective for a moment. "Now the churches are overwhelmed," he went on. "They have to listen and be silent now at what is actually being done. You see, the Peace Mission Movement is not an organization; it is a Movement, the same as the Christian Movement or the Jewish faith. But the Peace Mission Movement embodies both the Jewish faith and the Christian Movement. It does not take away from either, but it embodies the two and makes it what it is."

"You mean that you accept both Christian and Jew in your Movement? Also Moslem?"

"Certainly!" came the emphatic reply. "I have often said that if each person would be true to the religion under which he was christened and live it and express it in all conscientiousness and sincerity, the very spirit of the Christ within would lead that person to a higher light."

"Does anyone ever preach for you, Father?"

His reply was vague but informative. "I have assistants at practically all of our churches. There are some who are spiritually awakened and qualified otherwise from an intellectual point of view. And there are some who are ordained of different churches and they come and join and participate in the services and become part of the work."

While discussing financial features of the Peace Mission Movement, Divine informed me with a sense of justifiable pride that his churches were free from debt and clear of all mortgages.

"Yet," he added wisely, "we have never taken up a collection and have never done any soliciting."

"This has aroused considerable speculation among journalists, Father. Do you have time to read all the things that are written about you?"

"I bear no record of the things that are written about me!" he said with emphatic sweetness. "You see, a good many of these writers try to write about me but have never contacted me. They go by hearsay."

Suddenly he asked if I would like a cup of tea. Almost before I could answer, the door opened mysteriously and four girls came in carrying large silver trays weighted down with heavenly food: fried chicken, riced potatoes, fresh vegetables and fruits, tea, hot rolls, and a choice of pie. An immaculately dressed elderly woman spread a linen cloth on the table.

"Why, Father," I exclaimed as calmly as possible, "I thought you said 'tea'!"

"The Lord is never stingy!" came the pleasantly suave reply.

He ate sparingly. As far as I was able to learn, he does not drink and, unlike "de Lawd" in *Green Pastures*, does not smoke.

"What I ask of my followers," he says, "I expect of myself."
What does he ask? Miracles. The miracles of changed lives.

The kingdoms are full of former prostitutes, gangsters, thugs,
sneak thieves, drunkards, and the less professional sinners.
Through the Divine preaching and the Divine example, all
are made to feel that here is someone who loves them and
is interested in them. He wants them to put God to a test.
But first they must do something on their own. They must
obediently retrace their steps and clean up their past. Restitution is the door into the kingdom. No other religious
group takes this word so literally. Conscience funds throughout
America have been swelled. Bad debts have been paid. Old
wrongs have been righted. Criminals have voluntarily given
themselves up to the law.

One woman told me: "Twenty years ago I stole a hundred dollars from the lady I was working for. When I heard
Father God I knew I had to make that good even though
nobody knew I had stole it. I earned a hundred dollars. Then
I went to look for the lady I worked for. She had died. I told
Father. He said I had to give the hundred dollars somewhere
just the same because it didn't belong to me. I said I'd give the
hundred dollars to him. He refused it. I looked around where
to send it and thought that there wasn't anybody who had done
more for me than my country. So I sent the hundred dollars to
the Treasurer of the United States."

The Treasury Department has acknowledged that this has
happened many times. Thousands of dollars have been received,
not only as conscience payments but as gifts of gratitude to
"God's country." Father says, "Christianity and democracy are
one."

Souls are not reborn in the kingdom of the "true God Father Divine" without restitution. This is the highly specialized method by which he has dug acres of diamonds from the rough. His office is the clearinghouse for sin. His people sit down with him and draw the ground plans for a new destiny. For most of them, "God's" assignment becomes a lifework. Or it may happen like this: "I thought I had thought of all my sins," said a follower, "but one day while I was carrying home some groceries I remembered how, years ago, I beat a grocery store out of a bill. Was I glad I thought of that! It gave me a chance to erase out another old sin, just like God would want me to do."

The kingdom files are fat with evidence that here is one small spot in the Christian world where the doctrine of restitution is a mania and a passion. The convert sends his restitution payment to the individual or the concern to which he is indebted, asking that Father be notified that payment has been made. This double-check system brings the acknowledgments to kingdom headquarters. Here are a few letters selected at random from thousands. A New York firm at 364 West 121st Street, New York, advises Father:

This is to acknowledge with grateful appreciation the sum of $310 paid to us by Ruth Smile on the 13th day of August. This was a debt all but forgotten....

Here is one from the Unity School of Christianity in Kansas City:

Dear Father Divine:
At the request of Miss Glory Sun, I am writing to acknowledge receipt of a money order from her for $25 in complete

payment of a debt she felt she owed Unity School although we had released her previously from any further obligation. . . .

Goodwin and Goodwin, New York realtors, write:

Dear Father Divine:
We are pleased to inform you that one of your followers, Faith Faithful, has paid up an old debt of back rent. . . .

"If Father hadn't done anything else," said one of the reborn, "all those payments alone would prove that he's God. Where else does anything like that happen?"

Divine chuckles wisely. "The outer expression of things is but the condition of the mind within."

That is the secret: change the mind within. As to the actual manifestation, there is no prescribed form. People "get changed" under the Divine influence in various ways. Some sing and shout and dance. Some weep. Some become hysterical. Others go quietly about the business of effecting a practical adjustment. Spiritual names are selected, designating the spiritual change. They run a merry gamut: Pearly Gates, David Peace, Live Dove, Noah Frankness, Virgin Rose, David Consolation, Violet Ray. One of the men told me his reborn name was Joyful Job and added, "In Bible days great changed lives always brought along new names—like Saul who became Paul, like Peter who became The Rock and like Jacob whom God named Israel after his wrestling match with the angel."

Joyful Job had his struggle with God in a Harlem tenement house, but it was as real for him as though he, too, had been traveling on toward Canaan with Jacob the wretched. His wife, who is not a Divinite, said, "If he wants to be called Joyful Job, let him be called Joyful Job. He is a changed man, that's sure, and no religion helped him till he met Mr. Divine."

There are many Joyful Jobs in the Peace Mission Movement. They are growing in number like the green bay tree, and Mrs. Joyful Job is no doubt right when she says that no other religion helped her husband.

If a follower wishes, he may aspire to angelhood. It doesn't mean wings; it means work. It means closer fellowship with Father, full-time service, and a home in the kingdom. It means a new moral code: no more smoking, no more drinking, no more sexual intercourse. I did not learn just how far this matter of celibacy is carried, but I know that in the rooming houses provided for the angels, men and women are strictly segregated. An investigating committee reported "thousands of broken homes" as a result of angels giving up husband or wife. Angelhood also means giving up the right to one's own will, time, desire, and name. It is modern monasticism beyond the pale of the church. The religious of this order once wandered in the neglected ranks of unchurched America. They had been left for the law, but a black shepherd came along and rounded up the lost strays. He built an unorthodox fold to keep them in, but I am glad he came because they had been nibbling along the edges of our unbalanced social system long enough.

I saw these lost sheep safe in the fold. I saw the green pastures and followed them beside the still waters. I saw Father restore their souls. I sat at the table he had prepared for them. He called the affair "Holy Communion." But if this is communion, a Thanksgiving dinner is just a snack. It was a banquet of sixty courses free to all who would receive it.

Father and I came out of a kingdom office at ten-thirty P.M.

Crowds stood on the stairs and in the halls. They melted tight against the walls when Father approached, and some of the women made a London Bridge for us to walk through.

A young female angel, dusky and pretty, flung open the doors and we entered the Divine banquet hall. I had expected another courtly corner of the kingdom, but I was not prepared for such Olympian extravagance. The huge U-shaped table that filled the beautifully appointed room was richly set—glistening linen tablecloths, luxurious stiff linen napkins, brightly polished silver, fine dinnerware, an abundance of fresh-cut flowers. All was magnificently impressive. A corps of immaculate waitresses stood at attention. What kind of church dinner is this? I thought. Had cafeteria style gone by the board? Would nobody need to walk around with silverware protruding from lapel pocket, balancing coffee, water, and a man-sized dinner on a slippery tray?

We walked to the head of the table. At Father's place were twelve silver serving sets for coffee and tea. Beyond them, sixty serving forks and spoons were laid out in a shining V. Suddenly my eyes fell on the host's chair. On it three gold letters had been inscribed: G o d. Father smiled wistfully as he sat down. "Just the work of some enthusiastic angel," he seemed to say. For a moment he modestly betrayed that occasionally he was bored with being God. I was convinced that he would rather see his people live the idea than talk about it, and this has been the way with gods all through the ages.

From my place at Father's table I watched the lost sheep come in—Negro and white, young and old, rich and poor, good and bad, the high and mighty, and the humble and lowly. Dignified men of middle age touched shoulders with black boys who had

never had a square meal before their admission to the Divine
hierarchy. Sedate old ladies in aristocratic attire walked with
the girls who might have been their maids before the Lord
stepped in. Now they were all living together, happy and con-
genial since the Peace Mission Movement had wiped out class
and racial distinctions. The curious and the jackals were as
impressed as I and completely sobered by the princely proportions of the event. The ever-present secretaries took their
places on either side of Father. Across from him sat the "Rosebuds," the girls who make up the Divine choirs. When everyone
was seated, the doors were closed, and those who could not be
accommodated waited quietly in the halls for the second serving. It would be a long wait.

When the fabulous provider of his people's needs gave the
nod to the head waitress, the supernal fare was brought in on
silver trays. Each tray was first presented to Father who blessed
it with upraised hand, added a serving fork or spoon as needed,
and the trip around and across the tables began. Chicken—
fried, fricassee, à la king; meat—steak, chops, roast, cold cuts;
fish—there was perch fried in corn meal; potatoes—boiled,
mashed, creamed, scalloped, and yams; fresh vegetables to meet
every taste, and crisp cool salads of many varieties. It was like
a cutting from a Hollywood movie. It was fantastic, colossal.

"Don't take too much," warned my companion. "This goes
on for a long time."

She was right. For three hours the food kept coming with
the precision of a smoothly running machine.

"Will you take your favorite bread, sir?" asked a waitress.

"What would you like to drink?" asked another. "You may
also have your choice of dessert."

Through these waitresses we had access to the inexhaustible commissary of the living Fundamental. "God" was stintlessly providing for his children, good measure, pressed down, shaken together, and running over! One of the reborn sitting across from me chuckled. "God has done again upset the cornucopia of his horn of plenty!" Order, fellowship, and heavenly enchantment presided at this table of the "Lord." The Rosebuds sang happy songs about Father, about God, about the marvelous larder of the Dean of the Universe, about how wonderful it was to be at heaven's table! The event reached ecstatical heights. It was Christmas in the kingdom! It was homecoming in the promised land! Actually it was just an ordinary weekday evening.

"You can come back tomorrow night," said a Rosebud, sensing my enthusiasm, "and the day after tomorrow. Almost every night of every week Father has a banquet in Philadelphia or in New York!"

Everything is "on the Lord" in the Divine Peace Mission Movement. Why should "God" ask for anything since he owns the universe? Why insult "God" by passing a plate around for nickels and dimes? It is Father's pleasure to give, to give generously, extravagantly, omnipotently and with a loving hand. And when he has given once he gives again and again. Free schools! Free movies! Free church services! Free recreational centers! Free banquets! Free! Free! Free! That's God working!

"Send ME no money. It will simply necessitate MY sending it back." This is a stock line in Divine publications.

Yet Father confessed to me that he owned nothing in a "personal way." No one has been able to find a bank account in his name. There is no record that he has ever needed to pay income tax.

"My work is to give, not get," he told me one day. "I don't even own an automobile, but when one is needed it is always provided. I imagine that right now, because I need one, a car is standing at the door. Whenever I will it, one is there for me to use. Let's go and see."

We walked out to the balcony and looked down. At the curb stood a freshly polished Cadillac! This is the way he explained it: "I make real every assertion! I tangibilitate! I materialize every assertion, for God is the materializer of all of His Earth's Creation!"

When Father bought the fashionable million-dollar Brigantine Hotel near Atlantic City in 1942, he redecorated and reconditioned it and dedicated it as one of the better heavens in his kingdom. Then he started "visibilating." Some of the suites had previously rented for ten and twelve dollars a day, but Father scaled the whole lot down to a straight two dollars a week. Then he sent out embossed invitations and reopened the Brigantine with a banquet of a hundred and five courses—all free.

Such Holy Communions have dedicated Divine establishments throughout New York, New Jersey and Pennsylvania. Father is not statistically inclined, but the most casual investigator discovers that the extensive reaches of the kingdom are far from mythical. The Promised Land of the Peace Mission Movement is a chain of farms in Ulster County, New York. This agricultural department provides poultry, cattle and farm produce for the restaurants, hotels, and banquets in the Divine dominion. At the dedication of the Krum Elbow estate on

the Hudson, Father sounded the depths of his generous spirit
when he said to the thousands who had jubilantly followed
him there:

"Enter in, young men! Enter in, old men! Enter in, all
the inhabitants of the earth and become self-respecting,
self-supporting and independent!

"You call me God. It is because God in all evidence has
been discerned and nothing else but God is seen in me.
In all I am doing and in all I have done, there are those
who have known me for fifty years and more and will
tell you the same. Here is Mother Divine. She can tell
you, as she has told millions, she has never seen anything but God in me.

"Permit me to be transmittable, permit me to be reincarnatable, permit me to be reproducible. When this is
done you will see God in all mankind!"

In New York City thirty missions have been opened, in
Philadelphia twenty-five, in California seven, and others in
Connecticut, Maryland, the District of Columbia, Florida, Ala-
bama, South Carolina, Michigan, Minnesota, Iowa, and Washington. There are foreign missions in Canada, British West
Indies, England, Australia, and Switzerland. At the smallest
and most isolated post of the kingdom, the feeling prevails that
the great resources of their Father are always within easy reach.
The larger missions operate community Peace Centers with
recreational facilities, homes for the aged, orphanages, employment agencies, schools offering "all academic subjects, practical
courses in Americanism, Christianity, and Brotherhood, and
commercial training." Everything is free.

Such incalculable affluence has given rise to romantic notions concerning the source of supply in Divine's work. Father demands tithes of his followers, they theorize. People remember him in their wills. A rich anonymous philanthropist has subsidized the Movement. He gets his money from political sources. Followers scoff at such mundane suppositions. When "God" needs money he simply materializes it. He dips into the limitless reserve of his omnipotence. He draws his checks on heaven's treasury.

Such credulity is understandable, but as I looked beyond it I saw that "God" was but the incarnation of the co-operative efforts of a believing people. Father is the expression of their highest aspirations. He is the exalted director of America's greatest spiritual co-operative. The Peace Mission Movement is the practical unfolding of the dream he dreamed when, as an unknown and barefoot messiah, he surrounded himself with twelve disciples. They pooled their resources and trusted Father. He provided them with something better than money: "the Abundance of the Fullness of the Consciousness of Good, no Space is Vacant of the Fullness thereof." The master and his twelve have expanded into a congregation of the "seen and unseen actually living in the garden where the tree of life is blooming." Wherever the Movement takes root, it prospers through Peace Groceries and Markets, Peace Jewelers, Opticians, and Doctors, Peace Specialty Shops, Lumber Dealers, and Funeral Directors, Peace *Corsetières,* Laundries, and Radio Dealers. In New York and Philadelphia all the basic enterprises that provide the service needed by a city population are included.

This is a vigorous and successful application of the principle of the apostolic church. This is Christian communism, city style. Father's preachments, persuasion, and power give rise to more and more co-operatives constantly. Twenty started in one day. In them everything is cut-rate. Gasoline is two cents below standard price. Food and clothing of quality are ridiculously inexpensive. Beauty parlors run by Divine followers are so well kept and so reasonable that they have attracted a large white patronage. Peace restaurants serve good meals for ten and fifteen cents. A grocery dealer who ran an inch advertisement in a Philadelphia magazine now buys a half page because "Father advised me to lower my prices and I've never done so much business in all my life."

In these co-operatives many people willingly work for nothing because they want to "serve humanity." "Why not just work for God?" they ask. "What does life mean if it does not mean serving others? Money can't bring you happiness. Happiness comes from doing good." Unable to gain recognition in the great world, they become notable in the Divine kingdom. Finding inequality in society, they become a part of the microcosm of the Peace Mission Movement where there are no rich and no poor, where there is no racial or creedal discrimination, but where all are children of the one "True and Living God Father Divine." That is why Father says: "I have striven to UNIVERSALIZE ourselves by SOCIALIZING ourselves with others in the Abundance of the Fullness of the Comfort and Convenience and of the Food and Shelter we have about us!"

This may not mean much to the untutored! But to the true

followers it is a creed and a holy document. Whenever he speaks, a neology comes, cast in the bristling pattern of the Divine mold.

"What has Father done for you?" I asked one of the angels.

"What has he done!" was the rejoinder. "Let me tell you in his own words. 'That which is tangible was intangible at one time, but God, as the Tangibilator as well as the Creator, tangibilated that which is tangible, but at one time it was intangible, invisible, impractical, and unprofitable!' That's what he's done! Aren't you glad?"

Others may not remember his words, but they never forget the spiritual impact or the gleam in Father's eyes, or the thunderous sound of his voice when he wants it to thunder, or the fierce, impromptu, primitive passion with which he cries, "You are the personification of Life, Liberty, and the reality of Happiness!"

This thought is incorporated in the International Righteous Government Department, one of the basic units in the Peace Mission program. Father declares that through its operation a noble nation is arising, electrifying the atmosphere. The program, pointing to a new Americanism, has caught the enthusiastic response of the young people in the kingdom. They, more than anyone, have a fierce conviction that Father is what their world, this world, needs. He plays skillfully on their emotions. To them he is a youthful, forward-reaching prophet. He pushes back the horizons of their restraints and tells them about the glory of living under God's shadow.

He is their crusader: "It is immaterial to me what man or men may think or say. I am going on!"

He is their hope: "I have even greater discoveries for you than the Atomic Bomb!"

He is their wonder-worker: "I cause your prayers to be heard and answered before you pray them!"

He is their messiah: "I produce God and shake the earth!"

And he has told them that America is God's throne and democracy is His crown!

The contagion of Father's spirit has caught their hearts, and they give back to him all that he imparts to them. They work in the kingdoms. They conduct the services. They give testimonies. Their imagination and enthusiasm are reflected in the songs they sing. The old gospel stand-bys are never heard because new songs have grown out of the group consciousness. Songs that remind one of the "Ballad for Americans" or numbers from "We the People." Songs that bring religion out of a musty past.

> "We'll keep the Flag of Freedom and Liberty waving high,
> By living our Constitution and our Bill of Rights!
> By fearlessly standing for the rights of every man;
> By establishing Justice and Truth as Real Americans!
> Through expressing a citizenry of a True Democracy,
> We have the Force of Power that's international Victory!
> Eventually the symbol of the Flag of the Free,
> Will be seen in every land: *Americanism, Christianity,*
> and *Democracy!*"

But the Rosebuds are not content with simply singing their own compositions. They often stage hallelujah marches through the auditorium, clapping or waving their hands, singing spasmodically as the orchestra plays a lively number. They also express themselves through orations, pledges, and affirmations. One night a teen-ager sitting near me suddenly jumped to her feet and emphatically declaimed:

> "We, the youth of the Peace Mission Movement,
> And the enactors of the three great documents:
> The Declaration of Independence,
> The Constitution and its Amendments,
> And *Father Divine's* Righteous Government Platform,
> Demand the immediate passage of the *Antilynching bill!*"

Then someone started a song called "Down with Bilbo-ism!" Down with racial discrimination, race prejudice, hatred and inequality! Up with the antilynching bill, the brotherhood of man, the defense of America, democracy! Clean out the Senate! All of this is tossed into the religious hopper and becomes part of the Divine obsession. The people know what they believe. No hazy groping or outmoded clichés here. No uncertainty in the path of sinking traditions. "We believe in racial and social equality. We believe in the confiscation of all armaments and their destruction. We believe in the unification of North, South, and Central America into the United Countries of America with one flag and one language! We believe in Christian communism. We believe in buying for cash. We believe in substituting 'Peace' for 'Hello!' We believe that the Constitution is our protection, and that we are the protectors of the Constitution!"

To broadcast these basic tenets, Father publishes in Newark, New Jersey, a sensational fat tabloid called *The New Day.* The date line carries A.D.F.D. (Anno Domini Father Divine.) It is a weekly and sells at the nominal fee of five cents a copy or two dollars a year. Father's spiritual aliases, personal pronouns referring to him, and all references to Deity are impressively set in bold upper case. Divine's impromptu bursts of eloquence in sermons, office talks, and interviews are printed verbatim and consume the greater part of the fifty pages. Letters of restitution, together with Father's replies, original songs, and world news, are also published. Peace Co-operatives use this journal as their principal advertising medium.

One night during a Righteous Government meeting a sudden, hushed suspense gripped the crowd. Immediately everybody stood. Father had entered the auditorium and was ascending the platform unobtrusively.

"Peace!" he said, raising his hand.

"Peace, Father dear!" responded the audience.

"Peace, children!" said Father and sat down.

They wondered if "God" would speak. The stenographers waited, watching him, pencils poised. Out of the moments of Father's genius they had caught flashes of great wisdom. Accompanying him through crowded days, waiting upon him in his office, sitting near him at services such as this and at Holy Communion, following him on the roads to new kingdoms, they had been given the opportunity to record memorable axioms:

"Blessings are like things bought on the installment plan; when you stop paying for them they are taken away."

"How can unjust officials give you justice? They do not have it to give."

"See God in someone, for until you see Him in someone you cannot find Him in yourself. But when you find Him in yourself, you will see Him in all mankind."

"Men fight for democracy abroad and tremble at the fear of it being enacted at home."

Father nodded to the Rosebuds to strike up another song. They did. They intoned:

"We thank you, sweet Father,
For your love and care.
We thank you, sweet Father,
We know you are here!
We love you, we praise you,
We thank you, our God.
We live in secureness
By trusting your love!"

As Father listened his eyes drifted dreamily, trancelike, sadly over his people.

Presently I noticed that his chin had fallen forward on his chest. To all appearances he was napping! The audience noticed him, too; at first with wide-eyed wonder, then they nodded slowly, understandingly. Even "God" needs rest, they seemed to say, as tender smiles formed on their lips. The Rosebuds sang quietly, awed and reverent.

A brother got up to speak. I looked over at Father again. His eyes were open now. He motioned to me as if saying, "Come here a second." We were both sitting on the platform confronted by about three hundred people, but when "God" winks who am I to disobey?

I went over to Father's side and leaned toward him.

"Do you like to bowl?" he whispered.

"I beg your pardon?"

"Bowl," said Father.

"Yes, I like to bowl, but——"

He got up with a peremptory "Come along."

We left the congregation, the Rosebuds, the testifiers, and the reborn and started down the stairs into the basement of the church where there were two bowling alleys and a smiling Negro pin setter.

"Throw a few," said Father, and his eyes twinkled because he was proud of those two alleys.

I rolled a few bad ones. "How about your trying it?" I suggested.

"I don't bowl," Father said.

"Oh, take one," I urged.

He consented.

From the way he selected a ball, a light, three-fingered one, from his stance and delivery, I was sure he was no bowler. Yet, when that uncertain ball got within nodding distance of the pins, it headed straight between one and three for the prettiest strike I ever saw. Father's nonchalance was characteristic. He rubbed the soft palms of his hands together as if to say, "Well, what do you expect when the Lord rolls one!"

So I bowled with "God" and we went back upstairs where the service was being concluded. Crowds were gathering for another banquet. Once more a long row of uplifted hands made an imposing bower along the narrow corridor and up the winding stairs. Under this sheltering canopy, the "King of Kings" wended his humble way while his people whispered, "Peace, Father, Peace." Again his poise and bearing seemed refined within the crucible of his imposed divinity. That he had the capacity and temperament to fill this holy station perfectly, none would deny. If he had his moments of human suffering and fears, they were enshrouded by his magnanimity and submissive devotion. To those who trusted and loved him, "God" was passing by. And as he led on, smiling quietly, gently, I felt he was leaving with them his oft-repeated benediction:

> "I come to all men and all nations that they may be even as this leaves me, Well, Healthy, Joyful, Peaceful, Lively, Loving, Successful, Prosperous and Happy in Spirit, Body and Mind and in every organ, muscle, sinew, joint, limb, vein and bone and even in every atom, fibre and cell of My Bodily Form."

CHAPTER VII

THE BAHA'I FAITH

B AHA'U'LLAH!" They speak the name softly, accenting the second and last syllables. In spite of the foreign tang they make it sound beautiful, like the name Jesus for devoted Christians, like Jehovah God for the Witnesses on Main Street, like Father Divine for the reborn and angels in the Peace Mission Kingdom. Baha'u'llah is the "Splendor of God," the Persian messiah. He is more than that. He is the Great Prophet in whom all nations and all religions should be united. To three thousand Americans he is the "hope of the world." They are members of a "world religion" and call themselves Baha'is.

"Baha'u'llah!"

The name was dramatically brought to America with the World Congress of Religions in 1893, an occasion so in keeping with the message of Baha'u'llah that Baha'is feel it all belongs in a prophetic plan. Here, at the Columbian Exposition in Chicago, it seemed that all nations, tribes, and religions were brought together for the deliberate purpose of creating interfaith understanding. Oriental priests mingled with the clerics of the West. For two months Jew, Christian, Moslem, Hindu, Buddhist, Zoroastrian, Shinto, Taoist, and Confucian, together

with many lesser-known groups, sought a common denomina-
tor of belief which would unite all religions against irreligion.
On the thirteenth day, one of the delegates arose to say:

"In the Palace of Bahji, just outside the Fortress of Akka, on
the Syrian coast, there died a few months ago, a famous
Persian sage, Baha'u'llah—the 'Splendor of God'—who regards
all nations as one, and all men as brothers. He uttered senti-
ments so noble, so Christlike, that we repeat them as our
closing words: 'All nations should become one in faith and all
men brothers; the bonds of affection and unity between the
sons of men should be strengthened; diversity of religions
should cease and differences of race be annulled. Let not a man
glory in this, that he loves his country; let him rather glory in
this, that he loves his kind.'"

These words, although reflecting so perfectly the spirit of the
Congress, were lost in the sensationalism of the gay nineties'
"World's Fair." The representatives of the faiths of the universe went back home; the Torah, the Bible, and the Koran
were taken, each by his particular adherent. Missionaries returned to proselytize, each for his own belief. But a few
spiritual gypsies, remembering, looked eastward wistfully. They
believed that Baha'u'llah had not only an idea, but a divine
revelation. By a special providence and their own pursuing,
they got hold of his writings, "tablets," filled with wisdom,
symbolism, and authority. They translated from the Persian
such works as *Seven Valleys and Four Valleys,* a treatise on
the journey of the soul to its final unfoldment; *Hidden Words,*
a summary of the truths inherent in revelations; and the *Book
of Certitude,* in which was interpreted the oneness of all faiths.

For many Americans, these sacred writings had the spirit

and sweep of prophecy, and they were ready to accept
Baha'u'llah as the mouthpiece of God. These were not people
whom the churches had passed by; some of them had passed
up the churches, feeling that creeds and sects were narrow and
confining. To them Baha'u'llah's words came as a supreme
challenge, "O ye people of the world! The Religion of God
is for the sake of love and union; make it not the cause of
enmity and conflict! By My Word shall the diverse sects of
the world attain unto the light of real union!" Lured by this
utopian promise, well-to-do pilgrims set out for the Syrian
coast. There they found that the poor and the lowly were following the same star to the prison shrine of the Persian Sage.

"Baha'u'llah!"

I saw his words carved in the alabastrine arches above each
of the nine doors of America's most magnificent religious structure, the Baha'i House of Worship, in Wilmette, Illinois. I saw
people of many races and creeds enter these doors to worship
together, people who believed that the Prophet's dream to
unite all religions had been fulfilled. What was the line interrupted by my heckler friend in Hometown long ago? "Creeds
are but branches of a tree——" At last I had found a group
which claimed to be the primal point of unity for the diver-
gent branches of the world's tree of faith. They call their
temple the *Mashriqu'l-Adhkar,* a Persian word meaning the
"source of the mention of God." They call it the "Tabernacle
of the Great Peace" that proclaims the oneness of mankind.
They call it the "Portal to Freedom," and for one familiar
with Baha'i history there is no more descriptive term.

It sounds back through more than a hundred years to Mirza
Muhammad Ali. At sunset on May 23, 1844, this young re-

former, pursued by suspicious rulers and indignant religionists, arrived at Shiraz, Persia. A disciple was waiting at the
gates of the city. To him he confessed that he was the "Bab."
He meant the "gate" through which a great new prophet
should enter to unite all nations and all religions. In the
midst of the squabbles of Moslem, Christian, and Jew, he dared
accuse that all had forgotten their common origin. He contended that in the same Divine and Universal Will, God had
revealed Himself through Moses, Jesus, and Mohammed. These
prophets were equal. They were mirrors reflecting God's glory,
messengers bearing the imprint of the same Creator, torches
lighted at one immortal fire. In the Great New Prophet, God's
spirit would again be manifest. But Persia was not America
and Mirza Muhammad Ali was hated by all faiths. Like John
the Baptist, the voice in the wilderness, who prepared the way
for the Founder of Christianity, the Bab was destined for
martyrdom. He was jailed with his disciples in prison barracks in the city of Tabriz. The day of execution was set for
July 8, 1850.

When the guards came for the Bab he was seated at his
prison table talking to a disciple. He begged them to allow
him to finish his conversation. They refused. But as he was
dragged from the room, he cried, "No earthly power can silence
me until I have said all I must say to this disciple!"

Thousands of spectators crowded the roofs of buildings and
jammed the streets through which they hauled him. In a
gateway between two barracks, a crosspiece was fastened.
Seven hundred and fifty men with rifles were ranged in three
files for the killing. The Bab was lifted up. The heavy ropes
that bound his wrists were fastened to a spike in the crosspiece,

and he hung suspended above the ground. Orders for the killing were given in rapid succession; three times, two hundred and fifty rifles fired at the dangling figure. When the smoke cleared, the Bab stood on the ground unhurt. The gunmen's bullets had severed the ropes and set him free. There was a moment of fierce silence. Then the spell was broken by convulsive excitement. Spectators struggled in frenzied escape from this incredible portent. The would-be executioners cried, "Miracle! Miracle!"

Their frantic, disordered search led finally to the Bab's cell. There he sat with his disciple, speaking as calmly as though there had been no interruption. They stopped in the doorway, reluctant to seize him again. In a few moments he rose from his chair. Walking toward them, he said, "I have finished my conversation. Now you may fulfill your intention."

Once more he was suspended in the gateway before a new firing squad. The spectators climbed back to the roofs. For a moment the crowded street was hushed. Then the rifles spoke again, and the body of Mirza Muhammad Ali became a mass of bleeding flesh and shattered bone.

But his message lived. "I am but a letter out of that most mighty book and a dewdrop from that limitless ocean, but a Great New Prophet shall appear! Wait for him!"

Nothing could quench the messianic hope that had been awakened in the hearts of the Bab's disciples. Nothing could destroy the dream in which they saw mosque, cathedral, and synagogue blended into one house of worship to the living God. Known throughout Persia as Babis, they were subjected to imprisonment and death. Persian religionists felt themselves in danger of being absorbed and destroyed by this new and revolutionary faith. Political wrath burst upon the Babis when they were accused of plotting to overthrow the government. Ten thousand were killed between 1850 and 1860. Never since the time of the early Christians had followers of a new religion been so persecuted. If the Bab's "Promised One" did not come soon there would be none left to acclaim him, for the last remnant of those who believed were rounded up at Baghdad in 1863 to be shipped to a prison at Constantinople.

While waiting deportation in an abandoned wilderness garden called Redvan, a man of fifty-one years, greatly respected among the Babis, rose prophetically, summoned his comrades around him, and said:

"This is the Day in which mankind beholds the Face, and hears the Voice of the Promised One! The call of God has been raised, and the light of His countenance has been lifted upon men. . . . Great indeed is this day! The allusions made to it in all the sacred Scriptures call it the Day of God! Bestir yourselves, for the promised hour is at hand!"

Baha'u'llah stood before the Babis in the person of Mirza Husayn Ali. He had been a disciple with them for nineteen years. He had suffered with them in their persecutions, gone with them through their blood baptism, spent years with them in the wilderness retreats. The son of a wealthy Persian, he had abandoned the world to follow the teachings of the "Oneness of All Mankind." It was he who had exclaimed after the killing in Tabriz, "My head longeth for the spears! The blood shed in the path of the Bab is more precious to me than all else!" Now he was transfigured. He no longer spoke as a Babi. He no longer was a Babi; he was the "Splendor of God!" As Jesus in His day, as Mohammed in his, so now Baha'u'llah!

Babis who had been in hiding came fearlessly to Redvan. They wanted to be near him whether it meant deliverance or greater persecution. They were now Baha'is, the chosen of Baha'u'llah. For nine days in the shadows of this wilderness garden, the light of the "Splendor of God" shone upon their lives. For nine days, eighty disciples drawn from diverse faiths sat with their Master and heard his words of "hidden wisdom":

"Ye are the fruits of one tree, and the leaves of one branch. Deal ye one with another in the utmost love and harmony. So powerful is the light of unity that it can illuminate the whole earth!"

The glorious tryst at Redvan was ended abruptly by the intrusion of the persecutors. Baha'u'llah and his Baha'is were carted off to Constantinople, then to Adrianople, and finally to Akka, a prison city to which only the worst criminals were sent. The disciples never doubted that their leader could have delivered them all, but great prophets never employ miracles to save themselves from suffering. Baha'u'llah was to spend his entire life as a prisoner. He was thrown into a filthy dungeon, shackled with a heavy chain that locked him to his prison wall. His followers were forced to watch as he was whipped and dragged through the narrow barrack passages of Akka.

Prison walls could not conceal the "Splendor of God." In the wide stretches of the desert and in the busy market places, people heard that the Promised One had been revealed. Those who had looked for his coming made pilgrimages to the prison-temple. Not permitted to enter, they waited until he showed himself at the window and raised his hand in blessing. When they wept for him, he called assuringly, "Fear not. These doors shall be opened. My tent shall be pitched on Mount Carmel, and the utmost joy shall be realized."

The faithful returned to their homes comforted, while the abbatial blessings reached beyond the circle of believers. From the hand of Baha'u'llah came a resistless tide of personal epistles, bearing commanding salutations:

> *Hearken, O Sultan, to the speech of Him that speaketh the truth. . . .*
>
> *O King of Paris! Tell the priest to ring the bells no longer! The Most Mighty Bell hath appeared!*
>
> *O Czar of Russia! Incline thine ear unto the voice of God. . . . All the atoms cry aloud: Lo! The Lord is come!*
>
> *O King of Berlin! Give ear unto the Voice calling from this manifest Temple!*
>
> *O Pope! Rend the veils asunder! The Word which the Son concealed is made manifest!*
>
> *O Rulers of America and Presidents of the Republics therein! Hearken to the strains of the Dove on the Branch of Eternity singing the melody! There is no God but Me, the Everlasting, the Forgiver, the Generous!*

Some laughed derisively as they read these messianic edicts; others put them quietly aside. Queen Victoria of England pondered over the lines, "The Lord hath ordained as the sovereign remedy and mightiest instrument for the healing of the world, the union of all its peoples in one universal Cause, one common Faith."

"If this be of God," she observed, "it will stand; if not, there is no harm done."

No outward change was effected. The roads of faith still ran their separate ways. But the Great Prophet had challenged the world, and Baha'is felt a ground-swell stirring beneath the religious consciousness of men everywhere.

In 1870, Baha'u'llah, through the intercession of influential Persians, rode from his barracks in the carriage of a Mohammedan sheik to the palace of Bahji within the prison city. He was still a captive, but here in comfortable quarters he was united with his family. Sometimes he was permitted to journey to Mount Carmel where, in lonely meditation, he knelt where the future shrine of the martyred Bab should be. Was it here that the organizational plans for the world-wide Baha'i faith were born? Was it here that he received divine inspiration for his prolific literary works? There was little rest for him at Bahji, for the faithful and the curious milled about the palace grounds. Even the rulers who kept him imprisoned stood in awe at his popularity, wisdom, and works.

A noted Orientalist of Cambridge, who visited him, said, "The face of him on whom I gazed I can never forget, though I cannot describe it. Those piercing eyes seemed to read one's very soul; power and authority sat on that ample brow; while the deep lines on the forehead and face implied an age which the jet-black hair and beard seemed to belie. No need to ask in whose presence I stood, as I bowed myself before One who is the object of a devotion and love which kings might envy and emperors sigh for in vain!"

Despite this growing process of deification, Baha'u'llah, like a good steward, prepared wisely for death. Having lived to reveal his message, dying, he thought only of its dissemination. From the "station of his Deity" he drew up his final will and testament which left no doubt about the "plan of God" concerning his successor. His eldest son should no longer be called Abbas Effendi. He was now Abdul-Baha, the Servant of Baha, and upon him the Covenant of the Cause should fall.

Thus with Baha'u'llah's death on May 28, 1892, the inviolable apostolic succession of the Baha'i movement was begun. Enthusiastic followers immediately began to speak of Abdul-Baha as another prophet, a new Manifestation of God. They remembered excitedly that this son of Baha-'u'llah had been born in the very hour that the Bab first declared his mission. Aged disciples related how, as a boy of eight, Abbas Effendi was brought to his father's dungeon. In the deep shadows, his terrified eyes beheld the "Splendor of God" chained to the wall, his swollen and bleeding neck encased in a steel collar. From that moment the bond between them was more than that of father and son or master and disciple. At Redvan, as a young man of nineteen, he was the first to call his father the "Blessed Perfection." Along the flagging march to Akka, he followed the little exiled band and guarded Baha'u'llah's tent.

It was Abbas Effendi, as a mature disciple of the Cause of God, who persuaded the Persian sheik to effect the removal to Bahji. He had gazed so long upon the glory of his father that Baha'is now saw that glory reflected in him. He quickly suppressed all attempts at deification. As the Bab was the gate through whom Baha'u'llah appeared, so, Abdul-Baha contended, he was merely the interpreter. But his supreme authority was not to be questioned. Baha'u'llah had referred to him as "the Center of My Covenant." He had made the commands concerning him explicit, "When the Ocean of My Presence hath ebbed and the Book of My Revelation hath been completed, turn your faces towards Him whom God hath purposed, who hath branched from this Ancient Root!"

With this divine legacy, Abdul-Baha inherited his father's political and religious enemies. The accusation had not changed—the Baha'is were plotting to overthrow world governments and set up a theocracy. For forty years Abdul-Baha saw the world from behind prison walls. He saw ancient roads built for man's salvation so littered with strife, that they were leading to destruction. Pilgrims who came to him at Akka heard him say that it was not his intention to found another religion. There were too many already; there should be but one. All faiths should dissolve into the "Splendor of God." And there should be a temple, a home for the One Universal Faith. Such a sanctuary would be a mighty influence for the union of all men.

On his release from Akka bondage, August 31, 1908, when the Turkish revolution overthrew the Ottoman Empire and set all political and religious prisoners free, the man who had entertained pilgrims himself began a pilgrimage. He traversed his homeland, the Orient, and Europe in search of a suitable location for the first Baha'i temple. During the days of Baha'u'llah, Russian Baha'is had undertaken the building of a house of worship in Ishquabad. But was Russia the proper setting? True, the light of divine revelation had always risen in the East and shed its radiance upon the West, but Abdul-Baha found the East a mélange of national suspicion and international discord. There was enmity among men who preached good will and impending threat of world war. Wondering whether in his day the West should be the source of more than mere reflected glory, he turned his face toward America.

In the spring of 1912, the Servant of Baha'u'llah bade his friends good-by with these words, "I am going to the United States to establish the fundamental principles of our Cause and to proclaim the oneness of the world of humanity and the equality of all men."

For the next nine months a Persian seer was in the American news. He was now sixty-four, a man prophetic in body and spirit. His eyes had a sorrowful, quietly longing expression, as one who brought with him a gaze that had rested much on God and longed that every man might see Him, too. His beard was snow-white and his long hair was covered with a small felt turban. His face was slightly wrinkled but his skin was radiant. He was of medium size, very strong in form, muscularly built, yet sensitized by some mystical power. He traveled with a retinue of servants, secretaries, and devotees. He spoke no English, but in purest classical Persian greeted those who thronged about him in New York. A traveling companion interpreted his words, "I pray that you may be manifestations of the love of Baha'u'llah; that each one of you may become like a clear lamp of crystal from which the rays of the bounties of the Blessed Perfection may shine forth to all nations and peoples!"

He crossed the continent and visited America's great cities. Church, temple, and synagogue welcomed him. He met all creeds, classes, and races on their own level. Photographers persuaded him to pose for the press and the movies. He appeared in the Chicago Masonic Temple and in the Washington, D. C., Public Library Hall. He brought material and spiritual blessing to the slums of New York. He spoke in America's great universities. Columbia was impressed; the president of Leland Stanford said, "Abdul-Baha will surely unite the East and the West, for he treads the mystical way with practical feet."

His knowledge of world affairs marked him as a prophet. In Los Angeles in October 1912 he said, "We are on the eve of the battle of Armageddon. The time is two years hence, when only a spark will set aflame the whole of Europe. The social unrest in all countries, the growing religious skepticism antecedent to the millenium, and already here, will set aflame the whole of Europe. By 1917 kingdoms will fall and cataclysms will rock the earth."

He held out no hope that the Baha'i faith could stem the onrush of Armageddon. Instead he said that war was inevitable. The old world had failed to develop the spiritual powers of the human heart in proportion to the outreaches of science.

Editorial comments were generous:

"No religious movement of recent times is nearly so significant as that of Baha'ism."—*Portland Oregonian.*

"The religion of the Baha'ists has nothing of the eccentricity or faddism of so many modern religions and none of their shallow philosophy. It is simply a synthesis of the noblest ethics of the world around one common center—love and good will to all men."—*Boston Congregationalist.*

"Baha'ism should be welcomed as one more indication of the drawing together of races and the coming co-operation of man in the establishment of what in both Eastern and Western language is called the kingdom of God."—*The Christian Register.*

Criticism generally was not directed at Abdul-Baha but, rather, against the fanatical devotion with which he was hailed by American zealots. Wherever he appeared, someone in the crowds claimed that a glance from him had an electrical effect. Women came forward to kiss his hands. One enthusiast said that she "had seen God!" A minister, feeling the touch of Abdul-Baha's hand, said that his heart melted to tears, that his voice choked in his throat and that he could not have spoken a single word had his life depended on it. America was being initiated to a hypnotic spiritual power.

The climax of the grand tour was reached in Wilmette, Illinois, where an influential group of believers had selected a site for a temple. As early as 1903, a supplication had been sent to the Servant of Baha to which he had given his fervent assent. Abdul-Baha's endorsement of the "sacred spot" was graphically related to me as I rode up Sheridan Road one day with Albert Windust, one of the earliest American Baha'is.

"It was May first of 1912," he began, "that the Baha'is followed the carriage of Abdul-Baha along this very way. We had set up a tent on the temple site. Five hundred seats were arranged in three circles with nine aisles leading to the center area. That is the way he wanted it. We expected him to drive his carriage right up to the tent, so the people formed an avenue from the road to the entrance. But the Servant of Baha'u'llah surprised us all by getting out and walking briskly to the temple grounds. There, at high noon, he said, 'The power which has gathered you here today notwithstanding the cold and windy weather is indeed mighty and wonderful. It is the power of God, the divine favor of Baha'u'llah! Thousands of *Mashriqu'l-Adhkars* will be built in the Orient and Occident, but this, being the first one erected in the Occident, will be of greatest importance.' With these words, he took a golden trowel and broke the ground. Then he called for a workman's spade. After turning up some of the earth, he asked everyone to come forward and do the same. As they did, they announced their nationality. Thus, symbolically, all of us prepared for the ideal unity of which the Bab spoke and for which Baha'u'llah lived and died."

The record said that all of the major countries of Europe, the Near East and the Orient, the Jews of the world, and the North American Indians were represented that day.

In devout reminiscence, Windust went on: "When the last spadeful of earth had been turned, Abdul-Baha set down a common field stone and said, 'Now the Temple is already built!' "

To hear again of such indomitable faith made understandable the imprint which the son of Baha'u'llah left on American religious life. The temple was to cost over a million dollars, and in 1912 there was less than forty thousand in the Baha'i treasury. Yet he said, "The Temple is already built!" Did he mean the "Temple of the Word" in people's hearts, or did he foresee the response of a believing and generous segment of the American public? All of the money came through voluntary subscription. Contributions, generally, were not large, but they ran the range from a peddler's donation on Chicago's south side to a gift from the late movie actress, Carole Lombard. Soon, believers all over the world were sending their offerings. An anonymous giver sent a thousand dollars, simply addressed to "The Baha'i House of Peace."

Abdul Baha predicted that America, with this temple at Wilmette as headquarters, would lead all nations spiritually. He maintained that the American people were worthy of being the first to build the "Tabernacle of the Great Peace," and to proclaim the oneness of mankind. Baha'is felt that no greater commission had ever been sounded on American soil. From their temple at Wilmette a unifying truth should emanate to all the world.

The dome of the amazing structure now loomed in the distance. As we approached, I had to admit that it was indeed a composite of mosque, cathedral, and synagogue. The East was blended with the West in a magnificent allegory of architectural trends—Greek, Romanesque, Gothic, Renaissance, and Byzantine. It was the kind of temple one would expect to glimpse just inside the pearly gates. It was patterned motion, the Taj Mahal of the Americas. In spite of the majestic austerity of the great, towering three-storied nonagon, two galleries, luxurious in their simplicity of line, encircled all with warmth and quiet welcome.

I stood for a moment in front of this alabaster house of worship, somewhat overwhelmed. Nine great pillars of white quartz rise in the form of a circle from deep within a caisson. These pillars frame nine sections of intricate masonry with recessed windows and nine cathedral doors, one in each section. This comprises the outermost unit or the first story. Within this, offset from it, the design is repeated in a loftier nonagon which rises triumphantly to supersede the first and form the second story. Between these pillars are sections of concave arcs and crystal latticework. From the interior of this second unit, nine majestic pylons thrust upward for a hundred and sixty feet, resolving into a clerestory of brilliant white filigree. It is granite spun into a texture of fine lace, so that one feels not massive weight, but is reminded, rather, of painstaking needlework faithfully embroidered into some ancient ecclesiastical robe.

"The nine pylons," Windust explained, "symbolize the nine

living religions of the world. These, rising from a common base, the heart of man, reach upward toward God. The higher they rise, the nearer to one another they become, until, when they attain their highest goal, they become one. All great religions are unified in the Baha'i faith."

It would be difficult to find a nobler ideal than this at the heart of any American religion. And yet a spirit of loneliness pervaded the temple grounds, and a sense of waiting hung over the glory of the *Mashriqu'l-Adhkar*. Even though an occasional car stopped in the drive, the great doors seemed to call in vain to the races of men hurrying by. The feeling was so impelling that I turned to Windust and asked how he accounted for the fact that the Baha'i faith with its all-inclusive aspect was still a "little-known" religion.

"We have ninety assemblies with a total of three thousand members in the United States," he replied defensively. "But one cannot measure the scope of the movement by these figures. We have always realized that Baha'u'llah's ideals must come through a slow, evolutionary process. But we have proudly watched their development in the affairs of men. We are convinced that the United Nations Organization is a gesture toward the realization of Baha'u'llah's message. Woodrow Wilson knew of the sacred writings before he went to the Hague with his plan for a League of Nations. I think it is highly significant that many world leaders are using Baha'u'llah's ideas effectively even though they do not acknowledge their divine origin."

It was a good argument, yet I detected a note of pain in Windust's voice that suggested how keenly he felt the ineptitude of men to get hold of Baha'i teachings. It hinted of the tedious, stubborn manner in which humanity accepts all simple truths. But I knew that public opinion regarded the ninety assemblies, sparsely dotting the forty-eight states, as conclusive evidence of the limited progress of the American Baha'i community. This is further emphasized by a comparison with other groups dating back to the year of the World's Congress of Religions. Christian Science, whose birthday closely approximates the advent of the Baha'i faith into America, lays rightful claim to over 300,000 active members. I was ready to attribute such disproportionate growth, paradoxically, to the ambitious goals of Baha'u'llah's followers. The legacy of faith which he left to the world is definitely not egocentric. Personal emphasis in this religion is subordinated to the interglobal idea; salvation for the individual is attained by the vision of a common world citizenship. This would seem to be almost synonymous with the democratically interfaith platform of Father Divine; however, Divine's rugged, almost uncouth, appeal breaks with this world religion when he holds out unlimited glories for the individual. To the blackest sheep in his fold, he promises green pastures of peace, freedom from want and fear, and a ringside seat in the kingdom.

When I voiced these thoughts Windust contended that no one better supplemented faith with works than Abdul-Baha. During World War I, he so impressed British government representatives with his philanthropic work and sacrifices among the people of the Near East that a knighthood was conferred on him.

"His zeal for social betterment was perpetuated when he ordered that a community of peace should surround this temple," Windust persisted. "Baha'is will not rest until the vision of

Abdul-Baha is completely realized. There," he pointed out, "a school will be built, there a hospital, here a college. There will be laboratories for scientific research, dispensaries for the poor, and homes for the aged and the needy. Doesn't this sound like a personal appeal?"

"But actually, Mr. Windust, Christianity is more than that; it is a personal religious experience. Christians build their hopes around such realities as repentance, restitution, and spiritual baptism. But these words have little place in your sacred writings. The way I interpret it, you believe that the transformation of life and character is the result and not the beginning of salvation."

"On that point," admitted Windust, "there is a difference in emphasis. The message of Jesus was designed for the individual; that is what was needed in His day. But when Baha'u'llah was revealed the world was ready for international social emphasis as well as the need for personal regeneration. Work, in the spirit of service, is accepted as worship."

So I was again reminded that one becomes a Baha'i not for personal gain, but to serve mankind and to assist in the amalgamation of the many scuffling religious tribes of earth. The ideal is certainly not unworthy; yet, to the average American, it is likely to remain grandiose.

But I had come to Wilmette to meet the people who denied such contentions. I would soon know what these believers were like, for Windust had assured me that a cross section of American Baha'is could always be found here long before the hour of worship. A number had already gathered. They were walking through the grounds and lingering in the shadows of the temple.

"Let us go up," Windust suggested. "Here, you see, are eighteen steps which surround the entire temple. In his day, the Bab surrounded himself with eighteen disciples. Nine, and multiples of nine, have special meaning for us."

The meaning for me as we ascended was lost in the temple's overpowering beauty. As I neared the pillars and archways, their interlaced designs became more and more incredible. The great ribs of construction carrying the tremendous weight had the appearance of fragile tapestry. Light seemed to be transmitted from behind the white, sensitized surfaces.

Suddenly my silent admiration was interrupted by the captivating patter of a bejeweled devotee of the faith. "Oh, Mr. Windust!" she rhapsodized, "I have just returned from a visit with the Blessed Guardian!"

She rapturously clasped her hands in an attitude of devotion, but, to me, it was unconscious vanity, for the gesture showed off to tremendous advantage the dazzling brilliance of two huge diamonds. I questioned whether she would be the most typical Baha'i, but she would surely be among the most interesting.

"You know how you felt when you were with Abdul-Baha, Mr. Windust," the enchanted pilgrim continued. "It was the same with the Blessed Guardian."

Immediately I sensed that Baha'is believe that the power of attraction which was Abdul-Baha's was passed on to his successor, Shoghi Effendi, the grandson whom he designated as the "Guardian of the Cause" in his last will and testament. They accept the tradition of incarnated mystical power from the Bab to Baha'u'llah to Abdul-Baha to Shoghi Effendi.

"I paid my respects at the tomb of the Bab and at the hallowed shrine of Baha'u'llah," she was saying. "I visited all of our shrines on Mount Carmel. I was at Akka and in the Palace at Bahji. I walked in the garden at Redvan. Oh, but my visits with the Guardian of the Cause! There is a nameless something that comes over one when one sees him. His eyes! I have never looked into eyes like his in all my life.

"And, do you know, one morning I had the feeling that he was going to call me to speak to me privately? Why should he, I wondered, because there were surely more important people in the party of pilgrims than I? But, sure enough, a messenger came and said, 'The Guardian asks for you.' I walked on air! Almost his first words were, 'I have had you much on my mind. You are to carry a message back to America for me. Remind all of those who stand identified with the Faith of the Master's words, "The prime requisites for them that take counsel to-gether are purity of motive, radiance of spirit, detachment from all save God, attraction to His Divine Fragrances, humility and lowliness amongst His loved ones, patience and long-suffering in difficulties and servitude to His exalted Threshold."'

"He wrote the words for me, but, do you know, when he read them to me they seemed already to be written in my heart? I never forgot them. One day I walked with the Guardian in the beautiful garden. 'Have you learned the words I gave you?' he asked. I repeated them for him. He turned to me with the most beatific expression I have ever seen. 'Good,' he said. 'Good. You have learned them with love and purity of motive, and they shall be to you and all who hear them as the rays of an effulgent Light.'"

"Everyone who has met the Guardian comes away impressed," Windust responded with his usual quiet enthusiasm. "Of course, you remember how we are admonished in the will of Abdul-Baha to take the greatest possible care of Shoghi Effendi so that 'no dust of despondency and sorrow will stain his radiant nature,' and that he may become 'a fruitful branch on the tree of holiness.' "

Such sanguine sentimentality would have been shockingly out of place elsewhere in America, but here, at the door of the *Mashriqu'l-Adhkar,* it seemed a part of Baha'i liturgy.

"Oh!" came the emphatic response, "the Center of the Covenant required that to obey the Blessed Guardian is to obey God and to turn away from him is to turn away from God. But one cannot fully understand until one has seen him," she concluded as she turned to go into the temple.

Engraved in the monumental archway above the door were the words:

O RICH ONES ON EARTH! THE POOR IN YOUR MIDST ARE MY TRUST; GUARD YE MY TRUST

Just now they seemed so significant that I read them aloud.

"One of our fundamental principles is based on that text," Windust explained. "We believe that extremes of wealth and poverty should disappear, and that everyone should live in comfort. There are inspired utterances of the Great Prophet above each of the nine doors."

As we started around the temple I watched the people arrive for the service. I thought I must be seeing a small-scale reproduction of the World's Congress of Religions. Most of them entered through the "main door," which faces southeastward to Haifa. Above this door the "inspired writing" proclaims,

THE EARTH IS BUT ONE COUNTRY; AND MANKIND ITS CITIZENS.
The other inscriptions were equally worthy of remembrance:

THE BEST BELOVED OF ALL THINGS IN MY SIGHT IS JUSTICE;
TURN NOT AWAY THEREFROM IF THOU DESIREST ME

MY LOVE IS MY STRONGHOLD; HE THAT ENTEREST THEREIN
IS SAFE AND SECURE

THY HEART IS MY HOME; SANCTIFY IT FOR MY DESCENT

I HAVE MADE DEATH A MESSENGER OF JOY TO THEE;
WHEREFORE DOST THOU GRIEVE?

MAKE MENTION OF ME ON MY EARTH THAT IN MY
HEAVEN I MAY REMEMBER THEE

THE SOURCE OF ALL LEARNING IS THE KNOWLEDGE OF
GOD, EXALTED BE HIS GLORY

While we stood before the ninth door reading, BREATHE NOT
THE SINS OF OTHERS SO LONG AS THOU ART THYSELF A SINNER, a
young Negro greeted Windust. I again felt the enthusiasm of
belief reflected with genuine passion.

"Great words there!" said the Negro, putting his hands on
his hips and gazing up with a conquering air.

"Great words of a great man," I admitted.

"Baha'u'llah!" A light, satisfied chuckle accompanied the
word. "You know, my friends used to say to me, 'How you
goin' to learn all them foreign names connected with that new
religion?' 'What foreign names?' I says. 'Ain't I learned Bible
names all the time? Is Baha'u'llah and Abdul-Baha worse than

Melchizedek or Nebuchadnezzar? Is *Mashriqu'l-Adkhar* harder than Laodicea? When I think of Sunday-school words like the Edomites and the Jebusites, you think I'm goin' to have trouble with Babis and Baha'is?' These names are beautiful." He went on musingly, "Take the Baghdad garden, R-e-d-v-a-n. That's called Rizwan. Take Mirza Muhammad Ali. Mirza's Persian for mister. He was the Bab, you know. Bab means gate. He opened up for Baha'u'llah. Baha means splendor. U'llah means Allah, or of God. There you got Splendor of God. Take Abdul-Baha. Abdul means servant, servant of Baha, servant of God. He was the exemplar. And the present leader, Shoghi Effendi. Shoghi means teacher. Effendi means master. There you got master teacher. Nothing to it! And they say, 'How you goin' to learn all them foreign names?' "

"Foreign names!" Windust repeated, shaking his head despairingly. "When anyone says that, it merely indicates how far we still need to go before we realize the Great Prophet's dream. That is one of the reasons why we advocate an auxiliary universal language. That is why we are interested in universal education. The world can be harmonized only through our universal religion."

"But isn't there a danger that Baha'ism will always remain an abstract, visionary symbol rather than a practical basis for world unity?" I protested.

"No, it's all worked out!" exclaimed the Negro and, with a faraway look in his black eyes, he recited what might have been an assignment from the Baha'i catechism. "Unfettered search after truth and the abandonment of all superstition and prejudice. Religion must be a cause of love and harmony, else it is no religion. Religion must be in agreement with science, bring-

ing faith and reason into full accord. Then shall the world be
united."

He turned and entered the temple with a reverent pride
which convinced me that his new religion meant more to him
than merely a new vocabulary. He had conveniently blended
it with his American heritage.

"We have no illusions about the difficulties and work ahead,"
Windust hastened, eager to temper the idealism of the Negro.
"But we do have an organizational plan that will do the job.
Each year every Baha'i community elects a Local Spiritual Assembly. This is a board of nine that handles the affairs of the
community. Any Baha'i over twenty-one may be a member of
this Assembly. We have no nominations, and so there is no
electioneering. We vote by secret ballot, and the nine persons
receiving the most votes are elected. Above the Local Spiritual
Assembly is the National Spiritual Assembly found in every
country where our faith is established. Its members are elected
by delegates from local communities. Our National Assembly
now has its office in the building over there on the lake shore."
He indicated a modest white stone' building. "The National
Spiritual Assemblies will soon act as an electorate for the International House of Justice which will sit in Haifa as the legisla-
tive body for Baha'is everywhere."

Finally he concluded with an auspicious note in his voice:
"Think what will happen when, instead of a League of Nations
or a United Nations Organization, there will be an International House of Justice stressing the principles of the Oneness
of Mankind!"

"Do you really believe that the House of Justice has a better
chance than other organizations to unite the world?"

"I do, because Abdul-Baha promised in his will and testament that both the Guardian and the members of the House of Justice will be under the protection of God and, therefore, infallible. The Guardian was designated as the sole interpreter of the words of Baha'u'llah for the express purpose of preserving unity. This is the only way that sectarianism can be prevented. Of course, some, through a desire for personal leadership and power, have set up groups of their own, but they will fail."

I knew that this was a reference to the New History Society, a group that refused to obey Abdul-Baha's last will and testament.

"Isn't it possible that this will happen again when Shoghi Effendi dies?" I asked.

"I don't think so. Baha'is who were faithful to the will and testament of Abdul-Baha are determined to maintain unity. The first-born of the Guardian's descendants will be his successor unless he does not possess the necessary spiritual and intellectual qualifications."

"And who decides that?"

"The nine Hands of the Cause. You see, the Guardian will choose teachers and helpers from Baha'i communities throughout the world to assist in propagating the faith. All of these will be called the Hands of the Cause of God. This group will elect nine of its constituents to sit with the Guardian at Haifa. One of their duties will be to verify the choice of a successor."

As Windust completed his minute description of the Baha'i organization, a young Chinese greeted him.

Turning to me, Windust said, "You will be interested in meeting this young man; he is an exchange student at the state university."

"And what is your chief interest in the Baha'i faith?" I queried.

"It is all good," the young man answered precisely. "It is the only basis of understanding between the East and the West. My interest was first aroused when I learned that Abdul-Baha had said, 'Whatever the intelligence of man cannot understand, religion ought not to accept.' The religion of my people was made up almost completely of practices and beliefs which I could not reconcile with science. That is why I could never feel that our forms of worship gave us what we needed. But I have found this great world faith in complete accord with science. That is as it should be, because religion and science cannot be separated. They are the two wings by which humanity rises."

In a lighter mood, he continued, "Of course, I like to play around with the numerological aspects of the faith, too!"

He smiled broadly as Windust raised a mildly restraining hand and, with a sweeping gesture that took in the temple, went on, "Nine concrete piers sunk ninety feet below water level. Nine pylons. Nine columns with nine arches. All set in a nine-acre park with nine sides, nine avenues, nine gateways, and, some day, nine fountains! According to the Mohammedan calendar the Bab appeared in the year 1260. One—two—six—zero—that adds up to nine! According to the Christian calendar Baha'u'llah appeared in 1863; that is a multiple of nine. The Spiritual Assemblies have nine members. Nine Hands of the Cause will sit in Haifa. Nine is the number of perfection and, according to a Mohammedan tradition, nineteen represents the unity of all knowledge! The Bab had eighteen disciples. Counting him, that makes nineteen. Baha'u'llah made his pronouncement in Redvan nineteen years after the Bab's prophecy. The new Baha'i calendar will have nineteen months of nineteen days each. And, Mr. Windust, did you ever stop to think that Louis Bourgeois, who designed the temple, died on August 19, 1936!"

Windust showed friendly interest in this speculation. "There is no doubt that the science of mathematics was given to the world through divine inspiration," he agreed warmly, as we started toward the door.

Here he introduced me to Edris Rice-Wray, a young medical doctor of Evanston. She was one of a volunteer staff of trained guides who conduct visitors through the temple and are equipped to interpret any aspect of the Baha'i belief. I learned that visitors numbered 27,559 during the previous year. Among them were representatives of every state, practically every Latin American country, five Canadian provinces, and eighteen other countries. Two hundred ten thousand nine hundred and thirty have been registered since the guiding service was introduced in 1932.

I detected the same devotion in my guide that I had found in Windust. Her enthusiasm was even greater. She escorted me into the huge "lobby" which is formed by the convergence of the avenues leading from the nine doors. I was immediately struck by the unfinished aspect of the interior. Naked steel supports were in austere contrast to the intricate beauty of the galleries outside. Yet the upward sweep of the delicately perforated dome was breathtaking.

"Think how beautiful it will be when the glass dome is in place, catching the light diffused through the perforations," my guide envisioned. "The walls when finished will give the same effect."

She explained that this spacious lobby would serve as an auditorium reserved for worship only, but always open to the public for meditation and prayer.

"Services here will open with a cappella singing. Then there will be readings from the Words of God—the Torah, the Bible, the Koran, and, of course, the sacred writings of Baha'u'llah through whom man's redemption will come in our day."

And so we came to the stumbling block in the Baha'i road. In singular contradiction to unifying all religions, the Baha'i faith is asking the world to accept another prophet. Would the Jews acknowledge the "Splendor of God" as one equal to Moses? Would Christendom ever accept the claim that Baha'u'llah is the fulfillment of the prophecies concerning Christ's second coming? Could the Buddhists recognize him as another Gautama, or the Moslems another Mohammed? Would not all organized religions see in him a threat to their own prophetic messiahs? The fear that faith will be eclipsed rather than strengthened is the logical reaction of faithful adherents to other religions.

As if reading my thoughts, Dr. Rice-Wray was saying, "Of course, this may sound impractical to you, but wait." She touched the arm of a stooped old man. "Meet my Jewish friend," she said to me. "You were a shirt salesman in the South, weren't you, Sam?"

The man chuckled and said, "Many a Christian accused me of driving a hard bargain."

"And how did you feel about the Christians, Sam?" I asked.

"I hated them," came the honest admission, "just as I hated Jesus. Often when I said the name, I'd spit."

"And now——?"

"I do adore Him," and he nodded in deep sincerity.

The next person I met was a Baha'i-Christian. She spoke to us about the blessings she had received at the recent Feast of Nawruz, the Baha'i New Year celebrated in late February, and the Feast of Redvan, an anniversary observed on March twenty-first. My guide explained that both are solemnized by the giving of gifts and ministering to the poor and the sick. The newcomer spoke so enthusiastically about the joy of these days and the nineteen fast days preceding them that I thought she must surely be a member of the Spiritual Assembly.

"I'm really a Baha'i-Methodist," she acknowledged, transferring a copy of Baha'u'llah's *Hidden Words* to her left hand and extending her right in greeting. "You know, none of the Baha'is have ever asked me to give up my church affiliation. To me this demonstrates what we really mean by the unity of all faiths. I'm a good Methodist and a good Baha'i. You know, the Baha'i faith is a spirit. I think it is the only spirit that has the answer for all problems. I talk about it wherever I can—even to my missionary society. It is surprisingly easy to merge Methodism into the larger unity of Baha'i beliefs."

"I don't suppose you have ever been accused of being a better Baha'i than a Methodist," I chided.

"I wouldn't say that." She laughed. "There was more than a bit of criticism when my son was married in a Baha'i ceremony. But, you know, I've never been sorry. It was such a beautiful, simple service."

"But since you have no ministers, what was the ceremony like?" I asked.

"There was piano music and readings from the inspired utterances. Then my son took his bride's hand and and said aloud, 'We are content with the Will of God.' She completed the ceremony by saying, 'We are satisfied with the Desire of God.'"

"Is such a ceremony legally accepted by the state?" I asked.

"In certain states the secretary and the chairman of an incorporated assembly may perform a marriage," Dr. Rice-Wray replied.

"I am sure all of the states will recognize it some day," the Bahai-Methodist avowed. "The combination of religious and civic orders must come before the world can have peace. As Abdul-Baha once said, 'We must come to the truth of God wherever we behold it.'"

When she left us, my guide candidly observed, "Many Protestants are like that when they first become interested in the Baha'i faith. But eventually they find that church membership is binding. One cannot remain within the limits of denominationalism after becoming a part of this great World Religion."

"Was that your experience?"

"Not exactly. I was born in a Baha'i home. My stepfather was a Unitarian minister until he met Abdul-Baha. But after that both he and my mother were approved by the Spiritual Assembly to give Baha'i lectures wherever they were sent. You would call this missionary work, but it is a common service of the loyal Baha'i, and we do it without thought of remuneration."

We had now reached the reception room downstairs where

there was a generous display of Baha'i publications. The books were for sale, but my guide hastened to assure me that purchases were completely voluntary. She emphasized that some of their books had been translated into over forty languages.

Recorded classical music from Foundation Hall announced the beginning of the service. While I consulted my program, Dr. Rice-Wray eagerly supplied interesting personal descriptions for the names I read. A "charming fashion artist from Marshall Field's" was in charge. We were to hear three speakers: a "brilliant Latin-American fellow" on *The Unity of Religions;* a "clean-cut American law student" on *Peace Plans;* a "dainty, flowerlike Persian girl" on *The Spiritual Challenge of the Baha'i Faith.*

"It's really a typical program," she ended. "Young America— young people of the world standing together in the fulfillment of the Lord's Prayer, for the Baha'i faith is His kingdom come, His will being done on earth as it is in heaven."

Surrounded by the hundred or more worshipers, I felt that this was a microcosm of the great world of believers which Baha'u'llah had envisioned in his day. Baha'ism had not made the strides forward which other modern faiths had made, but the representation was, nevertheless, significant. Orientals, Negroes, and white representatives of who could tell how many nations and faiths; the Baha'i-Methodist, clasping her copy of the *Hidden Words;* the bejeweled pilgrim with the words of the Blessed Guardian in her heart, quietly zealous Albert Windust—young and old waited with eagerness and confidence beneath the eternal vigil of the "Splendor of God."

When the music stopped, his words were read in quiet, chanting tones:

"Blessed is he who proclaims the doctrine of spiritual brother-hood, for he shall be the child of light. Blessed is he whose heart is tender and compassionate, for he will throw stones at no one. Blessed is he who will speak evil of no one, for he hath attained to the good pleasure of the Lord. Blessed is he who teaches union and concord, for he will shine like a star in heaven. Blessed is he who comforts the downtrodden, for he will be the friend of God."

Blessed are the beatitudes of Baha'u'llah.

CHAPTER VIII

UNITY

K ANSAS CITY, PLEASE! VICTOR 8720! A midnight call
from a dormitory at a state university. "I need help!
I am going blind! The doctors say they can do
nothing! Can you help me?"

Victor 8720!

A young wife explains that her husband is a pilot. "He's
overdue at the airport. He's flying bad weather. He needs your
guidance."

Victor 8720!

"I am playing my first concert tonight. I want to know that
you are with me. It must be a success. Please help me at eight
o'clock."

Victor 8720!

A businessman is negotiating an important transaction. "I
must have prosperity thoughts. Please send them through at
two o'clock eastern standard time!"

Day and night it goes on!

Day and night there is someone on duty at 917 Tracy Street,
Kansas City, Missouri, to answer:

"Silent Unity. . . ."

More than half a million requests annually—telephone calls, letters, telegrams.

Day and night prayers are continuous. A hundred and four workers, mental messengers for God, watching over the spiritual horizons of America! The hundred and four are multiplied many times by others throughout the world who "hold thoughts in silence," collectively affirming health, prosperity, spiritual illumination, social adjustment and religious truth. Ten thousand letters a week are answered, covering every subject that plagues or prospers mortal man.

Long ago, on a spring day in 1891, Charles and Myrtle Fillmore sat in their home on Wabash Avenue with a small group of "divine science" scholars. From this Society of Silent Help mental and spiritual rays were being sent to those in trouble, sickness and poverty. Suddenly Charles Fillmore broke the sanctity of the moments with a whispered exclamation, "Unity!" The silent experimenters opened their eyes to him questioningly. "Unity!" he repeated. "That's the name for our work! The name I've been looking for!"

Elaborating on the revelation, he asserted, "It embodies the central principle of what we believe: unity of the soul with God, unity of all life, unity of all religions, unity of the spirit, soul and body; unity of all men in the heart of truth!"

Myrtle Fillmore, better than anyone, knew that this was another milestone on the long, hard road leading to the beginning of a new American faith. Eleven years before, she, a victim of tuberculosis, had married crippled Charles Fillmore. He was a freight clerk in Denison, Texas; she, a school teacher. As a girl Myrtle Page of Pagetown, Ohio, had united with the Methodist

Church and attended Oberlin College. In contrast, her husband, born on the frontier near St. Cloud, Minnesota, in 1854, was not "biased on the God-question by an orthodox education." While still a youth he had wondered about the possible existence of a divine law which a man could apply in moments of extremity. He had dabbled in spiritualism and had been fascinated by books on esoteric systems of religion.

The Fillmores made their first bid for fame in religious history in Kansas City during the depression years of the late eighties. The family, consisting of two boys, Lowell and Waldo Rickert, was in tragic circumstances. The father, having failed in real estate, was broke, sick and faced by debts and disaster; the mother, expecting a third child, was given little hope of recovery from the advanced stages of tuberculosis. The desperate couple began an impassioned study of the mental healing cults of the day. They attended classes conducted by Christian Scientists. They were seen at lectures on New Thought and at institutes of metaphysics. Unmindful of the mockery of neighbors, they continued their search for the keys which these cults promised would unlock the treasures of the inner life and restore them to health. Slowly a "supreme power operating by a fixed law" unfolded. It was a tremendous discovery. They found in themselves a limitless cosmic force. A power to heal! A power to overcome life's ills and trials! A power to meet every situation! A power to know God! Applied "in faith and faithfully," it set aside all destructive agencies.

The "truth" came first to Myrtle Fillmore. It was crude, unscientific, simple. It was the establishment of a healing consciousness through the constant repetition of an affirmation, "I am a child of God and, therefore, I do not inherit sickness."

Gradually, powerfully, the strength of this positive mental pattern evoked a regenerating and unshakeable faith. She applied the teaching in her own life. Inquisitive neighbors pried into the causes behind the noticeable improvement that followed. To them it was a miracle when the third son, Royal, was born a normal, healthy child. Soon they made of Mrs. Fillmore a willing practitioner of the self-demonstrable power. She called her treatment prayer and, while healing others, she herself was healed. In less than two years all consumptive symptoms disappeared.

Compelled to admit the efficacy of these healing demonstrations, Charles Fillmore began treating himself. Doctors said he was suffering from tuberculosis of the bone and that tube abscesses had developed in his leg. Insisting that either the principles would work for him or else they were fraudulent, he directed the power upon his withering hip. His technique was largely his own. He sought a quiet place where he could enter into the silence. Waiting upon God, he discovered that he could send spiritual impulses to any part of his body. He described these sensations as "crawly feelings." Each day he applied the life-giving power to his afflictions, "affirming health" in his abscessed leg. The silence became his rendezvous with the "Universal Mind." He began getting messages. He was "growing new tissue." His leg was lengthening. He discarded his cane. He no longer used the steel extension that he had worn since boyhood. He was beginning a complete body regeneration for which there was evidence in Scripture, "Be ye transformed by the renewing of your mind." In Fillmore nomenclature the process was described as the release through divine affirmations of electronic forces sealed up in the nerves.

Real estate was forgotten. Fillmore felt that he was at the heart of a gigantic discovery. Ideas grew wild and fast in his active mind. Throughout his life he had been battling against the windmills of fate when all he needed was to retreat into the calm of his own soul. The trouble had never been external, but internal. Life suddenly became adventurous. The determined little man believed he had captured a force that could beat back and conquer anything that stood in his way. It would bring him into a full and complete realization of the Kingdom of God. It was the Jesus-power and, upon the Jesus doctrine, the Fillmores began to build.

Skeptics now pointed to the house on Wabash Avenue with sinister gestures and patient smiles. Charles and Myrtle Fillmore advertised themselves as "Healers and Teachers." Every night at nine o'clock the Society of Silent Help met at their home and "worked miracles just by thinking." The report circulated that nothing spectacular happened. Everyone simply sat in silence for fifteen minutes concentrating on a positive thought—an affirmation frequently spoken audibly in prayer-like repetition. The Fillmores said, "To pray is to affirm."

And what was the result of this new spiritual science?

A Negro laundress was cured of asthma! An Irishman, crippled, walking on crutches, was healed. A boy threatened with blindness received new sight! Testimonies spread. The doubting came to sit in the circle of the Society of Silent Help, solemn-faced and hopeful. Accusing cries arose—superstition! magic! animal magnetism! All were repudiated with, "Where two or three are gathered together in my name, there am I in the midst of them."

In the fall of 1889 arrangements were made for a room to

accommodate the two hundred who had ventured into the cause of Silent Help and who, regardless of sect or creed, were devoutly seeking after "truth." The silence was as great as that of early Pietism, the testimonies as emphatic as a Methodist revival, the terminology sounded like Christian Science, and hints of the supernatural bordered on spiritistic phenomena.

The same year saw a small, unimposing monthly magazine among the farrago of journals of metaphysics and science of mind. It purported to be the voice of all souls seeking for spiritual light. It was, in fact, the voice of Charles Fillmore crying in the wilderness of the isms. The first issue of *Modern Thought* looked like a nerve center of the cults. There were articles on Spiritualism, Unitarianism, Rosicrucianism, Transcendentalism, Christian Science, and New Thought. Students of the occult referred to it as a new theosophy. Mystic and psychic wanderers saw in it a beacon glowing with the light of their own truth. Every issue brought the ministry of the Society of Silent Help to its readers. There were no financial involvements. Since God was doing the work, the service was free, but love offerings would be accepted.

Traditional churches watched the experiment with suspicion. Critically turning the pages of *Modern Thought,* they read, "He who writes a creed or puts a limit to revelation, is the enemy of humanity. . . . Creeds have ever been the vampires that sucked the blood of spiritual progress in the past, and life can only be kept in the present movement by latitude of thought tempered always by the power that moves the world, love. . . ." But the churches saw nothing to fear in a movement that had no name.

Modern Thought was never popular. Appealing to all mental-power groups, it satisfied none completely. Articles were accepted from anyone who had a religious ax to grind or a new faggot of faith to toss on the metaphysical fires. The subscription list never exceeded a thousand. Fillmore knew nothing about publishing. He bought the paper for the magazine an issue at a time as finances permitted. No one ever knew what size or what color the next copy would be. Looking closer at "Fillmore-ism," critics predicted that *Modern Thought* would not outlast the turn of the century. It would be wrecked in the miscellany of strange religions that had arisen out of the unbridled heterodoxy of the gay nineties.

No modern religion had a more laborious beginning. Every mile of the way was built upon a "miracle" or a "revelation." Every follower demanded a "healed life." Every publication of *Modern Thought* was a venture into the confused and obdurate stream of prejudice. The faithful, however, returned to their circle night after night patiently answering requests for personal aid. When Charles Fillmore shattered the silence on that evening in 1891, the lowly Society of Silent Help became Silent Unity, the stalwart champion of a new Christian cause. *Modern Thought* became *Unity,* now published by the Unity Book Company. But time was needed for the new name to be popularized. Unity lacked the dramatic effect of Christian Science and the romantic tone of Rosicrucianism. Some confused it with Unitarianism. Others remembered a Chicago magazine called *Unity.* Charles Fillmore parried by saying the name was a revelation. "It came to me as clearly as though someone had spoken it."

In 1903 the Kansas City group of Truth Students was incorporated under the name, Unity School of Practical Christianity, organized for the purpose of demonstrating "Universal Law."

Fillmore-ism was becoming exclusive. Charles Fillmore was no longer a spiritual free lance. He and his wife deliberately set about to apply modern organizational methods to a "practical, workable Christianity" securely integrated in a specific doctrine, audaciously affirming that "whatever man wants he can have by voicing his desire in the right way into the Universal mind." Making it clear that they had no quarrel with the mental cure groups, their friends of former years, they insisted that Unity was based upon a higher power than the intellect. Neither could they find latitude for their adventure within the confines of established Christendom. Fillmore explained, "The churches talk a great deal about God and about the past experiences of the prophets and the saints, but the power of God has seemed to have disappeared. We feel that we are to bring in a new dispensation with the power of the Spirit."

Still contending that their spiritual discovery was not another "religion," but only a practical philosophy to supplement the "faith you already have," Unity built a church. Dedicated in 1906, it was a great church combining a publishing house, a school and a health dispensary. Three years later an adjoining lot was purchased and an extensive building program was begun which continued throughout the next decade. At the heart of the growing organization was Silent Unity, a radiating center for the spiritual energy generated by modern mystics of a new school of thought!

Silent Unity! 917 Tracy Street! The address became the nucleus for an ever-expanding empire. In 1914 the name, Unity School of Christianity, was officially adopted to designate the world-wide spiritual, educational, and publishing aspects of this movement. Meandering through American religions, I met Unity at almost every turn of the road. In Los Angeles, New York, and Detroit—beautiful churches and large congregations. In every state—Unity Centers: twenty-one in California, twelve in Missouri, ten in Florida, nine in New York, nine in Ohio. Many loyal Protestants had given Unity literature a place beside their familiar denominational publications. In some homes the old church paper had been displaced. Did ministers object? Some did, complaining that the infiltration of Unity's printed word was subtle propaganda. Others conceded that they "used the stuff" in their sermons and it worked. The pastor of a large Methodist congregation had even introduced the use of affirmation cards. "Strictly Unity," he told me, "but my people like it."

Some liked it so much they left Methodism as well as other old-line denominations to become a legal part of the Fillmore faith. Reasons were kaleidoscopic:

"I was impressed by the sincerity during devotions. The people really seemed to be communing with God."

"Unity is practical. It can be applied to everyday life."

"I couldn't take the hell-and-damnation doctrine of my preacher any longer."

"My husband died eight years ago. I was lost until I found Unity."

"I got tired singing about the heaven to come. Unity showed me that heaven is here and now."

"My father was a minister, but he told me to do my own investigating. I did."

"Try holding a Prosperity Thought, then you'll know why I'm for Unity."

Because this one sounded much more like a business proposition than a religious experience, I demanded an explanation. "I never make a move in business without calling Silent Unity," the man flashed back. "Poverty is a disease and should be treated as such," he sermonized. "Each noon Unity holds a prosperity prayer service. At this meeting prosperity vibrations are set in motion and we tune in mentally. We all unite on the prosperity thought suggested monthly by Charles Fillmore." In a self-hypnotic manner, he closed his eyes and turned his mental prayer wheel on the current phrase, " 'With my mind's eye I see substance in Spirit, and prosperity is bountifully increased in my affairs.' Visualize prosperity," he went on. "Get the idea of thousands of other believers thinking the same thing. Keep in mind the Powerhouse on Tracy Street and get the feeling that this thought is coming out day and night over the spiritual airways."

The reliability of Unity's prosperity treatment was upheld by this man's success story. Yet it looked as if applied psychology, deftly spirited into sacred halls, was once more being canonized.

My landlady in Los Angeles was emphatic in her denial of such a hasty deduction. "It's the Jesus-doctrine," she said. "There's no psychology about it."

She was an "authority." For two years walking had been torture. She seldom ventured a step without her cane. But once when I returned after a summer's absence from Los Angeles, she greeted me with, "The most wonderful thing has happened!" She pirouetted carefully in the hallway. "Do you know what was wrong with me? I didn't like people! Now that I've begun liking people, see how I can walk!"

It was healing the Unity way. There was no mystery or magic about it.

"When I told the Unity worker about my condition," she confided, "all she said was, 'Give praise and thanks for perfection—give praise and thanks for perfection and healing and recovery will follow.' She said this over and over, then instructed me to make it part of my consciousness. Oh, it's really not a treatment; it's a prayer. I went into the silence fifteen minutes a day, always repeating, 'Give praise and thanks for perfection—give praise and thanks for perfection and healing and recovery will follow.' Make it a part of my consciousness? I couldn't. Always there was something in the way. My dislike for people. That was holding me back. But all day long I found myself saying, 'Give praise and thanks for perfection.' I wrote to Silent Unity and they helped me, oh, so much! One day in the silence I had the courage to deny that I really disliked anyone. That afternoon a feeling came over me that just can't be explained. It was a feeling of lightness, confidence. I took a few steps without my cane, and it went so much better that I kept on walking, always saying, 'Give praise and thanks for perfection and healing and recovery will follow!' It's really true!"

This incident persuaded me to track down other "miracles" among those who denied sickness and affirmed health. In a Midwestern town, I met a woman whose hearing had been impaired. Silent Unity suggested, "Praise and magnify the healing power of Spirit within, and good health is manifest without." She claimed perfect recovery. Another woman told me she had been cured of cancer. The doctors had said there was no hope. In the quiet of her hospital room, a Unity minister brought an affirmation, "Where the pain is, there is God." Her husband angrily insisted that she go to another hospital.

She refused. Two years later she was doing her housework. "What do the doctors say?" I asked.

"They wanted to examine me after I was cured," she replied, "but I wouldn't let them. What happened is between God and me."

Such conviction can hardly be accounted scientific. To the realist it is as fallacious as the "Red Leaf" artifice. This was a sheet of bright red paper which carried the much-publicized "Healing" and "Prosperity" thoughts, together with, "This leaf has been spiritually treated by the Unity Society members in Kansas City. It is charged with healing thought power and will connect all who use it with the Jesus Christ-consciousness. Hold it in your hands while repeating over and over the words of truth and you will feel the power of the Holy Spirit and the promise of Jesus Christ will be fulfilled in you according to your faith."

The "pagan innovation" stirred up a protracted round of acrid criticism. It was tagged a money-making scheme. Fillmore retaliated blow for blow; the "Red Leaf" had been charged with a spiritual, mental, and physical intensity that put those who used it into rapport with higher realms of consciousness. He compared it to the spittle with which Jesus anointed the blind and to the handkerchiefs blessed by Saint Paul. "Place it on the nerve center nearest the affected part and mentally affirm: 'Spirit-Mind Illumines and Heals.' Wherever the pain, there place the Red Leaf."

Behind it all I found a mental materia medica. *Divine Remedies,* a Unity publication, suggested a thought-cause for every ill. A condition of cross-eye is caused by an inner crossing of the thoughts. Selfishness clogs the ears and results in deafness.

A hard, unforgiving state of mind, hardheartedness, is often the cause of hardening of the arteries. Grief and bitterness are the root cause of gallstones. The central thought-cause of goiter is greed. Worry is the cause of Bright's disease. Cataracts are brought about by looking at the material world too closely. However quixotic and absurd these analyses sound, "miracles" rode across my skepticism by the sheer force of the believer's unconquerable enthusiasm and faith. I reasoned that a fair judgment must be based on the extent of personal adjustment effected in each case.

My attendance record at services covered the range from the thriving churches of Unity's leading exponents to the improvised centers manned by unordained ministers. The outstanding feature in every worship hour was the oft-repeated affirmation. Reverently heads were bowed and eyes were closed in silent meditation. Whether surrounded by thirty or a thousand worshipers, I always felt during these moments of silence that Unity Truth was striving for its greatest meaning. While all sought inner stillness and receptivity, indoctrination was going deep: God is Spirit—not a being or person, but the creative energy which is the cause of all things. God is that invisible, intangible, but very real thing that we call life! And I am life! I am a Christ, a manifestation of God!

The affirmation, spoken in unison, rhythmically, emphatically, intercepted the silence. It was repeated again and again with the same stress on the key words, like the well-rehearsed pattern of a verse-speaking choir. The purpose was to convince man's mortal consciousness of "truth." All services are unified to emphasize one constructive, positive idea. And the moments of unspoken meditation consciously relate the seeking soul to the watchtower of Silent Unity.

When I called at 917 Tracy Street I found a small chapel on the third floor fittingly dedicated to this mystical ministry. In a near-by office an elderly gentleman sat at a telephone. In adjoining rooms Silent Unity workers were stuffing envelopes with pamphlets and mimeographed form letters done in purple ink, Unity's symbol of power.

> *Dear Friend:*
>
> *You cannot know with what faith and love and joy we send this assurance: 'You are not alone. God is with you.' This is true—there is no aloneness; God is in all. . . . Use the enclosed words of prayer: "The healing power of God, through Christ, is now doing its perfect work in me, and I am made whole." Feel God's healing power at work. See His perfection made manifest in mind and body.*
>
> > *In healing faith,*
> >
> > SILENT UNITY

In an easily accessible office just off the main lobby, I met Lowell Fillmore, manager of the Unity School of Christianity and first son of its founders. At sixty-four, handsome, white-haired, he combines the realistic genius of a business executive with the wholly unrealistic naïveté of an ancient saint. He controls the plexus of the entire Unity system and its fifty departments. Energetically, two steps at a time, he led me up the stairs in the many Tracy Street buildings for an inspection of the smoothly working mechanism of his organization. The general activity of a going concern filled the corridors. Outside, the alleys were congested with delivery trucks and mail wagons. I began to realize that Unity headquarters dominated half a city block. Yet the sprawling structures were so over-crowded that Fillmore kept saying, "We've outgrown the place again, but wait till you see Unity City."

That the publishing department needed more space was ap-parent as we toured the basement. Wending our way through giant presses and linotypes, cutting machines and offset presses, we came to a spacious mailing room cluttered with every pos-sible Unity publication. Books with sleek, shining jackets called proud attention to titles and authors familiar to the Unity family: *Teach Us to Pray,* Charles and Cora Fillmore; *The Twelve Powers of Man,* Charles Fillmore; *Talk on Truth,* Charles Fillmore; *Christian Healing,* Charles Fillmore; *Christ Enthroned in Man,* Cora Fillmore; *Working with God,* Gard-ner Hunting; *The Sunlit Way,* Ernest C. Wilson, *Truth Ideas of an M.D.* by C. O. Southard; and the basic Unity text, *Lessons in Truth,* H. Emilie Cady.

Thousands of tracts, printed in practically every known lan-guage, were pigeonholed in long, high shelves. These com-pact, well-edited single sheets, together with small pocket pamphlets, are Unity's life line. Had any means of extricat-ing lost humanity from its complexities been overlooked? *Demonstrating Prosperity, Curing Colds Through Forgive-ness, As to Meat Eating, Casting Out Demons, Dreams and Their Interpretation, The Consecration of The Room, Human Relations, Health Through Body Renewal, Are You Getting All You Want From Life? Attaining Immortality, A Career of Friendliness is Open to Everyone.*

Lowell Fillmore's name recurred frequently among these tracts. Busiest man on the Unity staff, he finds time to compose numberless articles that are among the most popular in the repertory of the movement. In one of his lighter moods, he wrote, *Try It On A Fly,* an account of how he used Unity's teachings to control both himself and a buzzing fly during a church service. He is also the originator of "metaphysical gadgets," such as tithing boxes, thank-you boxes, letters to God, treasure maps, prosperity banks. These aid the movement and help the individual. But the nuggets from the rich mine of Lowell Fillmore's creative powers which have been most precious in tempering life's little annoyances are his thirteen "statement gadgets." He gave me a copy with the suggestion, "Try them sincerely and see what happens." The idea is to meet everyday situations with a well-tempered affirmation. When you have mislaid something and feel yourself becoming irked or distraught, say, "There is nothing lost in Spirit." In winning friends, hold to the thought, "I am a radiant center of divine love." Should a gossip or a bore mooch on your time, assure yourself that, "No man cometh unto me save the Father sent him." When answering the doorbell or on the way to an appointment, repeat silently, "I go to meet my good." Confront the pessimist and crapehanger who remarks that you are not looking well with the positive conviction, "I am Spirit, and Spirit cannot be sick." If you are caught in a storm or distressed by noise, affirm, "Peace." For heart trouble, repeat believingly, "My heart is right with God."

"Am I correct in saying that Unity aims at a personalization of religious truths and at a modernization of mystical religion?" I asked after reading my copy of statement gadgets.

He nodded thoughtfully. "Unity aims at a realization of the Christ within."

The metallic whir of the restless presses raised violent argument over the contention that the powerful effects of Unity are generated in silence. Out of the foment of mass publication comes nearly a million monthly periodicals spreading the gospel of the "everyday use of the Christ-principle." These are *Unity,* a magazine of Christian metaphysics; *Weekly Unity,* designed for the interested but uninitiated; *Wee Wisdom,* for boys and girls under thirteen; *Good Business,* success stories in applying the Christ-principle; *Progress,* more success stories; and *Daily Word,* a manual of daily devotional studies.

The incessant noises filling the printing establishment seemed to cry, "The printed word is the secret behind Unity's success! Day and night our wheels are spinning, our gears are grinding, our steel fingers are stacking page upon page! This is the clatter of Truth!"

Suddenly a gong sounded above the chanting steel. A workman pulled a switch. The presses stopped. Busy hands automatically paused in their work. Throughout the building—Silence. Silence broken by a prayer, consecrating and blessing the work, audibly transmitted over a loud-speaker. Then all the workers joined in the familiar, "Our Father, which art in heaven . . ."

Silent-70, the missionary sector of the movement, is built upon the inspiration of Luke 10:1, "The Lord appointed other seventy also, and sent them . . . into every city and place." This department is organized to distribute free literature to army camps, hospitals, prisons, libraries, orphanages, and other social institutions. Begun in 1910 with seventy workers, it now has more than seven thousand who take the responsibility for placing the material, five hundred thousand mailings a year.

Braille editions are made available to the blind through schools, public libraries, and homes. The work of Silent-70 is supported entirely by freewill offerings.

From the beginning it was a Fillmore innovation not to charge for spiritual services. They said, "The work is the Lord's and He will provide the means for its propagation." In tacit endorsement I had found a love-offering box at the door of Unity Centers everywhere. I had stood with believers and repeated with them the offering blessing, "I bless and give thanks to God for the privilege of giving my gift, which makes possible my greater receiving." Collection plates were never passed, but the persuasive blessing lingered, and offerings were placed in the conveniently located love coffer as the people went home. Each Center is an autonomous unit in the economic structure of Unity School, receiving no support from the Kansas City headquarters. All the local leaders whom I had met devoted full time to their ministry, "trusting to Divine law for finances."

The physical plant at Kansas City trenchantly confirmed the productivity of this principle of operation. Vituperators on the outside, however, have accused the Fillmores of supplementing the working of Divine law with promotional ingenuity typically Americanesque. Though Unity consistently stressed the no-cost-to-you idea, the need for adequate facilities to meet the demands of the growing clientele begat many novel stratagems. The first appeal for funds prior to 1906 was predicated upon requirements for the first building on Tracy Street. Subscribers to Unity publications were requested to send contributions. Each donation was to be accompanied by a blessing which would be placed in the cornerstone. It was about this time that the prosperity treatment was introduced with the exultant pronouncement from Charles Fillmore, "It is our right to be prosperous." This treatment, like all other Unity services, was free, but its triumph over poverty in the lives of individual believers was a profitable source of love offerings. But even this additional income was not sufficient to meet the cost of the construction program. An unwieldy debt hung over the building when it was completed in 1906.

The years that followed tested the Fillmore affirmations in their own lives. In the struggle to liquidate the debt, the pendulum of promotion swung to and fro from the mystical to the mundane, from affirming prosperity to the sale of souvenir china plates, from the radiation of prosperity thoughts to souvenir post cards, from the circle of silent help to a women's auxiliary. A young people's guild was organized to raise money. A pin with Unity's Winged-Globe emblem went on sale at a dollar. Gradually the Fillmores became aware of a new field of consciousness which the prosperity treatments had opened.

In 1908 *Unity* carried the announcement that a crisp new dollar bill would be sent to anyone who would agree to use it as a magnet for gathering prosperity thoughts and demonstrating prosperity faith. Experimenters were instructed to join with Silent Unity for a month in a daily prosperity affirmation. The dollar was then to be returned, together with the increase. About two thousand bills were requested; five thousand returned! The field was becoming productive. In a single month six thousand Prosperity Banks left headquarters. Recipients accepted these as another salient extension of the prosperity treatment. They willingly deposited a dime each week for ten weeks. Then back to Unity came the bank with a new name for the *Weekly Unity* subscription list. What others condemned, a generous diagnostician would have called Unity's growing pains. Or was it all the realization of the colossal statement with which Charles Fillmore had stormed the citadels of American faith: "Whatever a man wants he can have by voicing his desire in the right way into the Universal Mind!"

These words persisted tantalizingly as I stood on the mosque-like tower of a campanile in the heart of America. Around me lay Unity City, the culmination of the relentless pursuit of the Fillmores. In 1919 they had purchased a small acreage seventeen miles northeast of Kansas City. In subsequent years this modest "week-end retreat" expanded to thirteen hundred acres. At the official dedication in 1927, Charles Fillmore prophetically voiced the paramount ideal of his lifework: "We are setting up on earth the kingdom of the heavens."

From my vantage point on the campanile, it looked like a magnificent country-club estate. An exhilarating sense of freedom swept over me from across the rolling hills. The busy city's clangor intruded on Tracy Street, but here the blue of August skies quietly canopied Silent Unity. Out of the distance two highways emerged to cut across the palatial grounds. Intersecting, they seemed to symbolize the mystical and the practical of Unity's transversion.

Spying out the land from my post of observation ten stories high, I thought it must be the most ambitious project I had seen in all my ramblings on the roads to glory. There were vineyards, orchards, variegated patches of summer flowers, dairy cattle browsing on green slopes and fields of grain covering long farm acres. It was a land of milk and honey, lovely for situation. In the distance a rustic dam thrust giant concrete arms across a river, holding back a lake among thick foliage and deep lush grass. In a natural contour surrounded by poplars lay a large, sweeping amphitheater. Groups of buildings dotted the landscape, taking complete advantage of the freedom of space. Farm homes and utility structures commanded the outlying areas. Nearer the campanile, a cluster of native stone residences and cottages centered around a terraced tearoom, English style. Luxuriant vines clung to the low stone walls. The most imposing unit consisted of the training school and other professional buildings. But this was merely the beginning. The city was still in the making.

I looked out upon activity that was like a scene from the building of Solomon's temple. A new, revolutionary method, they said, years ahead of its time. Small crews of men hauled massive slabs of concrete with the aid of machines, slabs that looked like flat rocks hewn out of a great quarry. Days before, I had seen them cast in hulking molds. Embedded in them were steel claws which could be locked together, welded together to form a wall. The rigid, tense hands of the machine lifted them up, set slab upon slab. A workman in an iron helmet climbed alongside. Blue flames shot from his blowtorch. Another section grew—suddenly, imposingly. The machine shambled back to its roof-protected supply base, impatient for another load. A new printing plant was ready. A fashionable sanctuary for Silent Unity had been completed. The administration building was under way. Additional school buildings came next in the plans. 917 Tracy was moving into a greater glory. Unity City was going up in twentieth-century

Biblical style, "built of stone made ready before it was brought hither. . . ."

An elevator door banged behind me. A solid, genial, weathered man came to my side at the balustrade. Rickert Fillmore, manager of Unity City and second son of its founder, pointed out various locations with his battered hat. He was the dreamer and the engineer behind the building of this modern city of God. But he wanted no credit.

"Everything here, everything you see," he said with a smile, "is but the physical counterpart of the spiritual process of the teaching. Father says it's the fulfillment of prophecy."

"I wouldn't have believed that on my first trip out here twenty years ago," I replied. "A Kansas City minister brought me and some other fellows to see what was going on. We got stuck in the mud. All that I remember seeing was a small, hand-painted sign that said UNITY FARM. The minister pointed it out and predicted that nothing would ever come of things out here. He was stuck in the mud and convinced. When he said that Unity was just another mental cult, we believed him. And when he said that Unity didn't have the money to pay for the place, much less develop it, we believed that, too."

Rickert Fillmore laughed as I told the story, but when I finished he shrugged thoughtfully. "We have developed the land the Unity way. That is why people do not understand."

"Do what you see to do with what you have, and what you need God will supply?" I quoted questioningly. "Can it really be applied to a real-estate venture?"

"If it works at all, it works everywhere," he vouched. "When man works in harmony with God, the right things come at the right time."

O me of little faith, I thought. Is it possible that the Lord is a spendthrift? Is He actually moving through the earth seeking men who will exercise arrogant confidence in heaven's prodigality?

"Sometimes," my companion was saying, "I think Unity is like this campanile. Every once in a while some practical sight-seer asks, 'What's this tower good for?' I always tell them that it is a symbol of universal supply. Then I explain that it is not only a campanile, but also a water tower. We needed water to run the farms so we made the artificial lake over there. It covers twenty-two acres. When we had the water, we needed elevation and the pressure to distribute it. So we built this tower and camouflaged it. It makes available a continuous supply of a hundred thousand gallons."

"But if you needed water, why didn't you simply drill wells?"

"We tried that," he admitted blandly, "but we struck oil."

He went on to say that natural gas was available in all of the houses. Unity City was to be a self-sufficient municipality. Already it operated its own light plant, fire department, and street department. Even the chimes in the tower were built by Unity men.

We entered the elevator and started down.

"I want to show you some of our homemade furniture," he grinned. "The drought was killing off our walnut trees. They were beauties. But we cut them down and sawed them into boards. Now we have fifty thousand feet of black walnut lumber and it's seasoning wonderfully."

As we went from building to building it was evident that Rickert Fillmore's Unity was Unity City. He showed a boyish enthusiasm in the reams of blueprints and the artistic display of dioramas that transformed his office into an architect's paradise. When I asked about his training, he said with a perfunctory air that he had taken some work at the Chicago Art Institute. He glowed with pride when we went through the great tunnels which, though designed to put the gas mains and electrical conduits within easy reach, provide convenient pedestrian traffic lanes between the many buildings. Whenever we came upon groups of workmen who were turning his dreams into realities he paused, watching affectionately. "I put the men on their own and they get all sorts of wild and wonderful ideas," he said with characteristic self-effacement. "We work them out together." Rick, as the workmen called him, was living every moment in love with every inch of Unity City. In the large, efficient greenhouse, in the cider mill, in the ice-cream factory, and while we strolled the grounds, he told stories which were reminiscent of Unity's humble beginning.

He ushered me into a beautiful office with an adjoining kitchenette. This suite was for his father, he explained, but it was never used. Unity's founder preferred an old desk and a comfortable chair in his own home. Across the hall was another unused office, Myrtle Fillmore's sanctum until her death in 1931. In the quietly enshadowed prayer room, she had forged the principles of a living faith and fashioned the tools by which this faith could be applied.

When I asked about the philosophy and teaching of the movement, Rickert Fillmore usually smiled and with a wave of his hand said, "Talk to Lowell about that or wait until you see Father."

It was somewhat easier to follow "Rick's" engineering parlance through the architectural network of Unity City, than to
find my way through the metaphysical intricacies of Unity's
beliefs. My analysis suggested that it is an eclectic religion.
The entire field of metaphysics and mysticism yielded harvests
from which the Fillmores gleaned rare truths of the trans-
cendent nature of reality. The emphasis upon an inner light
and a spiritual interpretation of the sacraments reminds one
of Quakerism. Like Christian Science, Unity puts major accent
upon healing; like Theosophy it admits the necessity of reincarnation. Rosicrucianism anticipated the idea of cosmic unity
and spirit's enveloping principle. The astral or psychical self
harks back to Spiritualism. Vedanta's contributions furbish
Unity's idealism. "Home Blessings" and "Blessing of all mail
that leaves the Unity headquarters" fall into the long tradition
of Jewish history and Roman Catholicism. Instead of the
medal of Saint Christopher, the patron saint of travelers, Unity
issues a card blessing. Highways are sanctified with an affirmation, "All who travel this road are protected by the loving
power of God."

But despite all comparisons, Unity reiterates it is an independent institution, teaching anew the use of the Jesus Christ-
doctrine in everyday life. For the novice it has simple prayers.
"God is good—God is all." I had watched Sunday-school tots
at local Centers gather round the prayer box to affirm in childish
veneration: "The healing, cleansing power of Almighty God
is now flowing through you and in the name of Jesus Christ
you know you are whole and free now." Involved physiolog-
ical-religious designations are provided for the savant in such
works as Charles Fillmore's *The Twelve Powers of Man*. He

divines that the twelve fundamental faculties of the mind are related to the twelve apostles of Jesus, the twelve gates of the temple and numerous other symbols. Attempting to make his theory understandable, he has prepared a diagram which correlates twelve nerve centers in man's body with twelve spiritual impulses: center of brain corresponds to Faith and is exemplified by Peter; the loins, Strength, Andrew; the pit of the stomach, Wisdom or Judgment, James, son of Zebedee; back of heart, Love, John; root of tongue, Power, Philip; between the eyes, Imagination, Bartholomew; front brain, Understanding, Thomas; center-front brain, Will, Matthew; navel, Order, James, son of Alphæus; the medulla, Zeal, Simon the Canaanite; the lower part of back, Elimination, Thaddeus; the generative function, Life, Judas. Crowning this diagram is the aura of the "top brain," the "great I am," represented by Christ.

Classes of instruction to interpret these mysteries and doctrines have always been a part of Unity's system and are the vehicle on which the faith has gone forward. Neighbors meeting in the unpretentious Fillmore home during the nineties constituted the first student body. The curriculum was based upon courses in truth principles. Requests for instruction from subscribers to Unity publications gave rise in the spring of 1909 to the Unity Correspondence School. "Built upon faith, manifested by faith, and quickened by faith"—its growth was phenomenal. From an immediate enrollment of two hundred sixty-eight, it sprang to two thousand within two years. Charles Fillmore, who was in charge, declared it was a wholesome and harmonious way of disseminating the Christ-gospel of life. Eventually this extension service became a basic function. It stimulated religious thinking among students of many faiths.

It foreshadowed a logical method of training Unity teachers and leaders. Enrollees were invited to "chautauquas" and "healing meetings" in the early twenties. In such an atmosphere Unity's official training school was born in 1931, committed to the education of ministers for Centers "everywhere in the world." The school, conducted at Unity City from May to October, is organized on a four-term basis with six weeks to a term.

During my stay "on campus" I saw representatives of Unity's past, present, and future. The faculty consisted of men and women steeped in the traditions of the movement. Ernest C. Wilson, minister of Christ Church, Unity, Los Angeles, conducted a course, "Preparation and Presentation of Unity Lectures." An east-coast colleague, Georgiana Tree West of New York, lectured in the same course during a later term. The leader of South Side Center in Kansas City, Ida Palmer, taught "Spiritual Healing." Francis J. Gable, editor of *Good Business,* had charge of a class called "Spiritual Clinic" and lectured on "Human Relations."

The student body, preponderantly women, consisted for the most part of those preparing themselves for the Unity ministry. Requirements for ordination are the completion of the correspondence course, a methods-and-ideals course, two terms at the Training School and one year of probationary work at a Center. In addition to the ministerial candidates, I found a liberal sprinkling of men and women who were here solely for self-improvement. Mingling with them, I saw in this school the suggestion of a spiritualized course in how to win friends and influence people! To my surprise there were also a number of ministers who had come to consider the possibility of weaving some of the strands of this little-known group into the fabric of Protestantism.

The accolades of those who came and went to these summer terms centered around one man, Charles Fillmore. As the days passed, I found myself drawn into the prevailing belief that this bronzed and highly sensitized little old man, who walked with a slight limp, possessed an unusual spiritual prowess. Natural abilities had been indeterminately enlarged by an exalted faith which reached out to impress itself upon his students. They sat in his metaphysical classes: "Fundamental Unity Principles," "Prosperity," "How to Apply God to Everyday Living." They worked hard toward ordination, the day when he would usher them into the Unity hierarchy. He was watched and revered everywhere on the campus. Devotees persistently sought him out: "How are you getting along on your latest book, Mr. Fillmore?" "Papa Charley, they tell me you are going on another tour!" "You are looking younger every day!" "How is the Training School in Los Angeles, Mr. Fillmore?" "Your assembly message was such an inspiration!" "Mr. Fillmore, when will you come to our Center? Everyone is expecting you!"

Sometimes alert to every question, he listened patiently, quietly studying the faces about him. More often, lost in a spiritual hiatus, he seemed content to sit in the hopeful shadows of his ninety-two years. Startlingly free from the marks of age, here was a man who had deliberately worked at the business of staying young. He had achieved as much success in this as in his many other endeavors. Even his thinning white hair did not add age. His language was couched in the phrases that have made his books basic texts for Unity. "The superconsciousness of Christ in man has mastery and dominion over all conditions of mind and body. . . . Jesus was the result of a series of incarnations. . . . In the person of Jesus of Nazareth is manifested the highest state of consciousness. . . . His superconsciousness was His real self and through it He was able to redeem His body. . . . In like manner, when we learn the process we can transform and redeem our bodies into the Christ-consciousness. This age is ready for it and there are men and women who can achieve these things."

Frequently he emerged with a gentle shock of humor, but inevitably he came back to his basic precept, "We are on earth for divine self-realization through experience." His was still an extremely active mind with the drawing power that goes with the play of positive thought-forces. Among the leaders of America's little-known groups, I had found no one who seemed to apply himself more consciously to mental discipline.

Charles Fillmore's constant and faithful companion is Cora Dedrick, whom he married in 1933, when he was seventy-nine and she was fifty-seven. Having served as the Fillmores' secretary for many years, she had contributed much to the progress of the movement. In recent years she has extended, explained, and enriched many of the earlier writings of her husband, and they have collaborated on important publications. Their names appear together on the staff of the Training School. Cora Fillmore consistently reflects Unity refinement. Her philosophy, spirit, and talent qualify her to assume the responsibilities of leadership demanded of the wife of Charles Fillmore.

My retreat at Unity City was climaxed by a final luncheon

date with several Unity leaders. As our party gathered on the terrace, a workman passed by, singing a new doxology:

> "Praise God, from whom all blessings flow;
> Praise Wealth, which helps us here below;
> Praise Truth, the highest virtue known;
> Praise Health, which everyone may own!"

When Charles Fillmore mounted the stone steps leading to the tearoom, his hand resting lightly on his wife's arm, I was again reminded of a Hindu swami. He had the same expression of quiet seeking, seemingly indifferent to surroundings, naturally assuming the role of divine selection without posing as one of heaven's final saints.

It was at this luncheon that I fully realized the significance of the Fillmore triumvirate—Charles and his two sons cooperatively administering spiritual and material counterbalances to a modern ecclesiastical corporation. Another persistent family had established a big business according to the American tradition. They had developed a good religious product and had insisted on distributing it in the American way. Steadily Unity has grown. Steadily it has met and overcome the vicissitudes that beset any growing, competitive industry. Neither the raillery of the indevout nor the adulation of mercurial zealots has destroyed the value of the teaching. Patiently and tirelessly the Fillmores have nursed their philosophy. Today it is a thoroughbred in the green pastures of American religion.

Is Unity becoming a denomination? I asked Charles Fillmore. After yielding to a moment of reflection, he said, "Unity is a School of Christianity. As such it is an independent educational institution. All of our Centers are places of religious research for all. We have no creed, but we are eager to serve the people of every creed."

I was ready to insist that the students at Unity City and the scattered groups throughout America were united in a spiritual movement that would overrule Fillmore's contention. Creedal aspects in Unity have been apparent since the "vampire editorial," and its denominational ties are as strong as those of the seasoned old churches. The constitution and by-laws of the Unity Annual Conference, organized in 1933, provide ample proof that the once independent local Centers are now controlled by a centralized and theocratic executive board. The Field Department, begun in 1915 to "supervise field lectures and to assist Centers which ask for counsel," now functions as a checking agency authorized to approve or disapprove all local activities.

Unity, I was sure, had already turned the corner of denominationalism. But Charles Fillmore insisted, "Unity is just a school," and the world that is Unity will shape itself to his inner thought as long as he lives. I was never with him without wondering how long that would be. Like many little-known epistles, Fillmore documents are redundant with hints that the true adept may live forever. The death of Royal, the third son, in 1923 was accepted as inevitable. When Myrtle Fillmore died, a noted Unity minister said that she had left the world only because she willed to go. Of himself Charles Fillmore says, "My body is being transformed cell by cell. The ultimate development will be a completely new organism having ethereal life with all the perfections of youth."

When I saw him the last time, his hand resting upon the

arm of Cora Fillmore, I wondered if he meant he was looking forward to a subsequent reincarnation. Or would it be a progressive and incessant mortality divided as it now is between Missouri and California! As he paused to say good-by to a group of students who had just completed a term at the Training School, I was tempted to conclude that it was through them that he expected to gain an earthly immortality. They were returning to local Centers to perpetuate concretely the truths exemplified in the life of Charles Fillmore—truths that contain shallows in which a child can wade and depths in which a giant must swim.

CHAPTER IX

PSYCHIANA

I TALKED WITH GOD—YES, I DID—ACTUALLY AND LITERALLY! This sensational banner line, glaring from a page in the *Pathfinder,* set up another experiment in my observatory of "little-knowns." As I read the advertisement, linked with the mysteriously coined word, Psychiana, I knew that I was on the trail of a new star on the horizon of American religion. It was the "power of God" by mail with a money-back guarantee. It was the gift of Frank B. Robinson to the world. It was the most arresting advertisement I had ever seen, but my first reaction was completely unsympathetic. I questioned the propriety of anything religious appearing in such an irreverent setting, and, with growing concern, noted similar ads in at least a hundred newspapers and in scores of magazines. They had been appearing since 1928. Even though I knew that the "cults" were prospering, and many so-called "sects" proudly reported substantial increases in membership, I could not believe that fellow Americans would go in for religion by mail. Further investigation, however, revealed that an announcement of the gospel-according-to-Robinson had steered straight into twelve million homes each year for the past decade.

While I was building a case against Psychiana's monopoly of religious advertising, an AP news story broke upon me. The Church of England was earmarking four million dollars to match ecclesiastical advertising with the commercial advertising of the nations. The mystery man of Moscow, Idaho, anticipated the trend by twenty years, and this raised an interesting question. What would have happened if Frank B. Robinson had stayed in the established churches of Protestantism? In twenty years he has gained for Psychiana more converts than the Canadian Baptist denomination, which he disowned, has accumulated in nearly two hundred years of American history. My Reformed Church boasted a gain of fifty-eight thousand in the last census. Robinson would call that petty spiritual cash. And we have tradition! We go back to Zwingli and Luther and even farther than that. We have our roots in good old "Mother Church." We came over from Europe with the backing of the Reformation fathers and the endorsements of synods, diets and councils. We even brought the Heidelberg catechism, unabridged. But out in the solitary reaches of northwestern America, there is a lone figure who tarried only briefly in a religious school, who studied neither Luther's ninety-five *Theses* nor Calvin's *Institutes,* who never argued about the interpretation of the Lord's Supper, but who is dispensing spiritual vitamins to over a million souls.

I had heard him described as saint and sinner with equal vehemence. Some ministers told me emphatically that they were glad he had not stayed with the church. He was too much of an iconoclast. One bishop said, "That man in Moscow is antichrist!" The pastor of a large congregation confessed that he used Robinson's teachings in his pulpit but that he didn't want it to get out. Psychiana lessons were rolling out of Moscow like cars off an assembly line. Was it possible that there were still multitudes untouched and unserved by the churches? If so, it was a bitter commentary on the state of Protestantism. I was more anxious to believe that Robinson had tapped a rich vein in the gullible strata of the American public. Whatever the answer, this man had far outstripped all other religionists in sensationalism. It was evident that whatever had happened when he talked with God had made an impression that stuck. His name was in the American religious news for keeps, and someone was always coming up with the question, "What about Psychiana?"

Was he trying to start a new denomination? There was no talk about churches or societies. In 1938 the Moscow office suggested the organization of local study groups, but this plan was never vigorously pursued. Only twice did I hear of a convention—one in Portland and another in Los Angeles. There were no ministers, no missionaries, no fieldworkers. All that ever came through with any degree of clarity was the mystifying but positive statement: I TALKED WITH GOD—YES, I DID—ACTUALLY AND LITERALLY!

One night after an open forum on current religions, a gentleman called at my hotel to confess that he was a Psychiana student. "It saved my life," he affirmed convincingly.

"What do you mean 'saved'?" I asked.

"From being a misfit," he responded. "From failing in just about everything I ever tried, from discouragement and from losing faith in myself. I went along forty years without ever knowing what the real secret of life is. Now that I know, I'm successful. But it's more than that."

"How much more?"

He surprised me with a sudden flash of humor. "Twenty-eight dollars more," he said with a light laugh. "That's what it cost me to learn the great secret. I'll give it to you for less than that."

"Religion at cut-rate?"

"Free!" He was serious. "I'll tell you the secret of Psychiana. Dr. Robinson's teaching can be summed up in one line: the continual consciousness of the God-Power operating in your life."

He turned to go as if he felt that this was so profound that I would want to think it over.

Crudely maintaining a link between the commercial and the divine, I detained him to inquire about the twenty-eight dollars.

"Psychiana comes in a set of twenty lessons that cost twenty-eight dollars," he informed. "But if it had been twenty-eight hundred it would have been cheap!"

He said good night and I was left alone with this new puzzle of what people believe. A mail-order religion! A correspondence course in finding God!

What *about* Psychiana?

I put the question to the pastor of a large city church.

"Many in my congregation have been circularized," he admitted with a shrug.

"Did any of your parishioners ever enroll?"

"Only two."

"Are they still in your congregation?"

"Heavens, no! You can't reconcile Robinson's stuff with Christianity."

"Isn't it Christianity?"

"Certainly not!"

I elicited the names of the two apostates. One was a clerk in a department store. To her Robinson was a prophet and his correspondence course scripture that she could fully comprehend. There was no mystery about it, she said. One simply followed the lessons, believed in them, and life was changed; the presence of God was revealed and problems melted away. The influence of Robinson, whom she had never seen, was tremendous. For ten years, ever since she was thirty-five, she had been bothered with arthritis. Then she saw I TALKED WITH GOD—YES, I DID—ACTUALLY AND LITERALLY! Hoping that she, too, could get in on this heavenly conversation, she wrote to Moscow for information. Among the circulars she received was this testimonial: "Since writing of my daughter's illness, I have found the God-Power is actually working for me. She is much better, and her physician tells us now an immediate operation will not be necessary. That means only one thing: *The God-power is working. Since studying Psychiana I have an abundance of everything.*"

This persuaded the saleslady to become a student. After six weeks of Psychiana, her arthritis was gone. With a note of impatience she averred that anyone who could not find himself in this gospel was self-condemned.

"Haven't you ever seen the lessons?" she asked.

I had not, so she brought them out. There were twenty pocket-digest pamphlets with a personalized salutation: "Dear Friend and Fellow Student." Each contained about seven thousand words sparkling with spontaneity. Across each cover page ran the dauntless promise: THE POWER OF THE SPIRIT OF GOD

WILL REVEAL ITSELF TO EVERYONE WHO STUDIES THESE LESSONS CAREFULLY.

I thumbed through the pamphlets.

"You can't find out anything about them that way," the woman remonstrated. "You must read and study and apply every word of Psychiana, believing. You must follow the exercises."

"Exercises?"

Picking up the first lessons, she turned to a page which showed signs of much use and read aloud:

"Breathe slowly and deeply and then lay your lesson down. Close your eyes and repeat as many times as you care to, slowly and very quietly, the following sentence: *I believe in the Power of the Living God.* Then get on your feet and, standing erect, say the same sentence three or four times out loud if there is no one around to annoy you. On your way to work in the mornings or whenever you have unoccupied moments, repeat this sentence mentally as many times as you can."

"Isn't this just another Coué cure?" I proposed. "It seems to be putting religion in the field of the subconscious."

"That's the trouble with reading only the exercises," she sparred. "Psychiana teaches there is no subconscious. There is only God. You tap the God-Power and before you know it, things begin to happen."

This was also the opinion of the pharmacist whose name the minister had given me. Feeling that he was not getting enough out of "church religion," he decided to investigate Psychiana. He had seen at least twenty advertisements before he asked for a trial lesson. This answered his questions. He enrolled. He had now found a "religion untrammeled by any creed," and he kept repeating to me the term, "a practical viewpoint."

"If I ran my business the way the churches run theirs," he said with certitude, "I'd be bankrupt. Robinson comes right out and tells you what he has to give you and what it's going to cost you to get it. If it doesn't work, you can get your money back."

He showed me a membership application on which was printed, "If, after you have carefully studied these lessons you do not find the Power of God, you may return them, and, according to the terms of your membership application, you may have returned to you every dollar you have paid to us."

"Robinson knows he's got something," he reiterated, "and he's not ashamed to tell the world about it. He comes right out and says that if religion doesn't produce, there's something wrong with religion. I can understand that kind of talk. What I think the churches ought to do is call him in for consultation rather than oppose him the way they do. He's a great man."

"Have you ever met him?"

"No, and I don't suppose I ever will. He's practical in that, too. In his autobiography he says that he doesn't want to meet his students. He says we might look for some frock-coated, priestly looking fellow and be disappointed!"

This deliberate circumvention of the age-old precedent of amassing followers left me as baffled as that first Psychiana advertisement. All of the religious entrepreneurs whom I had met were usually on the road, on the air, or in the pulpit. Here was a man who deliberately absented himself from his disciples. He had repudiated all the methods popularized by the founders of other faiths. It was not through personal contact or human appeal that he built up his constituency. Standing alone and aloof, he depended solely upon advertising coverage and the power of the printed word to propagate his message and convert the world. Did he have a genuine antipathy toward meeting the people and handshaking them into his favor? Or was the mail-order approach the subtle system of a religious capitalist?

An extended study of the Psychiana clientele led me to the office of a prominent chiropractor in Madison, Wisconsin. Robinson's autobiography had a special table in his reception room because it was a "positive approach to God." A storekeeper in St. Louis displayed twelve of Robinson's books on a shelf over his cash register so that his customers could see that he "wasn't ashamed" that he belonged to the movement. In a farm home near Fairview, Kansas, I saw, thumbtacked on the dining-room wall, a "Procedure for Psychiana Students."

1. Before beginning the day's work, close your eyes and say, "Spirit of the Living God, I begin this day recognizing your presence in me. I'm going to let you guide my every movement through this day. Thank you for being so close to me."
2. At breakfast, smile.
3. At noon, repeat the statement made earlier and express gratitude to God for being so close to you.
4. In the evening read your Psychiana lesson and recognize that the Spirit of God is in you.
5. Before you retire, don't get down on your knees and ask God to forgive you all the sins you have committed that day. Thank Him that you have committed no sins for which you need to ask pardon. You can sin if you want to, but if you do, don't come sneaking around to God at night and ask forgiveness. If you

really are sorry for what you've done, *you won't do it any more*. Then, before you retire, think of a few names of those you have spoken to about Psychiana or those you know would be interested in having our lessons started to them.

In Cleveland, Ohio, I met a student (formerly a Protestant) who studied his lessons in a Catholic church near his tire shop! Here he sat, reading material which was definitely tabooed by that church's hierarchy, "finding God" by the paradoxical combination of the votive light and the inspiration of Robinson, who once wrote, "When I put aside the idea that Jesus Christ was God, I immediately felt a sense of great relief."

It was this heretical thesis that evoked the fury of orthodox churchmen. But the "tire man," impervious to the blast of criticism, read into the statement his own unimpeachable interpretation. It was he who first explained to me the significance of the word "Psychiana" and how it came into existence. With pretentious faith, he said:

"You see, when Robinson was looking around for a name for his teaching of the Power of God, he put that Power into practice. One night before going to bed, he placed a pencil and a tablet on his night stand. He dreamed that he was in a room with a dead man. Standing over the dead man was a stranger, who was making signs over the corpse with his hands. Dr. Robinson asked him what he was doing. The stranger said, 'Why, Dr. Robinson, you ought to know. I'm using Psychiana to bring life back to a spiritually dead world.' Robinson came out of that dream and wrote the name Psychiana on the tablet."

"Well, that's a great story!" I acknowledged politely.

"Great story?" exclaimed the tire man. "That's only half of

it! About a month later, Dr. Robinson happened to walk past the desk where his staff opens the mail. A photograph fell out of an envelope. It was the stranger who was in the dream. He lived 'way over in Alexandria, Egypt. His name was Geoffrey Peel Birley and what do you think happened? Dr. Robinson decided to test the dream by asking him for forty thousand dollars to help Psychiana get started. Mr. Birley sent it!"

"How do you know all this?" I asked, deciding that this was one story with which I would someday confront Psychiana's founder.

"Why, we students know all about Dr. Robinson. He tells us what he is and what he was and that's the way religion ought to be."

From this credulous believer to a churchman who held his nose in a gesture of disgust, I met no one who had seen the Moscow messiah. Even the journalists who attacked him in popular and professional magazines rarely thought it necessary to look him up. His friends were content to believe that he was as great as any saint of the past and a good deal more practical; his enemies put him down as a religious racketeer. Entertaining these two opinions, I started for Idaho to talk with the man who had "talked with God."

Prejudice went with me, for I had secured a copy of *The Strange Autobiography of Frank B. Robinson,* a potpourri of intimate confessions, prophetic encyclicals, and philosophical flights. Unfortunately, an exalted self-esteem intruded persistently throughout the three hundred pages. The man was struggling valiantly to make his religious experience articulate. He was constantly hammering away at the idea that what he had found would inevitably shatter the "impotent religions of the world." He was willing to battle America's two hundred and eighty religious groups on this issue. He believed himself to be heaven's advocate of a new religious order. This unshakable conviction made his writings conspicuously egocentric. Yet a primitive, brutal passion surged through the story. Nothing that he said was passive or commonplace. I saw in him a Paul Bunyan of the creeds, stalking through the religious timber, hacking out a marker, tossing aside a lean-to, blazing a trail with an utterly ruthless disregard for the forest's beauty.

He was, indeed, "down on the churches." He accused his father, a Congregational minister in Northumberland, England, of being a profligate. He told of beatings he received and let his readers in on carousals in the manse. Harsh denunciations attacked both the morals and the entrenched opinions of old-school religionists. Caustic charges bristled from the pages of the *Strange Autobiography*.

"I have seen lots of 'religion' in my day. I have seen religion in action. I saw it nearly beat its own sons to death. I saw it guzzling beer. I saw it having illicit intercourse with members of its own church. I saw it lie, under oath. I saw it steal. I do not want that sort of religion, for religion, or what masquerades as religion, has not changed for the better since my boyhood days. It has gone so far that the whole world knows it for what it is—a ghastly sham perpetrated on the world by the church in the name of God. I do not care what religion did to me, and it marred me. I do not care how I have suffered through religion. I am only glad to realize and know at last the actual truths of the Great Spirit. God is beginning to dawn on this earth. What a day! What a responsibility! Trying times lie ahead. Many hard battles remain to be fought. These battles, however, will be won, for I have learned well the lesson: Be still and know that I am God. The call is clear. The objective is God. The Power comes from God. How can I fail?"

The scant biographical data winnowed from such lines did not seem to warrant the "strange" appellation. As in the case of many religious leaders, there is mystery surrounding Robinson's birth. Was he born in New York City, Halifax, or Stratford on Avon? Circumstantial evidence could support either of these locations, but Robinson is not sure which is correct. There is no record of his birth. To the inhabitants of the Psychiana paradise the question is irrelevant; they neither romanticize nor concern themselves with solving the riddle.

More important, since it points up the unquestionable destiny of their leader, are his experiences. His boyhood was spent in Halifax where, after his mother's death, life became unbearable with a chameleon stepmother and his hypocrite father. In 1900 he was shipped off to Canada with a brother Sydney. They had passage on the steamer *Parisian,* about five dollars spending money, and a letter of introduction to a Baptist minister at Belleville, Ontario. Their reception by the Reverend Henry Wallace showed that there were other ministers as "irascible as the Reverend John H. Robinson." Wallace turned the boys out of his house with the suggestion that they throw themselves for relief upon the Salvation Army. When Sydney contracted pneumonia and hospital care was needed, Wallace refused to help. Frank wired his father for money. The reply was laconic: "Secure best medical advice. Sorry cannot help financially."

Today in Belleville, old-timers recall how, after Sydney recovered and left town to be heard of no more, Frank stayed on. He owed a debt and he worked it out. They remember him as the boy in his teens who drove the first rubber-tired hack, hired out as a farm hand, worked for a time as a drug clerk, and beat the head off the drum at Salvation Army meetings. It was no surprise when the news reached Belleville that Frank B. Robinson had started a new religion. He had always been looking for God. It was the story between Belleville days and the appearance in Moscow, Idaho, that was inexplicable.

That story began in a Bible Training School in Toronto where Frank had been sent by a Baptist philanthropist who saw in him evangelistic potentialities. What he had not seen was the deep spiritual unrest that made Frank Robinson a new phenomenon among those who stirred up the sawdust trails.

Here was a seeker who claimed that he made an honest attempt to find God according to the Protestant formula. He had "an insatiable desire to actually know who and what God was like," an impatient longing for a tangible spiritual something that he believed the ministers themselves did not possess. Even his own premature ordination failed to produce the evidence of God that he was looking for. Whatever he did was fundamentally vigorous but few believed that his "quest" was respectable. Here was a man who threw himself upon the church and the clergy as if to test their armor and to challenge their influence.

In a rebellious moment at the Bible School, Robinson concluded that organized religion could never point the way to God. He left the school and, in quick succession, there followed periods with the Royal Canadian Mounted Police, the United States Navy and Army, a job as a drug clerk in Portland, and as a whistle punk with a lumber company near Klamath Falls,

Oregon. Throughout this interregnum, Robinson was still seeking God. Sporadically, he tried again the well-beaten paths of Christendom. But he charged that whenever he needed help ministers disappointed him and Christian organizations offered him stones for bread. He tabulated his indictments. Ten of them. They were "magnificent and bitter disillusionments" and included: the preacher father who beat him until the blood flowed; a Salvation Army lass who tried to seduce him; a church elder who, when asked for advice about entering the ministry, said, "Frank, you never appeared to be much of a damned fool, but you're certainly making one out of yourself now."

Frustrated by hapless attempts to find God, he became a social and religious misfit. For twenty-five years he was more often Mr. Hyde than Dr. Jekyll. One night he poured out his heart at a rescue mission; the next day saw him on a drinking spree. One week he pounded out gospel hymns on the YMCA piano; the next week he was thrown into jail as a vagrant in Vancouver. When he at last "found God" he lambasted the churches with a broad generalization drawn from his own experience: "You cannot find the Power of the presence of God through anything any church teaches, for the simple reason that what they teach is not of God."

Was I about to look in on some divine immensity or was I approaching the gateway to America's most successful grudge story? Whatever the answer awaiting me, one thing was certain: Robinson was no longer a religious vagabond. He had boldly written his name into the chronicles of American religion, and I had heard that he was the richest man in Idaho.

Moscow is a town of six thousand. As I stepped onto the platform of the modest little station, I greeted a workman with an inquiry about the founder of Psychiana.

"You mean Doc?" came the rejoinder. "Yes, he's in town as far as I know."

"Doc" was the sobriquet based on a doctorate in psychology from the College of Divine Metaphysics in Indianapolis. The University of Idaho, located in Moscow, has never seen fit to honor him with a doctorate. Among the faculty, opinion about the Psychiana initiator is divided. They admit that he has a constellation of ideas on the workability of the God-Power, but his ways are "unacademic," and his method will not be circumscribed by convention or ordinary logic. Remembering the character of the *Strange Autobiography,* I imagined that Robinson would scoff at degrees.

When I called him from my hotel and asked about an appointment, he replied, "I happen to be coming over that way. I'll meet you in the lobby."

Expecting an anemic sentimentalist, I was surprised when a broad-shouldered, six-foot Westerner in a big Stetson walked in. He had the square jaw of a fighter and a grip that said, "Put 'er there!" When we reached the street, he waved impatiently at his shining Cadillac, saying, "Let's walk. It'll do us good."

I fell in with his long strides.

"A few weeks ago they brought me from Seattle in an ambulance." He spoke with intensity. "Three doctors stood over me one day. One, a close friend of mine, said, 'Frank, I think tonight will be your last night on earth.'" His words were accentuated by emphatic nods. "'I shall live until I have accomplished what I have set out to do,' I told him. Now, don't get me wrong. I'm no miracle man. But I do believe in the power of the Living God. Like Paul, I am fully persuaded that what I have committed and consecrated to God will be abundantly taken care of. I stand on the Power. It is wonderful. It is beautifully sweet. It brings results. How I wish the Christian church would understand it! The Spirit of God, the Spirit behind all creation, lives on this earth. It says, 'Come, take, use!' "

Passers-by greeted him with a nod or a friendly "Hello, Doc." He lifted his hand in businesslike responses without pausing in his peripatetic address. "God lives now. I rejoice in that Power and Presence. The world is ripe for this revelation. It will not come through crucified gods. It will not come through resurrections. It will come when men and women recognize the fact that the Power that created us still lives in us, and is, here and now, fully and totally available to us all."

We were passing a drugstore. He suggested that we have a soda, adding the usual, "It's a warm day." A more typical American setting could not have been found for the unfoldment of a drama of American faith: a soda fountain in a corner drugstore where Robinson came to work as a clerk in 1928.

He did not want to reminisce, but since I was eager to supplement the story of his life and learn just how he "talked with God," I began, "Was it here you had your religious experience?"

He shook his head as if the term smacked too much of churchianity and was inadequate to describe what had happened to him. He conceded, "No, that happened before we came to Moscow."

"We?"

"There were three of us—Mrs. Robinson, son Alfred, and I."

"Why did you come to Moscow?"

"This drugstore closed at six o'clock, and I wanted time to work on the greatest religious teaching in the world, Psychiana."

"You had already talked with God?"

He nodded.

"Didn't you ever think about following the conventional method and preaching about it?"

"I knew that wouldn't work. In the first place, you don't preach about God. You *live* God's power. Besides, the soapbox method would have been too slow, too small. I chose the mails as the only feasible way. I decided to charge a small fee and if the teaching didn't work, I'd refund the money. If it works, I said, some wealthy man will endow the movement and I'll give it free to the world."

"One of the things I wanted to ask you about was Birley and the forty thousand dollars," I spoke up.

Robinson told the story in detail, even more dramatically than I had heard it from the student. "It will take a good deal more to endow Psychiana, but that will come, too," he ended confidently.

"About talking with God——"

He eyed me suspiciously for a quick moment. In the penetrating flash, my sincerity was weighed in whatever omniscience he possessed.

He pushed back his chair.

"I'm interested in the truth of Psychiana, Dr. Robinson," I hastened to add, "and I'll leave it to you how to proceed."

"If you've finished," he said, "we'll walk over to the office."

The Moscow street with its cars and young people, shopkeepers standing in open doorways, farmers, women window-shoppers, and newsboys was a summer Main Street anywhere in America.

In 1928, when Robinson walked here, he carried a small note-book. Sometimes townspeople saw him stop and make a nota-tion. "Funny for a drug clerk," they said. "Always writing. What's he figuring out?" He wrote during his spare moments at the store. Neighbors talked about a light burning after midnight in the Robinson home; sometimes it burned all night.

"He pounds the typewriter hunt-and-peck till his fingers bleed. Then he tapes them up and types some more."

"He borrowed the typewriter from Carey Smith, the clothes presser."

"Mrs. Robinson is as bad as he is. They're both hepped on whatever it is."

"He's crazy."

Nineteen twenty-eight—Amos 'n Andy, flagpole sitters, Babe Ruth, Red Grange, Lindbergh, talking movies. A drug clerk rented the dining room of the Moscow hotel for a series of lectures on "The God-Power."

"Ladies and gentlemen of Moscow! I talked with God—yes, I did—actually and literally!"

A prophet had spoken in his own country. The University of Idaho suggested that its professors stay away. Townsfolk tapped their foreheads significantly as they left, but a few believed and said they would come again.

All that night and throughout the following Sunday, the drug clerk beat out a steady tattoo on his typewriter. He brought the pages to his wife.

"These are good lessons," she said. "They will change the world if only we can start their distribution."

"We'll start it," vowed the drug clerk. "Twenty-five hundred dollars will do it."

He had twenty-five dollars; he had been in Moscow less than ninety days. But by nightfall a farmer, a road commissioner, a grocery clerk, a bookkeeper, and a bank cashier had pooled the required amount. Robinson was putting the "God-Power" into practice. He was applying one of the major premises of his new faith: Trust the Spirit of God by taking aggressive action.

It was now necessary to compose the advertisement. While working on it, a thought came through: "Don't write an ad; simply tell the people what happened to you." A Spokane advertising agency refused the copy with "We can't handle that kind of stuff. No one will answer an ad like that." The drug clerk sent it direct to *Psychology Magazine*. The investment, $400; the proceeds, 5,300 replies. *Physical Culture* brought 13,000 replies; *The Pathfinder*, 23,000. Wherever it appeared it had the same startling compeller line: I TALKED WITH GOD—YES, I DID—ACTUALLY AND LITERALLY! Applications for the God-Power lessons began coming in. Moscow's citizens saw mail sacks hauled to a small office over the drugstore. There at night, a grocery clerk, a bank cashier, a road commissioner, a bookkeeper, a drug clerk and his wife stuffed envelopes with lessons on the art of tapping the "Power of the Great Spirit." Robinson gave up his job in the drugstore, bought a second-hand multigraph machine. The world was ready for a new revelation of God. Psychiana was born.

I saw the name on a substantial two-story brick structure as we turned the corner. It was an office building, nothing church-like about it.

"This is building number one," explained Robinson. "We built it eight years ago after outgrowing rented offices all over town. We bought another building recently. Our staff is now well over a hundred."

In a room fronting the street, a group of about twenty women were busily assembling bulletins for mailing. The clangor of printing presses came from an adjoining room. Robinson picked up a four-page folder from a tall stack on the working table and passed it to me. "More than a million of these will go out," he said casually, but not without a pretentious note.

Expecting a lesson on the "God-Power," I was struck by a screaming multicolored broadside aimed at the Better Business Bureau! A tornado of charges roared out of the pages.

"Others are coming," Robinson assured me as we proceeded to his office. He whipped more copy out of a desk drawer. Red and black captions left no doubt about the matter:

WHEN JESUS CAME TO EARTH

When Jesus walked the earth some two thousand years ago, He brought to humanity a message of staggering import. He brought the very same message that Dr. Robinson is bringing today. But "reformers" crucified him. They never let up until he was safely in the tomb. They thought they were doing good, because Jesus Christ was certainly unorthodox, just as Dr. Robinson is unorthodox.

I don't believe there was a "Better (?) Business Bureau" operating in that age; had there been, you may be sure it would have been in the vanguard of those misguided people who, because Jesus refused to operate according to their traditions, killed him. Had there been a private, membership-selling scheme called the "better" (?) bureau then, it probably would have asked Jesus to file a financial statement with it. And Jesus would have refused, just as The Psychiana Religion refused. For, like Dr. Robinson, Jesus was afraid of no one. He never gave or took a bluff. He cared little what the surface indication of an organization was—*he looked into it and saw the truth.*

"The Bureau has insinuated that Psychiana is a racket," said Robinson. "But here are the facts." He brought out the rough draft for another attack. There were statements about the BBB from Congressman A. J. Sabath; President of the Consumers' League of America, E. C. Reigel; Honorable Charles U. Becker; F. Odell Adams, secretary of the Manhattan Board of Commerce, and others. Bracketed in a conspicuous paragraph was this statement: "In Washington not long ago, the Postmaster General said this to Dr. Robinson: 'We have never, in seventeen years, received one complaint from a member of your organization.' "

"America is going to hear about this," Robinson vowed, and it was no overstatement. I learned later that these printed bombshells had exploded in a million homes and business places throughout the nation.

The telephone rang. A boy came in with a telegram. Robinson showed it to me. A student in New Jersey was inquiring about lesson seven. It was overdue.

"He sounds as anxious about it as if it were money from home," I commented.

"It is," Robinson said without a smile and communicated with the mailing department for a checkup on lesson seven. While I sat with Psychiana's founder on our first afternoon, he received eight telegrams asking for advice and help, or requesting interviews.

Two contrasting items stood out prominently in Robinson's modern well-appointed office. One, an axiom tacked to the door, THE GREATEST TRUTHS ARE ALWAYS THE MOST SIMPLE, SO ARE THE GREATEST MEN. The other, a large portrait of my host all decked out in the clericals and ring of a high church official.

His fine, clean-cut face, with not a wrinkle, his consistently wholesome expression, and his eyes hinting of something mysterious going on in his mind, suggested that he deserved the embroidered accouterments; but, remembering what he had written and said about church organizations, I blinked incredulously. I never expected to see the jeweled cross upon the breast of Frank B. Robinson!

"Byzantine American Catholic Church—Eastern Rite," he said, as he cut open a telegram. "The apostolic succession goes back to the first church in Antioch, founded by St. Peter in A.D. 38."

"But doesn't the ring signify that the wearer is wedded to Christ?" I asked, attempting to eke out a confession.

Robinson circumvented with "Catholic means universal, unimpeachable."

"But I'm really interested in knowing why you wanted such a consecration."

His reply was straightforward. "It was by invitation, and it links me directly with a hundred million Eastern Catholics."

He laid his work aside and sat for a moment in thought.

Then he said, "No churches are necessary for a concept of God. No theology is necessary; no rite, no creed, no article of faith. God knows nothing about these things. What God knows all about is life—human life. For where there is human life, there is God right in the middle of that life. Jesus was no more than that—a human life acting out the God-Power."

As I listened I caught my first glimpse of the gap that separated the man Robinson from the ruthless religious anarchist of the *Strange Autobiography*.

"I have been called antichrist," he went on, "but that is part of the persecution I expect. I have put my finger on the sickness of the churches and they hate me for it. Billy Sunday once wrote me and said, 'For God's sake, stop driving men and women out of the Kingdom of God. Just as fast as I save them, you drive them away.' I told him I disputed his claims to leading people into the Kingdom of God and offered to meet him in public debate anywhere he suggested. He never accepted. As for my ideas about Jesus, I think He was the greatest of all spiritual pioneers. I cannot and do not accept the immaculate conception, the virgin birth, or the vicarious atonement. I doubt whether Jesus would have accepted them himself. The poor, lowly, lovely Nazarene never wanted any man to build a monument to him. What do you think Jesus would say if He returned to earth and saw cathedrals built in His name while people lie sick and diseased in sin? What would He do if He saw men and women prostrated before His statues without recognizing the Power of God which He tried so desperately to bring to them? For this Great Master did know spiritual truth. His message was so potent that had not the churches cast it aside and worshiped the Messenger instead, the world would now know God. People are sick of traditions about Jesus. They are sick of church theology. They want God. They want a spiritual Power they can use now."

Throughout this short exposition of the state of the church, he was rummaging through a pile of transcriptions. "For five years I was on the air over eighty stations," he explained. "This will give you an idea of what the broadcasts were like."

He put a transcription on the record player and leaned over the console to listen to his own voice. Egocentrism? Yes. But I felt that it could be explained by the fact that his conception of God, "a divine personal revelation," had become the pervading force in his life.

"God is the life principle behind every created thing," said the record. "When we recognize the stupendous fact that life which is God is the invisible motivating impulse dwelling in this body of flesh, then the entire human personality is illumined by the ever-present existence of the invisible Spirit. All that a man needs of God is hidden in his own soul."

At this point Robinson cut in with "That's it! Listen! That's what I mean!"

"At no time has God, nor will God, manifest Himself on this earth or anywhere as a person," continued the transcription. "The twenty crucified gods that line the pages of religious history were all human beings. I am aware that this is against the teaching of many churches. The world must decide who is right, but unless it accepts Psychiana's teaching of God as a life principle, as a vital, usable force—it will collapse."

Western Union intruded with another wire. Robinson read the message as if Psychiana stock had again gone up. He gave me the telegram, which carried a Denver, Colorado, top line:

WISH TO REPORT ON RECOVERY OF MY CHILD. CHILD IS ENTIRELY
WELL. CANNOT EXPRESS MY THANKS.

"This seems to refute your denial of being a miracle man," I
smiled. "I don't suppose this is the first——"

"Nor the greatest," he finished. "In Manila the death certifi-
cate of a student had already been signed. Another student
asked to be left alone with the 'dead' man. The man recovered
and, according to last reports, is still alive. In the last eighteen
years we could have recorded five hundred thousand miracles
effected through the God-Power."

"You don't keep the records?"

"We don't keep a miracle file; that would be impossible. But
if you're interested in testimonials, come along."

We walked together to Psychiana building number two, and
Robinson explained that it housed the correspondence study
and accounting departments. When I asked if all of his employees were required to take the course, he replied in the
negative and added sagaciously, "Only about twenty-five per
cent do. Sometimes the nearer men are to truth, the less they
appreciate it."

I was beginning to see that Psychiana operated as an industry. The manager-employee relationship was founded on friendliness and good business principles. The workers told me that
"Doc" had always been reasonable in his demands and consistently fair in his practices.

At building number two, I met Elmer F. Anderson, account-
ant and Robinson's close personal friend. He was the bank
cashier in the quintet that raised the initial capital for Psychiana, Incorporated. In the early days of the experiment, he ran
the multigraph after banking hours, helped out with the book-

keeping, and pinned his well-balanced faith on the reality behind the phrase, I TALKED WITH GOD—YES, I DID.

Anderson was opening a huge pile of incoming mail when we arrived. He sorted the testimonials from the letters with checks appended. While "Doc" stood over his afternoon mail, I felt that he had a genuine pastoral affection for his unseen congregation. He picked up a card.

> *Dear Sir:*
> *I want to tell you how wonderful your lessons are....*

He let it fall, picked up another, then a third and fourth, glanced at them, and let them drop back into the disordered heap.

> *Dear Doctor:*
> *Words can never tell you how much you have done for me....*

> *Dear Doctor:*
> *I am so happy I can hardly write. You have saved my family....*

> *Wonderful Teacher:*
> *As I told you in my last letter, I have bought a little home, thanks to the great God-law. I was a drunkard, but no more. Thanks to you....*

He laid the card back on the pile and walked slowly out of the room. Anderson said nothing.

"Do you mind if I look at some of these?" I asked.

"Not at all."

The sprawling words on a card peeped out of the pile.

*"Damn you, Robinson! When I stand before the judg-
ment throne, I hope you'll be there when I am. I hate
your ads. I hate your guts. Damn you, Doc!"*

Handing it to Anderson, I asked, "Is this unusual?"
"We get all kinds," he replied good-humoredly. "But you
won't find cards like that from students."

I riffled through hundreds of letters and cards. The post-
marks were a cross section of America. Anderson said the
morning mail would be heavier. When I admitted that these
far exceeded my expectations, he led the way into an anteroom.
Here was a bale of letters.

"I was planning on burning these," he said. "Bushels of letters must be burned frequently because space does not permit
keeping them. Dr. Robinson used to read all the mail; now he
can no longer pledge himself to that. We receive at least a hundred thousand testimonials a year."

Left alone with the sacred trust, I found incredible
addresses: "The Man Who Talked with God, Idaho." "Doctor
Robinson, Idaho." "Psychiana, U. S. A." Salutations were senti-
mental: "My dearest Teacher," "Dearest Doc," "My kindest
Helper," "Man of God." There were crudely scrawled letters,
professionally typed ones, and telegrams. The more I read, the
less I questioned the authenticity of the documents. One, from
a man whom I later interviewed in Kansas City, testified, "My
life has been changed completely, and I have gained untold
personal wealth of great good." He said that since taking the
Psychiana course, he had started "getting the breaks." His surroundings proved it.

An R. F. D. letter from Iowa said, "I am enclosing a check

as an appreciation for all your wonderful teaching has meant
to me." The amount, one thousand dollars, was penciled in at
the top of the letter. Many students expressed eagerness to
spread the God-Power through personal missionary effort.

From Seattle came a letter saying, "Sir, I am considering at
this very moment seriously and with earnestness of lecturing on
the Philosophy and Psychology of the Power of God in Man,
and I desire your written approval to use and express the great
good of Psychiana for man's needs. Sir, I shall not go forth
upon this new and wonderful work without your express per-
mission granted me in writing."

An ardent, down-to-earth epistle from Montgomery, West
Virginia, began, "All Hail to the Spirit of Life! Your wonderful teaching has blessed me with a typewriter maching i dont
know much about typeing so please excuse all unspelt words.
Writing to try to express my thanks for *the man of God who
delivereth us from poverty and want through teaching of that
great providing spirit of life in us.* it has been manifested and
proven to me and they all around me can see how prosperious
i am since ive been taking these lessons. they make remarks
about it i got a referagtour two weeks ago and they all ask me
how is it that you can get a new fridadair and no one elce here
can. i ancered well i trust the GOD who never did die and he has
all things in his hands. say some of them call me crazy and
others believe. there is something to the majourty that believes.
no doubt that i shud have written befoure. i have many nabours
and friends i wood like to just go and tell them about this
wounderful teaching. i plan now to buy me a lot on the suburb
of this town and build me a cheep house to start with and have
me a school of reality have all the scollars to inroll with you and

compleet their course direct from you and meet with me to discus and testify. *Tell me what do you think of my progect in every way i want to apoint the people to you like john pointed them to Christ i can say i am not he i am only the voice crying in this wilderness prepair ye for the religeon which has a reality of works both in meteral things and devine spiritual inspiration of noledge. this is your humble servant and scollar. p.s.* if this shall be satisfactury with you all my husband and i will go to work at once and we will reserve room at the best hotel in our town and prepair the way if you will come for us to receive you and e.c.t. while on others thou art smiling do not pass me by."

My curiosity about Psychiana coverage and reception was satisfied. Evidently the "Great Law of Abundance" was no respecter of persons. It worked wherever applied in the Psychiana way and kept a flood of mail flowing both in and out of Moscow. When the movement began in 1928, the local post office was second class; today, first class. Robinson attributes this directly to his activities. He reports that last year $100,000 of the $160,000 postal receipts were from Psychiana.

The accounting department adjoining Anderson's office makes such a figure understandable. Rows of card cabinets tabbed with the names of states and metropolitan centers lined an entire wall. As we walked along these files, Robinson pulled out drawers at random and flipped through the cards, saying, "You can see that we are spread out pretty evenly in all sections of the country. Our students are scattered over more than twelve thousand cities. Our lessons are also mailed to seventy foreign countries. The headquarters for foreign distribution is The Hague."

Test-checking revealed 612 students in Des Moines, 9,632 in

Seattle, 13,641 in Los Angeles; Dallas had 1,827, Birmingham 12,902, Detroit 18,124, Boston 9,945, and New York 23,814.

Seeking other data, I discovered that women students number equally with men, that there are more urban than rural enrollees, and that, in a Psychiana survey taken ten years ago, eighty-nine per cent of ten thousand students had an income of over three thousand dollars a year.

"We have ministers, congressmen, college professors, housewives, students from every walk of life; rich and poor, good and bad, wise and otherwise," Robinson reported.

"Satisfied and dissatisfied?"

"I wouldn't say that."

"Have you ever had any student who enrolled for the course and then took advantage of the 'satisfaction or money back' guarantee?"

"Never."

"How about a person who can't afford the lessons; can he get them free?"

"Let him say so and he'll get them. A few years ago the postage on the free lessons was greater than that on the paid. Lessons go free into every penitentiary in the country. I never refuse anyone, but nowadays get few requests from people who are broke."

The clatter of bookkeeping machines and typewriters kept telling me, "This is big business." At a mechanically rotating "Lazy Susan" a group of women were assembling lessons. They snapped up the material from the printed stacks revolving with the table.

Every student in Psychiana automatically becomes an associate member of the Psychiana religion. This is provided for in the bylaws of the religious corporation. Robinson made clear that the movement is not organized for profit. Neither can the receipts from lessons meet the operating costs and the enormous advertising expense. At present fifteen hundred newspapers, including the *American Weekly*, and two hundred fifty magazines, practically all pulps, carry the ad, I TALKED WITH GOD— YES, I DID. Robinson, well-to-do friends and associate members are continually subsidizing the work.

My days at Moscow revealed the qualities of Robinson as a civic leader as well as a religious pilot. Moscow's well-equipped Youth Center was "Doc's" idea. He and his students paid the bill and wrote above the door, "You can't go wrong doing right."

"If we published our benevolences in the yearbook of American churches, we'd be known as Idaho's biggest charitable organization," Robinson told me with pride. "But we don't and people rarely hear about our charities. Perhaps that is why Psychiana has been called a religion without social significance. They say that students who have no local organization fail to fulfil their obligations to their communities. Nothing is farther from the truth. We set the example here in Moscow by frequently giving a ten-dollar basket of groceries to every indigent family in Latah County. Our associate students are in on this, and you can be sure they carry on in the same way at home."

The most lasting expression of "Doc's" community spirit is beautiful "Robinson Park" with its lake and one hundred sixty-four acres of timber. Private interests were bidding for the tract, but Robinson outmaneuvered them, purchased it, and presented the deed to the county commissioners.

It was in this park that I learned from Robinson some of the deeper philosophy which he has tested and found practical. "The energy which is God is best found in quiet," he mused. "Like the tornado with the space of calm in its heart, so the restless, ever-throbbing and heaving rhythm of God is eternal peace when understood. You will never know the fullness of the Power of God until you get to a place where you need that Power to protect, guide or help you. It works best in an emergency. When my enemies hauled me into court accusing me of falsifying on a visa, when they sent out postal inspectors to investigate Psychiana, I suppose I was the least excited of anyone. My friends often said to me, 'Frank, how can you sleep, how can you think, with all this going on?' They did not know how often I came out here and just waited quietly on God. There are no greater words in the Bible than these: 'Be still and know that I am God.' I knew that all of these affairs were just an attempt to stop Psychiana. There will be other attempts, but I know that the Power I use will wipe out of the way any and all efforts to stop this teaching."

When I asked him how the movement would be perpetuated after his death, he said, "The Spirit of God will take care of that. I don't lead. I follow. The Spirit of God will work through this Movement until the whole world knows what I'm talking about."

In later conversations with Robinson and people about town, I heard so much about his son Alfred, a lieutenant in the Air Corps, that I wondered if he might be the logical successor. My surmise was strengthened one day by Robinson's remark, "Alfie knows as much about the God-Power as I do."

The longer I extended my visit with the master mind of Moscow, the more I wondered about the difference between the character I saw in him and the one so blatantly depicted in the *Strange Autobiography.* I finally concluded that the torrent of execrations sweeping through his published works was the result of an undisciplined enthusiasm that followed hard upon the spontaneous success of his God-Power project. A passionate conviction of his prophetic mission had impelled him to ride roughshod over the prejudices and cherished traditions of the institutionalized churches. I felt that he regretted more than he would say that he had permitted some of his early sensations of glory to break over into unbridled invectives. His relationship to organized religion came up in practically every interview. A born fighter, he knew how to deal with the charges of the Better Business Bureau and postal investigators, but to be maligned by the churches was an unresolvable conflict.

He wishes now that Protestantism would investigate his teachings. The misunderstanding which exists brings something akin to suffering to this man whom enemies describe as cold-blooded and indurate to public opinion. They say he is a strange mixture of naïveté and cunning. Even many who come to Moscow have been thrown off the track by his bluff, aggressive, self-centered manner. Churchmen always single him out and suspect him of deliberately trying to destroy their faith.

Yet I saw behind all the vitriolic offensives an impassioned, though ill-directed, desire to empower denominations for their work. His lust for God had brought a cry of racketeering and heresy upon him from those who never looked farther than the puissance whipped up by the whirlwind of his advertisements. Yet these flames were but the reflection of the fire of his convictions.

However he may have romanticized an experience which

other men have encountered since the beginning of time, the calendar of his life began when he talked with God, actually and literally. I waited until my last day in Moscow to get this story from him and, while it may have been colored by the surroundings of the Robinson home, I consider that in the telling he dug deeply and sincerely into his soul.

The living room of the modest brick home at 122 South Harvard Street is equipped with a two-manual pipe organ. The traditional repertory of gospel songs provides pastime and inspiration for Psychiana's leader whose strong frame is refreshingly contrasted with his tender melodies. On this evening he played his favorites, "Lead, Kindly Light" and "O Love That Wilt Not Let Me Go," as well as "In the Cross of Christ I Glory," and "Jesus Calls Us o'er the Tumult." Their rendition would have persuaded his worst critics that he has not disowned the church or Christ as completely as his sensational literature seems to indicate. While the soft music entreated understanding, I felt that he was basically in accord with Christian ideals of beauty and truth.

Florence, the fifteen-year-old Robinson daughter, was entertaining friends on the lawn. With us was Mrs. Robinson, a charming woman, devoted to "Robbie" by a bond that has been forged in many Psychiana trials. Perhaps she had evenings such as this in mind when she prefaced the *Strange Autobiography* with "We live happily. I know of no family more completely in love with each other than this family is." The scene was as typically American as Psychiana itself.

Robinson now led me into the arcana of his experience. "It happened in a little room at 500 Laurel Avenue in Hollywood. I had been to church that morning, the beautiful Methodist

Church on Wilshire. There in those magnificent surroundings I counted twenty-six people. That's all who had come out for the service. Now, remember, I'd been looking for God a long time. I'd been looking for God all my life. I thought God ought to be something that would do great things in people's lives. None of this make-believe stuff for me. I wanted a workable, usable God. Here were twenty-six people. I listened to the sermon. I'd heard hundreds of sermons. None of them had ever brought the real power of God into my life. Please believe me, I had tried to find God in the church many times. It had not worked for me. It may for someone else, but it didn't for me. The plight of churchdom cried out to me that morning. 'God, God,' it cried, 'where are You? You exist, You are a Power, why can't man find You?'

"That Sunday afternoon in our little home, I went into a room and closed the door. I wanted to think this thing through. I was forty-two years old and the thing I wanted most in life had always escaped me. God was the unknown quantity. I believed He existed. Let's say I *knew*. But the fact had never been demonstrated convincingly. I didn't want to go through life and miss the greatest Power that a man can possibly have— the Power of God.

"It was with this kind of seeking that I stood in that room. I lifted my eyes and said aloud, 'Oh, God, if I have to go to hell, I'll go with the consciousness that I went there earnestly trying to find you!' I spoke to God aloud. Remember this! You must speak to God aloud. Whenever Jesus needed the God-Power, He made His request audible. That is a great secret."

He paused in a mood of deep seriousness.

"You spoke to God aloud," I prompted quietly, "and then God spoke to you?"

"A remarkable thing happened," he went on tranquilly. "Instead of feeling condemned for denying that the church had helped me find God, there came to me a feeling of wonderful rest and peace. Something said——"

"A voice?"

He shook his head. "Something," he repeated. "You can describe it only as a sense of power and right. It was like a flash. I spoke to God aloud and the answer came in a vivid conviction that something possessed me in its grasp. It led me back—back through the churches and all my experiences—to the God of my childhood. I had a feeling of perfect, unquestioning confidence and conviction that God is not known through creeds or churches but through a childlike faith. I won't even call it religious emotion. The Spirit of God is a *Law*. It has no emotion. It is the Power of God and it exists in us to the degree that we will call upon it and use it. It only operates when called upon. The Spirit of God has never operated on its own. It always takes the spoken word. I have learned to speak that Word of Power into existence. Think of Jesus in terms of the 'Word' and you will better understand the Power of Jesus. It is the same Power that I have found and that all men can find if they will earnestly seek it."

"You always find it by speaking aloud and then a 'feeling' returns to speak to you?"

"I cannot tell you in one evening all that I have learned in twenty years. We find God and become expert in God only after years of actual participation in the practices that reveal

God. But from the moment of the experience, life changes. From that Sunday afternoon on Laurel Avenue I began an upward climb. It has led me from failure to success, from defeat to triumph. But God is not found without seeking nor realized without the use of a workable technique. That is the heart of Psychiana's method.

"Alfred can play on the organ a Bach fugue from memory. But I remember years ago how he used to sit at that organ by the hour, doing scales. What was he doing? He was impressing upon the Spirit of God that he wanted to play Bach, and, more than that, he was using the invisible Power of God to impress upon Him that he could play Bach.

"The ascent into the Spiritual realm is not haphazard. It can be instantaneous, but, outside of an emergency, it never is. For, in traveling the Spiritual Highway, it is good to know every step and take those steps consciously. Then, if one's foot slips, one knows the way back, and has not lost what one has learned about God. Remember, once a spiritual experience is attained, it can never be lost. It is there. It is part of life. No one can ever take it away."

When I recalled these words on the next day while I waited for my train, I was reassured that they were true. Piled high on a platform wagon were huge mail sacks, the stamp of Robinson's achievements. More Psychiana fires would be lighted throughout the world.

And as I boarded the train I had the feeling that Frank B. Robinson had talked with God—yes, I did—actually and literally!

CHAPTER X

HOMETOWN

📖

I RETURNED from my trip among the "little-knowns" like one who has taken a refreshing walk on the open road. I had heard the resounding tread of a nation finding God. I had seen the close-up of a people's faith. I had felt the heartbeat of the second freedom—American religion. A moving, living force that strikes us all and lures us on! A highway, a search, a consuming passion, a longing for a workable meaning of God! An everlasting attempt to get the most out of this world and the eternal hope for a world to come!

The people that I had walked with for a little while had made religion their adventure. They had dared discover in their own way what God is like and where He dwells. Loosed from traditions that did not seem right, bound by nothing that did not seem good, they had turned aside from the old ways and charted their own short cuts to glory.

Climbing with the faithful up new summits that lift men heavenward, I gave little thought to my own religious identity. Neither was I asked about it. It was blended with the sacred beliefs of my fellows. But the deep roots of my evangelical background were clawing at new earth. And all the time the spirit of the faiths—all two hundred eighty of them—beat in my heart like the sheltering wings of God's everywhereness.

I found a parable one day in a lake among the mountains of eastern Oregon. Mirrored in its depths I saw the blue sky and the timbered slopes. The motionless waters reflected perfectly a sheepherder passing that way with his flock. So, mirrored in the depth of personal experience, I saw the passing parade of America's "little-knowns." Strange, expletory religions! Profound in their claims, extravagant in their testimonies, mystical in their faith, modern in their methods—yet in all I saw truth and beauty. They were the children of the Bill of Rights, flying messengers bearing the eager voice of a new Reformation.

An indefinable and confident air of authority and inner discovery was the common characteristic. What do they have that the churches do not have? Nothing—and everything. From what they believe we can learn very little; from *how* they believe we can learn much. All their merits are inherent in the established churches; the difference lies in the degree of vitality with which they are employed. We take our religion for granted; their religion is the most thrilling experience of life. Our faith tends to be natural, commonplace; theirs is supernatural, special. Critics of historic denominations allege that there is little evidence of a transfer of Christian principles from pulpit and pew to life. While walking the modern roads of faith, I heard the incessant refrain, "Religion must be lived or it will be taken away."

The old churches are committed to a symbolism of language that has very little meaning for contemporary ears. Is this the reason that their members have only a nebulous notion of denominational precepts? It is difficult to perpetuate undefined religious philosophies. Among the new groups each member is positive that he holds the keys of the kingdom. His is a loquacious gospel! To believe it is to talk about it—every conversation is an opportunity to witness. I have often wondered if the difference between the two lies in the regular serving of quotable lines which the new prophets pass out with such consummate skill—not a liberal helping, a precious morsel as if each word were calibrated to the needs and tensions of the moment. The average worshiper, no longer quoting from the Bible, has nothing left with which to hold his offensive except his own ideas. But the "little-knowns" have a corner on sly spiritual slogans which, when heard and used, will change one's life because they change one's mind.

The democracy of Protestantism, which allowed every man to become his own priest, made no provision for the people who want to be told precisely what to believe and exactly how to believe it. They go, therefore, where they can find prescribed techniques. In almost every modern movement the ideal of a social religion is subordinated to an emphasis on the individual. Every seeker is convinced that there is something within him to which a direct revelation of God can appeal. Then follows a continual sense of wonder at his own spiritual development. The commonest blessings suddenly become "gifts from God." In return for these he is attached by a new allegiance of service to the organization. The smaller the group, the greater his loyalty.

And behind it all I saw the active minds and the indefatigable hands of aggressive leaders. These men and women are obsessed with an uncompromising fidelity that hints of the stubborn dogmatism of the early martyrs.

Again I wanted to say, "All roads that lead to God are good——"

But even while I sat beside the placid waters of my mountain lake, it was suddenly lashed into rampant waves of restless foam. The beautiful reflections were lost in the surging body of temperamental waters. How like the public mind when judging the "little-knowns"! Prejudice and intolerance distort the calm reflections. Blind waves of criticism beat against each other and sweep impartially over the innocent shores.

They're all rackets!

It's heresy!

Divine revelation ended with Jesus.

They're made up of disgruntled Christians.

They offer an easy panacea for all the problems of life.

They're religions for the frustrated, appealing only to the emotions.

Folks follow for the loaves and fishes; they're out for material blessings.

The people who leave the churches to go culting are looking for a place in the sun.

To me, these were wild shouts from a pharisaical segment of the public. Having walked with the people, I understood how such snap judgments could arise. But any man who approaches these groups objectively will qualify each accusation with a sympathetic admission of their social and spiritual work. In my observations the commendable had outweighed the questionable. But misunderstanding and bigotry were also apparent among the "little-knowns." On every road I heard the ultimatum, *"This* is the way; walk ye in it!"

This flaunted affirmation, too, was in the American tradition. Religious tolerance was the unknown quantity in the early colonies. The promise of freedom of worship which lured the persecuted across the sea proved for many years to be a fable. New York barred Catholics from citizenship; Penn's holy experiment excluded "papists" from political offices; North Carolina demanded that all public officers profess a Protestant faith. The Anglicans were as unwelcome in the North as the Puritans were in the South. Massachusetts inflicted criminal punishment upon those who broke Puritan decrees; Maryland set the death penalty for those who denied the Trinity. Arrest, torture and execution were ordered for men and women who had professed special revelations or who had "familiar spirits." But Americanism broke through the welter of intolerance to forge a mighty document, the Bill of Rights. This made possible a people's unhindered and sensational search for God, a phenomenon unique among the nations.

Judging from the chronicles, the unpredictable "little-knowns" of today will take their places with the well-knowns of tomorrow. Though some religious movements have burned themselves out as the years went by, the enthusiastic sensationalism of most groups has leveled out into complacent denominationalism. Observers in their day thought them transient and insecure. They failed to see in the suffering and hope the birth pangs of another great American faith.

1668—A nonconformist in Salem, the Puritan theocracy defied, excommunication, banishment, a log hut in the wilderness, a Great Awakening, a sect of sinners: the Baptist denomination today leads the field of Protestantism.

1750—Broken windows in New York, hysterical camp meetings in Kentucky, an unhappy love affair in Savannah, mobs under the frenzied spell of the spirit at Whiteclay Creek, cries of hypocrite and charlatan in Philadelphia: Methodism, present membership seven million.

1828—A Vermont farm boy, visions and angels, a book of gold, riots in Missouri, a killing at Carthage, flight from Nauvoo, a handcart brigade across fifteen hundred miles, the miracle of sea gulls, lawless polygamy: the Church of Jesus Christ of Latter Day Saints with one million adherents.

1832—*Vermont Telegraph* publishes: Mathematical Proof... Jesus is Coming ... March 21, 1844. Ascension robes prepared in New England, New York and Ohio. Correction: Jesus is Coming . . . October 20, 1844. Disillusioned Millerites. Today the Adventists have two hundred thousand members.

1879—Faith cures, cries of mesmerism, hypnotism and animal magnetism; a revelation, *Science and Health with Keys to the Scriptures;* cries of antichrist, insanity, the heresy will not outlive the heretic: Church of Christ, Scientist, present membership three hundred thousand.

More than ever I wanted to say, "All roads that lead to God are good——"

In spite of the wide gulf between the various "little-knowns" and the even wider gulf between them and the traditional churches, I saw in all a common cause. They were simply varying aspects of one great truth, a truth so rich and unconfuted that it could be broken and scattered along many beautiful trails. Selecting the way best suited to his needs, man sets forth with the profound assurance that the new faith will accomplish for him what all others have failed to accomplish. But when he finds truth, he discovers it is God—hidden in his soul from the beginning of time. Each denomination, sect and cult has the same real value to different believers, and, perhaps, to be truly effective, religion must be as multifarious as the people it serves. It is too much of a living, growing thing to be closeted in a single interpretation. It is but a means by which men and women at different stages in life's development have sought to find God in their own way. Quarrels and misunderstandings revolve around the means; the goal is seldom argued about. The essence of the spiritual outreach is liberty; therefore, we can expect the continually evolving process of spiritual democracy to go on. "Lesser-knowns" are always breaking off from the "little-knowns." Every new cult immediately sprouts its own seedlings which, regardless of the weeding out of time, reach maturity in the fertile soil of Americanism.

In none of the groups did I meet leaders who had deliberately set out to "start a new religion." In every instance, they began by saying, "We have found something that will enrich and supplement the faith you already have." They claimed only a modern method of reaching out and using the same old saving power. They all followed the pattern of a new denomination emerging out of a voluntary association of like-minded believers. Soon a headquarters is established. Followers are drawn from two sources: a million every ten years from the churches and a million from the disorganized ranks of those whom the churches pass by. Eventually the United States Bureau of Census finds another name to include in its tabulation of Religious Bodies; technically, the movement is no longer a sect or a cult. It has shifted into the denominational bracket.

After years of prospecting along the new-made trails, I returned to the old home church. Each stroke of the bell on this

Sunday morning was freighted with remembrances. Back through the years—Sabbaths and holy days, Easter baptisms, confirmations—it was ringing for them all. Long ago I stood at the parsonage window while the bell tolled out Uncle August's eighty-two years. A great man had died. The black-plumed horses, the mourning congregation, school dismissed for the day. . . . By the time I grow up, I thought, everyone will have religion and there'll be no need for preachers and churches any more. But the bells were still ringing across America. And there were also the "little-knowns," who had discarded such tradition with other "superfluous ritual." Oddly, while I was among them I had not missed this nostalgic call to worship. Now, in my father's house, I wondered how I had escaped a mild sense of loneliness. The bell was reassuring. The old faith still lived amid the flaming prophets of new religious orders.

Mother led the way to third pew front, center section. The congregation was not the same; there were new names on the church roll, new worshipers around me. I had always contended that a great deal is lost by staying too much under one's own roof, but life was pulsing here. Hometown was still listening to the voice of a personal God. Had I missed something by walking too much on the open road? These people were so engulfed by their ideals that the stampede of "little-knowns" passed over them unnoticed. Nothing had disturbed the practical value of their faith. The order of service and the sermon were carbon copies of Uncle August. Nothing about the worship hour had changed except the perceptibly shorter prayer. It was traditional religion from the Doxology to the final Amen.

If what happened later that day was a rehearsal for the big show on its way to the arena of American faith, we are headed for an exciting season. That afternoon with an astonishing absence of bitterness and suspicion, the Roman Catholic priest and our young minister stopped to chat on our front porch. Expecting and respecting differences, we sipped homemade wine and ate homemade cookies. How impossible a scene when I was a boy! The benign Catholic father, the oracular minister with my mother reflecting the summation of his beliefs, and my dad, still a question mark among believers—all listening to me, a religious cosmopolite. Vividly I talked about Psychiana and the God-Power, Buchman and the four absolutes, Spiritualism and materializations, Unity and its science of life, the Foursquare Baptism of the Holy Ghost, Jehovah's Witnesses and their Theocracy, Father Divine and his kingdoms, the Baha'is and their world faith!

How did my audience react?

The priest: "I always maintained that when Luther and his crowd began their nefarious business, they started so many sects that soon nobody will be able to count them!"

My dad, sitting quietly with a blanket over his lap: "All those religions! It would be exciting to find out about them all. But by the time a man learns how to live, it's time to die."

The minister: "Churches fail when they lose their authority over the people. I'll never believe that the cults have anything that we don't have. I'm going to keep on preaching the same old gospel."

And Mother? She said, "Let me fill your glasses again! There are also plenty of cookies!"

What a blessed sacrament! As we touched our glasses I felt courageous enough to say:

> "All roads that lead to God are good;
>   What matters it, your faith or mine;
>   Both center at the goal divine
> Of love's eternal brotherhood.
>
> "A thousand creeds have come and gone;
>   But what is that to you or me?
>   Creeds are but branches of a tree,
> The root of love lives on and on.
>
> "Though branch by branch proves withered wood,
>   The root is warm with precious wine;
>   Then keep your faith, and leave me mine;
> All roads that lead to God are good."

THE END